On Fighting Poverty

I. On Understanding Poverty: Perspectives from the Social Sciences
    Edited by Daniel P. Moynihan

II. On Fighting Poverty: Perspectives from Experience
    Edited by James L. Sundquist

*Volumes in the American Academy
of Arts and Sciences Library*

PERSPECTIVES ON POVERTY

II

On Fighting Poverty

PERSPECTIVES FROM EXPERIENCE

Edited by

JAMES L. SUNDQUIST

with the assistance of Corinne Saposs Schelling

Basic Books, Inc., Publishers

NEW YORK / LONDON

© 1969 by the American Academy of Arts and Sciences
Library of Congress Catalog Card Number: 75–78452
Manufactured in the United States of America

The members of the
American Academy of Arts and Sciences
Seminar on Race and Poverty
respectfully dedicate this work
and its companion volume to
Martin Luther King, Jr.
1929–1968
and
Robert Francis Kennedy
1925–1968

⊄ The Authors

ROBERT COLES is a research psychiatrist on the staff of the Harvard
University Health Services. A child psychiatrist, he has done extensive
field work with white and Negro families in the rural south, in
Appalachia, in a northern ghetto, and with migrant farm workers,
studying their lives from a medical and psychiatric point of view.
He is a contributing editor of *The New Republic* and on the editorial
board of *The American Scholar*. He is author of *Children of Crisis:
A Study of Courage and Fear, Dead End School,* and *Still Hungry in
America.*

GREGORY FARRELL is Assistant Commissioner of the New Jersey
Department of Community Affairs and Director of the New Jersey
Office of Economic Opportunity. From 1965 to 1967 he was Executive
Director of United Progress, Inc., Trenton, New Jersey, the local
community-action agency. He also served as Community Field Repre-
sentative of the New Jersey Office of Economic Opportunity in Tren-
ton and was Urban Affairs and Education Reporter for the *Trenton
Evening Times.* He is the author of *A Climate of Change: The New
Haven Story* and "The War on Poverty: Where To Now?", for the
New City Foundation in *New City.*

SANFORD KRAVITZ is Associate Professor of Social Planning, The
Florence Heller School for Advanced Studies in Social Welfare, Bran-
deis University. He has been Associate Director, Community Action
Program, Research Demonstration, Training and Technical Assistance Projects Office of the Office of Economic Opportunity. He also
served as co-chairman, Urban Areas Task Force, President's Task
Force on the War Against Poverty. He is author of "The Community Action Program in Perspective," in Warner Bloombert, Jr.,
and Henry Schmandt, eds., *Power, Deprivation and Urban Policy.*

ROBERT A. LEVINE has been Assistant Director for Research, Plans,
Programs and Evaluation, Office of Economic Opportunity. He is now

working on poverty and related matters at the Urban Institute on a Ford Foundation grant. He has also been Chief, Research and Plans Division, Office of Research, Plans, Programs and Evaluation, Office of Economic Opportunity; Senior Economist, The Rand Corporation; and Research Associate, Center for International Affairs, Harvard University. He is author of *The Arms Debate,* and "Rethinking Our Social Strategies."

PETER H. ROSSI is Professor and Chairman of the Department of Social Relations, The Johns Hopkins University. He was Director of the National Opinion Research Center, University of Chicago. He is author of *Why Families Move* and *The Politics of Urban Renewal* among other books.

WILLIAM C. SELOVER is State Department Correspondent for the *Christian Science Monitor.* As the *Monitor's* specialist in government antipoverty programs, he has followed the Economic Opportunity legislation in Congress and has written numerous articles on the legislative development of the program. He has also conducted field investigations for the *Monitor* which resulted in several series on the administration of the Economic Opportunity Act of 1964. He was a Maxwell Graduate Overseas Fellow in India.

JAMES L. SUNDQUIST is a senior fellow of the Brookings Institution, Washington, D.C. While Deputy Under Secretary of Agriculture, he was a member of the Task Force that wrote the Economic Opportunity Act of 1964. Earlier he served as a staff aide on Capitol Hill, where he helped develop and steer through Congress the Manpower Development and Training Act, the Accelerated Public Works Act, and other precursors of the War on Poverty. He also served on the President's Appalachian Regional Commission. He is the author of *Politics and Policy: The Eisenhower, Kennedy, and Johnson Years.*

JOHN G. WOFFORD is Director of the Urban Mass Transportation Study at the Harvard Law School and was formerly Associate Director of the Institute of Politics of the John F. Kennedy School of Government, Harvard University, of which he had been a Fellow. From 1964 to 1966 he was Staff Assistant to the Director of Operations, and then to the Deputy Director, of the Community Action Program of the Office of Economic Opportunity.

ADAM YARMOLINSKY is Professor at the Law School of Harvard University, Chairman of the Urban Legal Studies Program Committee, and a member of the Institute of Politics of the John F. Kennedy School of Government. He served as Deputy Director of the President's Task Force on the War Against Poverty in 1964 and was Principal Deputy Assistant Secretary of Defense for International Security Affairs in 1965 and 1966. His recent publications include "Legal Aid for the Struggling Cities," "Trouble in the Cities," and "The Great Society—Another American Dream."

☞ *Preface* TALCOTT PARSONS

The two volumes growing out of the Seminar on Race and Poverty sponsored by the American Academy of Arts and Sciences in 1966 and 1967 come to press at an opportune time. There is a new administration in Washington that must make a new set of policy decisions in this area. The authors of the first volume, *On Understanding Poverty*, edited by Daniel P. Moynihan, addressed themselves to the diagnostic problems of the poverty questions as social scientists. In the present volume James L. Sundquist and his co-authors deal instead with the development and consequences of government policy in the field. Together these volumes should have a particularly important impact.

For the American Academy, publication of this volume documents another stage in its initiative in facilitating discussion among scholars and policy-makers of what have proved to be the most acute internal social problems of American society. In my preface to the first volume, I called attention to the role of the *Daedalus* study of the Negro American from 1964 to 1966 in the background of the Poverty Seminar.

Almost immediately following the completion—but preceding the publication [1]—of the Negro-American study, there occurred the major crisis in the civil rights movement which followed the shift of the "storm center" from the rural South to the urban ghettoes and was dramatized in the conflicts which emerged in the White House Conference on Civil Rights of 1966. The "War on Poverty," as formally declared by President Johnson, was of course most intimately connected with the racial problem, but was influenced by a variety of other factors, social, political, and intellectual. For example, attempts to explain the greatly accelerated demand for enhanced participation and community control raise complex problems for the sociologist and the historian. As Sundquist points out, the expectations and the related political processes have been exceedingly different from the last massive attempt to deal with the problems of the disadvantaged in American society, namely, in the New Deal period.

How much does the far greater involvement of race contribute to the difference between the 1960's and the 1930's? How much is attributable to the sociological theories of community solidarity which Moynihan emphasizes in a recent book and which are referred to in the first volume in this series? How much results from major structural changes in the position of industrial labor and the trade unions?

This volume gives perhaps the most solid and careful review of the development of policy in the war on poverty, the clash of different groups urging different courses and the problems of evaluation, which is yet available. The American Academy is proud to have sponsored the project and is especially grateful to James Sundquist and his co-authors for their contributions.

Note

1. Talcott Parsons and Kenneth B. Clark, eds., *The Negro American* (Boston: Houghton-Mifflin, 1966).

Acknowledgments

The editors of the two volumes "Perspectives on Poverty" wish to express their appreciation to the authors included in this volume, to other participants in the seminar, and to the Academy staff. In addition, they thank the Research Funds Committee of the American Academy for providing support to initiate the seminar on poverty and the Stern Family Fund for its grant to the American Academy which has helped make this publication possible.

Contents

On Fighting Poverty

Chapter 1

❦ *Introduction*

JAMES L. SUNDQUIST

A STORY IN SUPERLATIVES

America's War on Poverty is a story in superlatives.

It was the boldest national objective ever declared by the Congress—to do what no people had ever done, what the Bible says cannot be done—to *eliminate* poverty from the land. It was reviewed by the Congress with the minimum of care, in the shortest of time, and with the least understanding of what was about to happen. It granted the broadest of power and discretion to a single adminis-trator—Sargent Shriver—to upset and remake, if he could, the insti-tutional structure of community after community across the land. It became—and remains—the most controversial of all the domestic programs of the Kennedy-Johnson era.

No, nothing about the War on Poverty is commonplace. In the zeal of its administrators, in the freshness of their ideas, in the inno-vations of organization and policy approach, it stands alone—even in a period when many New Frontiers were being crossed and a Great Society was being born. No matter what may happen to the Office of Economic Opportunity (OEO) and the Economic Opportunity Act their influence upon American institutions will have been profound.

This book is about that War on Poverty—how it came to be, where it was supposed to go and where it went, the groping, the turmoil, and the upheaval—as told by those who were on the scene. Some were participants who pause now to tell their own stories with perspective and detachment. Some were close observers who now offer syntheses of what they saw.

Most of the papers included in this and a companion volume (*On Understanding Poverty*, Volume 1, edited by Daniel P. Moynihan) were presented at a series of seminars held at the House of the American Academy of Arts and Sciences in 1966 and 1967 under Dr. Moynihan's chairmanship. The papers were then revised and brought up to date during the first half of 1968.

How did the War on Poverty begin? The next two chapters place the War on Poverty in its essential historical perspective: President Johnson, when he proclaimed the War on Poverty, knew where he wanted to go but had no idea how he was going to get there; Congress took the whole program essentially on faith. The Democratic majorities in Congress would have found it impossible, even had they been so disposed, to challenge the central objective of a new and still-popular President of their own party who had assumed office under tragic circumstances and who was now their leader in a presidential campaign year. My own chapter traces the origins of the War on Poverty and of the various programs that went into it. Adam Yarmolinsky describes how the bill that became law was assembled by the task force in which he played a leading role, what were the crucial policy issues, and how they were faced.

At this point we leave the War on Poverty as a whole and focus on the Community Action Program, which became the poverty war's pre-eminent experiment in politics, public administration, and social change (although, says Yarmolinsky, it was initially considered to be of secondary importance to the Job Corps). Sanford Kravitz reviews the evolution of the community-action idea from the early settlement house and charity-organization movements and offers a critical review of its development under the auspices of OEO. John G. Wofford tells, from the viewpoint of the Washington insider, how the new agency launched community action, what questions arose in the shaping of the program, and how they were settled.

What happened in the communities? While the headquarters of Washington agencies have a life of their own, it was in hundreds of cities, towns, and counties that community action took form. Two chapters capture the ferment and the conflict that comprise community action. Robert Coles gives us a picture, supported by tape-recorded reports, of its impact on individuals in the isolated reaches of Appalachia and the South. Gregory Farrell, who was not a member of the seminar but who was asked to write about his experiences because they would greatly enrich this book, narrates the birth, growth, and achievements of the community-action agency he directed in Trenton, New Jersey—not a typical agency, to be sure, because there is no typical one, but assuredly one of the more successful.

Meanwhile, back on Capitol Hill, what was the reaction as congressmen viewed the consequences of their handiwork? William C. Selover, again not a member of the seminar but an experienced political observer, looks at the politics of the War on Poverty, analyzes the growing disillusionment of both the Congress and the administration, and recounts the events of 1967 when community action was continued only on condition of its being tamed, contained, and subjected to the control of the political power structure in each community that chose to so control it.

What is it all accomplishing? Robert A. Levine, assistant director of OEO, summarizes the efforts to evaluate the various elements of the War on Poverty and presents the results of the evaluation. Peter H. Rossi looks intently at the problem of the evaluation process itself, both in general and with particular reference to OEO.

Finally, is the whole experiment now to be brought to an end? What will be the strategy of the War on Poverty as the Republican party—whose spokesmen have questioned, criticized, and in many instances opposed the way that war was being waged—assumes responsibility for it? What should the strategy be? What, in particular, should be the disposition of that ingenious, lusty, but divisive institution that is the symbol and heart of the war on poverty— the community-action agency? The closing chapter highlights some of the strategic and policy questions that confront Richard Nixon as his presidency begins. It is a compound of the views of the members of the seminar with some perspectives of my own.

Chapter 2

⊂⊃ Origins of the War on Poverty

JAMES L. SUNDQUIST

The congressman was puzzled.

> I thought we had been working against poverty since the beginning of this country. I thought many of the programs, the Manpower Development and Training Act, vocational education, unemployment compensation, all kinds of measures of this sort were trying to keep our economy strong . . . Why, at this particular point, are we going ahead with a poverty program as such in an omnibus bill?

The question, directed by Representative Robert Taft, Jr. (R., Ohio) to Sargent Shriver during the opening hearings on the Economic Opportunity Act (EOA) in 1964, was appropriate. A few weeks earlier, in his State of the Union Message, Lyndon Johnson had added the word "poverty" for the first time to the lexicon of recognized public problems when he proclaimed, "This administration today, here and now, declares unconditional war on poverty in America." Until 1964, the word "poverty" did not appear as a heading in the index of either the *Congressional Record* or *The Public Papers of the President*. Had a new problem really been discovered? Was the War on Poverty a new idea or simply a new name for old ideas?

Sargent Shriver responded to Taft: "It is a question of timing . . . There is a time when the timing is right to bring things together to go ahead and solve the problem." [1]

This chapter is condensed and adapted from Chapter 4, "For the Poor, Opportunity," from my *Politics and Policy: The Eisenhower, Kennedy and Johnson Years* (Washington, D.C.: The Brookings Institution, 1968).

The notion that the timing was right occurred first, apparently, to John F. Kennedy. The War on Poverty did not arise, as have many great national programs, from the pressure of overwhelming public demand; the poor had no lobby. Nor was it proposed by the staff thinkers in government agencies who are paid to conceive ideas. It began when President Kennedy said to his principal economic adviser, Walter Heller, chairman of the Council of Economic Advisers (CEA), during the year-end review of economic conditions in December 1962: "Now, look! I want to go beyond the things that have already been accomplished. Give me facts and figures on the things we still have to do. For example, what about the poverty problem in the United States?" [2] That comment set in motion the staff work that, more than a year later, took concrete form as the War on Poverty.

Heller remembers that the President asked at the time for copies of *The Other America* by Michael Harrington and a study of poverty by Leon Keyserling.[3] Arthur Schlesinger, Jr., believes that Harrington's book "helped crystallize his determination in 1963 to accompany the tax cut by a poverty program" and that he was influenced also by John Kenneth Galbraith's *The Affluent Society*. By the spring of 1963, writes Schlesinger, Kennedy

was reaching the conclusion that tax reduction required a comprehensive structural counterpart, taking the form, not of piecemeal programs, but of a broad war against poverty itself. Here perhaps was the unifying theme which would pull a host of social programs together and rally the nation behind a generous cause.[4]

The key words are those that express Kennedy's dissatisfaction with the nature, scope, and accomplishments of his, and his party's, program as it stood in 1962—his desire "to go beyond," his concern with "the things we still have to do," the reference to "piecemeal programs," the feeling that something "broad" was required. One can read in these phrases the normal yearning of an idealist for ideas, of an activist for action, or the search of a politician facing a re-election campaign for a measure that will dramatize his principles and bear his name. But they express also an attitude that had become pervasive in the Washington climate as the Kennedy administration entered its third year, a feeling that the "New Frontier" was made up mainly of old frontiers already crossed and that all of those old frontiers, all of the innovations conceived over the course of a generation and written into law, would not, singly or collectively, change the gray face of the "other America." The Kennedy piecemeal programs, built on those of his predecessors, were reaching toward the substratum of the population in which all the problems were concentrated but somehow not making contact, not on a scale and with an impact that measured up to the bright promise of a New Frontier. The measures enacted, and those proposed, were dealing separately with such problems as slum housing, juvenile delinquency, unemployment, dependency, and illiteracy, but they were separately inadequate because they were striking only at some of the surface aspects of a bedrock problem, and that bedrock problem had to be identified and defined so that it could be attacked in a concerted, unified, and innovative way. Perhaps it was Harrington's book that identified the target for Kennedy and supplied the coordinating concept; the bedrock problem, in a word, was "poverty." Words and concepts determine programs; once the target was reduced to a single word, the timing became right for a unified program. That the word itself embodied various definitions, each leading logically to its own line of attack, only became apparent as the War on Poverty developed.

FAILURE AND FERMENT

The sense of failure had grown among participants in each of the major fields of public action that reached most deeply into the lives of the poor, among persons concerned with how poor people lived, how they worked, how they survived when they did not work, and how they conducted themselves in relation to the rest of the community—in other words, housing, structural unemployment, welfare, and crime and delinquency. Welfare programs were not decreasing the incidence of dependency; indeed, they seemed to be compounding it, as dependent daughters grew up to be dependent mothers in what Oscar Lewis has labeled the "culture of poverty." The rise in the volume and the violence of youth crime revealed in terrifying terms that programs to fit slum children for the middle-class world were falling short. Urban renewal, like public housing before it, had proved to be no solution; it was merely pushing the poor from one slum to another. The latest and most heralded measure to combat structural unemployment—retraining of the jobless—was foundering on the fact that many, perhaps even most, of the hard-core unemployed lacked even the basic qualifications to enter training.

Traditionally, the reflex action to failure on the part of each profession had been to demand more and better-trained professionals: teachers, social workers, counselors, policemen, probation officers, and others. But somewhere within or on the edge of each profession were those who said that more of the same was not enough, that new methods and new approaches were needed, too. The private foundations, as well as federal agencies with funds for research, listened to those who urged that new ideas be tested, and the result was an interacting sequence of theory, experiment, and demonstration that produced new strategic and tactical concepts for what became the War on Poverty.

In the atmosphere of dissatisfaction and criticism in each field, the streams of innovative thought and action arose, grew, and gained momentum. No one can say how much of the new thought and experimentation had made an impression directly on President Kennedy by 1962 or 1963, but some of it had been sponsored or subsidized by the Federal Government, and as a senator and as chief executive he had undoubtedly brushed up against it. Certainly, many of his close advisers had—including his brother, Attorney General Robert F. Kennedy, who was chairman of the President's Committee on Juvenile Delinquency and Youth Crime. In any case, the sense of failure and the resulting ferment created the intellectual climate in which the War on Poverty was born; they made the timing right. And when the War on Poverty took form, those streams converged and provided most of the new program components that gave it substance.

STREAM ONE: MENTAL HEALTH DISCOVERS
"THE SICK COMMUNITY"

President Eisenhower first expressed the Federal Government's concern with juvenile delinquency in a message to Congress on the subject of health.[5] That may seem odd, but nothing could be more symbolic of the way in which the problem was regarded. Juvenile delinquents were, in one way or another, sick. They were deviants from the healthy norm. Their moral or emotional sickness should be, like a physical sickness, diagnosed—the earlier the better—and then treated.

The President's proposal, submitted to Congress in January 1955, was for a national program of grants to the states to assist them in combating juvenile delinquency, at an annual federal cost of $5 million. The grants had been recommended by a national conference on the problem, called by Health, Education and Welfare (HEW) Secretary Oveta Culp Hobby at the suggestion of the Children's Bureau. So minor a bill, costing so little, and traveling under so hallowed a banner as child welfare, might have been expected to have smooth sailing. But such was not to be the case. The Eisenhower measure, and a competitive one sponsored by Democratic senators, became bogged down in a whole series of conflicts—between the Children's Bureau and HEW, between private and public welfare agencies, between the Democratic Senate and the Republican administration, and between liberal Democrats and their conservative elders in the House—that lasted throughout the Eisenhower years.

But the years that were devoid of legislative product saw progress of another sort. Out of the biennial testimony of professionals and theoreticians, the redrafting and refinement of competitive bills, and the pulling and hauling of public and private interest groups came a gradual shift in concepts and approaches. Implicit in the 1955 bill had been the assumption that existing state and local programs were wisely conceived; all that was needed was more money. By 1960, the emphasis was on research and demonstration, on the need for new approaches. And the language of medicine—early detection, diagnosis, and treatment of the individual case—had given way in large part to the language of community organization. Dr. Leonard S. Cottrell of the Russell Sage Foundation painted the contrast vividly in congressional testimony in 1960:

. . . the treating of a delinquent as a sick person who infects others with sickness is an important arm of treating delinquency. We have got to treat more people and finance more clinical guidance and better trained teachers . . . But, beyond that, and what we have not yet learned to do, is to treat the sick community as such. That is to say, we need skillful persons who can mobilize the resources in the community.

. . . It would be a grave mistake—and I repeat, a grave mistake . . . to think that you are going to deal or cope with this problem effectively if all that you can offer is an individual approach in psychology, psychiatry, and social work treatment.[6]

In the same year, Richard Cloward and Lloyd Ohlin of the Columbia University School of Social Work published a slim volume that laid the theoretical base for those who espoused the community-organization approach. In *Delinquency and Opportunity,* Cloward and Ohlin analyzed juvenile delinquency not as individual pathology but as community pathology and saw the delinquent not as a deviant but as a conformist, one who conformed to the patterns of a subculture that was as a whole deviant. The source of the trouble was not to be found in the individual or even in the subculture but in "the social systems in which these individuals or groups are enmeshed." The target must be "the social setting that gives rise to delinquency." The major effort should be directed toward "the reorganization of slum communities." The Columbia sociologists already had found the means to put their ideas to the test. Under the leadership of the Henry Street settlement house, an organization called Mobilization for Youth (MFY) had been formed on Manhattan's Lower East Side. MFY engaged Cloward and Ohlin to develop a research design, obtained a two-year planning grant from the National Institute of Mental Health, and retained the two sociologists as consultants in the administration of the grant.

Within a week of the 1960 election, President-elect Kennedy and Robert Kennedy asked an old friend and campaign associate, David Hackett, to organize the administration's efforts against juvenile delinquency. Hackett arranged a conference of experts on March 16. Among those present was Ohlin. Hackett later remarked, "I quickly learned from the March meeting that you can't get consensus among professionals, so I had to pick one of the best and rely on his judgment." He picked Ohlin.[7]

By 1963, the work of the President's Committee on Juvenile Delinquency and Youth Crime had become, in the words of one observer, "a $30 million test of Ohlin's 'opportunity theory.' "[8] The committee awarded research grants to MFY and to organizations in a dozen other communities for developing comprehensive plans of community organization to attack the causes of juvenile delinquency. The definition of comprehensiveness might vary among communities, but a community's program should "have identified many sources of the problem and have proposed to seek changes in many institutions." [9] No element of a comprehensive plan would be put into operation until all elements were ready to go. Because of the time required to create comprehensive organizations and prepare comprehensive plans, the committee by the end of 1963 had financed action programs only in New York City (MFY), New Haven, and Cleveland. The MFY demonstration included employment programs, work preparation, evaluation and guidance, skills training, anti-discrimination activities, remedial education, home visits, and neighborhood-service centers that provided an array of services.

STREAM TWO: URBAN RENEWAL DISCOVERS PEOPLE

By 1959, the old city of New Haven, Connecticut, had already become celebrated as the country's pacemaker in urban renewal. Under the restless leadership of a mayor, Richard C. Lee, who was himself a product of the city's working-class neighborhoods, New Haven had laid out a ten-year plan to become the nation's first city to be completely rid of slums. New Haven quickly achieved—and still holds—the distinction of winning more federal urban-renewal grant money, on a per capita basis, than any other city. To the more timid of his contemporary mayors Lee demonstrated that the bold rebuilding of an entire city was good politics, too: He had been re-elected each two years with increasing majorities and his 65 per cent of the vote in 1957 represented a margin even greater than the city had given Franklin Roosevelt.

It was perhaps to be expected, then, that New Haven would emerge again as the most imaginative of American cities when Mayor Lee turned his attention to the deterioration of the social structure, as distinct from the physical structures, of New Haven's slums. As elsewhere, urban renewal had begun in New Haven as an effort to revive the city's central business district and build its revenue base. But with the clearance of the first slum in 1956, "the 120 families who lived there thrust their miseries for the first time before the eyes of the city." [10] Funds were obtained for a social worker to counsel the displaced families, and he and the director of the redevelopment agency, Edward Logue, began to talk of the need to combine with the comprehensive physical redevelopment of the city an equally comprehensive and concentrated effort to deal with the social problems of the slums.

Meanwhile, the thinking within America's largest philanthropic organization, the Ford Foundation, had undergone a corresponding evolution. The foundation had taken an interest in urban problems and in reforms like urban renewal, but the head of its public-affairs program, Paul N. Ylvisaker, had come to the same conclusion as Logue: that the weakness of urban renewal was that it did little or nothing for the displaced. Ylvisaker began to protest "dealing with cities as though they were bricks without people . . . trying with massive programs to perfect physical form and material function while merely dabbling and extemporizing with the city's humane and civilizing purpose . . ." [11] As early as 1957, he was looking for a new and broader approach to the social as well as the physical problems of the urban "gray areas."

Hearing of Ylvisaker's interest, Logue met with him in December 1959 and was encouraged to develop a specific proposal. New Haven's planning was delayed, but eventually, in April 1962, its application for funds was approved. During the interval, Oakland, California, whose interest originated in a concern with juvenile delinquency, had moved ahead of New Haven to obtain the first Ford grant. Later in 1962, Boston and Philadelphia joined the program, and in 1963 a state-wide program was initiated in North Carolina under the leadership of Governor Terry Sanford. These five projects, which made up the foundation's "Community Development Program," had been awarded a total of $12.1 million.

Except for Oakland, where the city was the recipient, each grant was made to a new corporation designed to coordinate all agencies in the community, public and private, whose activities impinged upon the poor. The specific activities to be financed were agreed upon by the community sponsors and the foundation staff. In theory, the community agencies made their own analyses of the problems and proposed the remedies, but in fact they had a sharp ear for suggestions as to what was most likely to be approved.[12]

The community-action agency, which was to become the central instrument of the War on Poverty, was thus brought into being, not deliberately but inductively—and reluctantly. Said Ylvisaker in 1963:

We would have preferred not to have been party to the creation of still another community agency . . . But in three of the four culminating experiments we have helped launch . . . the only way open to fulfilling the broad objectives . . . was the building of a new instrumentality.

There is some feeling that this decision to establish new instrumentalities is an attack on the present system of community health and welfare councils. If so, it came not by intent nor with malice, but as a commentary on the gap that exists between the job to be done and the capacity of our urban communities as presently structured to accomplish it.[13]

When Abraham A. Ribicoff was Governor of Connecticut, he was as disturbed as every other budget-conscious governor by the steadily rising costs of public welfare. Since 1956, state and local expenditures classified under that heading had risen relentlessly at the rate of $300 million a year—from $3.1 billion to $4.7 billion in five years. Federal expenditures for public assistance had been rising at about the same 10 per cent annual rate, going from $1,558 million to $1,969 million in the 1957–1959 period alone.

Even before being sworn in as President Kennedy's first Secretary of HEW Ribicoff had promised a complete restudy of the federal public-assistance programs. President Kennedy reiterated the promise in his economic message of February 2, 1961. They had a special reason for the promise: The President was requesting at this very time a further liberalization of aid to dependent children—the category accounting for a large part of the total increase in public-assistance costs—by extending it to children of able-bodied but unemployed parents. As soon as that measure was passed, early in 1961, Secretary Ribicoff appointed twenty-three leaders in the social welfare field to an "Ad Hoc Committee on Public Welfare."

Hardly had the committee met when the subject of welfare hit the headlines. The depressed Hudson River town of Newburgh, New York, announced a thirteen-point crackdown on "welfare chiseling," aimed largely at what were described as "undesirable newcomers" to the city. The Newburgh actions, sponsored by City Manager Joseph McD. Mitchell, were denounced by Governor Nelson Rockefeller's state board of social welfare as violating state laws and regulations, contravening the "cumulative wisdom and experience" of the years in welfare administration, and infringing on the constitutional rights of welfare recipients. It accused Newburgh of embarking on a "publicity campaign" and added caustically: "Newburgh may have some governmental problems but public welfare is not one of them." Governor Rockefeller personally backed up his welfare board with a statement endorsing "the human values underlying our social welfare laws." But Senator Barry Goldwater hailed the Mitchell action as "refreshing as breathing the clear air of my native Arizona" and invited Mitchell to a well-publicized meeting in Washington. "I'm tired of professional chiselers walking up and down the streets who don't work and have no intention of working," said Goldwater after the conference.[14]

Secretary Ribicoff's ad hoc committee saw a chance to turn the Newburgh ruckus to constructive use. As practitioners in the field of social work, its members were convinced that the road to reducing the incidence of family breakdown and dependency lay through the expansion, upgrading, and more intensive use of their profession. In 1956, the profession had succeeded in writing into the law a provision that covered within federal matching provisions the cost of state services aimed at helping public-assistance recipients achieve "self-care," independence, and more stable family life. But the provision had been little used by the states except in experiments and demonstrations.[15] Now, in the glare of Newburgh, the committee took the occasion to place heavy emphasis on the need to accompany financial assistance with adequate rehabilitative services. Otherwise, said its report, delivered in September, such expenditures "may actually increase dependency and eventual costs to the community." Individual states and localities had "convincingly demonstrated" that skilled rehabilitative services could return a large number of families to self-support. "The application of these findings should be extended to recipients in all parts of the country. This cannot be done without greatly increasing the numbers of qualified staff." The committee endorsed community work programs within the context of rehabilitation and with appropriate safeguards to placate organized labor.

During the fall, the report's central ideas were incorporated by HEW into "The Public Welfare Amendments of 1962." Rehabilitation was the focus of the bill. The "community work programs" of the report were converted under the guidance of Wilbur Cohen, an assistant secretary, into "community work and training," with carefully worded safeguards. The Bureau of Public Assistance became the Bureau of Family Services. When President Kennedy sent the bill to Congress, he said that

public welfare . . . must be more than a salvage operation . . . Its emphasis must be directed increasingly toward prevention and rehabilitation— on reducing not only the long-range cost in budgetary terms but the long-range costs in human terms as well . . . The prevention of future adult poverty and dependency must begin with the care of dependent children.

Anticipating the rhetoric of the War on Poverty, he said the goal must be "to create economic and social opportunities for the less fortunate." In communities in which rehabilitation had been tried, he said, "relief rolls have been reduced." [16]

Speaking for the National Social Welfare Assembly, Robert E. Bondy saw the shift in emphasis as epoch-making:

. . . the Social Security Act, back in the mid-1930's, was a landmark, the opening of a new epoch in making minimum provision for the care of people in need. Likewise, the enactment of H.R. 10032 will open another epoch, the epoch of prevention and rehabilitation.

This is a shift in emphasis from public assistance as the center of our American plan for care of people to that of helping people to help themselves to independence and self-sufficiency with public assistance as an indispensable resource to that end.[17]

The reorientation of the country's welfare programs encountered no opposition in Congress in 1962—as it had not in 1956. "The most far-reaching revision of our Public Welfare program since it was enacted in 1935," President Kennedy called the measure.

STREAM FOUR: RETRAINING DISCOVERS ILLITERACY

By 1961, politicians who disagreed on every other subject were in consensus on one point: The unemployed must be retrained. Liberals who favored government spending to create jobs looked on retraining as a necessary *supplement* to enable the unemployed to fill the jobs. And conservatives who preached "fiscal responsibility" tended to seize on retraining as a *substitute* for vigorous spending measures. If the economy did not need stimulation to absorb the unemployed, they found themselves arguing, then jobs must in fact exist—if only the people out of work were competent to fill them. If the fault were not in the economic system, as the conservatives had been contending, then it must be in the people. In 1961 and 1962, accordingly, the Manpower Development and Training Act (MDTA) was written and enacted in an atmosphere of rare bipartisan harmony.

But when the MDTA had been on the statute books barely a year, its warmest supporters were acknowledging that the act was failing in one of its major purposes: It was not reaching the long-term, chronic unemployed.

"We in South Bend are disturbed," an Indiana editor testified, "because at present we know of no way to train approximately 60 per cent of our unemployed." [18]

A Michigan professor agreed: "A substantial portion of the 'hard core' unemployed are functionally illiterate and in the position where they cannot qualify for training," he told a House Subcommittee.[19]

Labor Secretary Wirtz described the retraining of the poorly educated as "one of the most intractable problems of unemployment." Twenty per cent of all the unemployed had less than an eighth-grade education, but only 3 per cent of MDTA trainees were drawn from that group. Among unemployed Negro workers, 44 per cent had completed fewer than eight years of school, but only 5 per cent of Negro trainees under MDTA were in that category.[20]

Accordingly, President Kennedy proposed in 1963 that MDTA be expanded to permit training in literacy and basic work skills in addition to the regular occupational training. The recommendation, significantly, was contained in a message on civil rights and job opportunities for Negroes sent to Congress on June 19 after a series of White House conferences on racial tension.

In the hearings on this proposal, from which the above quotations are taken, the director of the Department of Public Aid of Cook County, Illinois, which includes Chicago, gave eloquent testimony of the success of a basic education program in that city. In March 1962, the department had announced that all of the 50,000 to 60,000 able-bodied adults who were receiving general assistance would be required not only to participate in a work program but to enroll for basic education if they were functionally illiterate. The director, Raymond M. Hilliard, told the committee that compulsion had proved to be unnecessary—"the response . . . to this proffer of education had been tremendous, in fact, overwhelming." Attendance was excellent. Discipline was no problem. The "eagerness to learn . . . amazed and gratified" the teachers. Hilliard went on:

In carrying out this program, I have witnessed some deeply moving scenes. I think of the boy who brought his father for the first night and who helps him with his homework and also of the 50-year-old man writing his name for the first time and then writing it over and over again. Or there is the father of 13 who dropped out of school 38 years ago in the third grade and who entered our literacy program, and in the space of 5 months raised himself or was lifted to a point where he passed an eighth-grade examination and was awarded his elementary school diploma. On his graduation night, he remarked, "No kid of mine will ever drop out of school." He now has a good job and is also attending high school where in night classes he hopes to get a diploma in two years.

. . . I wish that you could have been with me to see 25 men go off relief in a body, at a graduation exercise of a class where they had learned to become Yellow Taxi drivers; 266 former recipients have now received this training and 215 are currently employed.

Hilliard urged a "massive attack" on illiteracy as a basic cause of dependency. On Chicago's relief rolls, he said, were "the dropouts of yesterday. And our rolls of tomorrow are going to be made up of the school dropouts of today unless we do something about it." [21]

A minority of committee Republicans, in each house, opposed the idea. But the basic concept of MDTA as an alternative to "handouts" still commanded the wide bipartisan support of the year before, and the bill was passed by a voice vote in both houses in December 1963.

One provision of the 1963 amendments lowered the minimum age for the payment of training allowances in order to induce more unemployed youth into MDTA courses. Originally, as the Democratic program for unemployment had evolved, the young were to be served primarily by another measure—the Youth Conservation Corps (YCC), which was modeled on the Civilian Conservation Corps (CCC) of the 1930s and which had passed the Senate in 1960. By 1963, however, it was clear that YCC had fallen upon difficult days. Upon sober second thought, influential persons in the Kennedy administration had come to share the reservations that had been expressed by the Republican opposition in the Senate debate in 1960: Would a YCC of up to 150,000 men—costing over half a billion dollars a year—be worth the investment? Was a period of employment and training in a national forest or national park the best preparation for a young man who, when his YCC service was ended, would be back on the city streets? Awaiting President Kennedy when he took office was a Bureau of the Budget staff paper suggesting that the CCC of depression days was not a suitable model for the 1960s. The conservation agencies championed the YCC, but President Kennedy—who had supported the proposal as a senator and as a candidate—compromised on the side of the Budget Bureau. He would support only an experimental YCC of 6,000, with another 50,000 to be employed in local public service and on-the-job training programs. The House Education and Labor Committee doubled the size of the Youth Corps, but the measure died in the House Rules Committee in 1962, and another bill proposing a somewhat larger YCC was lodged in that committee when the year 1963 ended.

THE WAR IS DECLARED

By 1963, the streams of thought and action traced above had already begun to flow together. The Ford Foundation and the President's Committee on Juvenile Delinquency, in particular, were pursuing parallel courses. When David Hackett called his meeting of experts in March 1961 to consider the Kennedy administration's approach to juvenile delinquency, it was David Hunter of the foundation who prepared the basic discussion paper. Hunter was among those who had drawn Hackett's attention to the work of MFY and introduced him to Lloyd Ohlin, who became the committee's theoretician. When the juvenile delinquency act was passed, the President's Committee made grants to each of the community groups that the foundation had brought into existence. The foundation in turn made a grant to MFY. Later, the Labor Department made grants to the same bodies for research and demonstration projects under MDTA. The committee and the foundation were agreed, too, on the organizational approach to combating poverty: a coordinating body that would have the power, through the leverage of money, to mobilize and redirect the energies of existing public and private bodies. Thus, before the War on Poverty was declared, some highly organized preliminary skirmishing was underway. MFY, New Haven's Community Progress, Inc., and their counterparts ultimately provided an arsenal of weapons for the War on Poverty—although it is fair to say that the arsenal was not really discovered until after the decision to declare war had been made.

After President Kennedy's conversation with Walter Heller in December 1962, Heller assigned one of his staff, Robert J. Lampman, to assemble the available data on poverty in the United States. In the press of current business (the tax cut battle was then beginning) the subject did not have high priority, but by May, Lampman had prepared an analysis of income statistics that revealed a "drastic slowdown in the rate at which the economy is taking people out of poverty." During the years between 1956 and 1961, the proportion of families with money incomes under $3,000 had declined by only 2 percentage points—from 23 to 21 per cent. The absolute number of families living in poverty had actually risen. Heller sent the memorandum to the President.

A month later, Heller was stimulated to further action by an article in the New York *Herald Tribune* reporting that the Republicans were planning an anti-poverty program. At that point, he asked Lampman and others to consider what might constitute "a practical Kennedy anti-poverty program." He sent their response to the President and received encouragement to proceed. During the summer, the CEA staff continued to analyze the problem of poverty statistically and conceptually, and as early as August had in draft a proposed chapter on the topic for the 1964 Economic Report of the President.

As the time came, in the fall, to crystallize the 1964 legislative program, the President's decision became firm. Sorensen says that Kennedy "started us working" on a "comprehensive, coordinated attack on poverty" more than a month before he went to Dallas—or some time in October.[22] Schlesinger details a series of specific instances in October and November indicating that the President had decided that an assault on poverty "would be the centerpiece in his 1964 legislative recommendations." [23] "By October," recalls Heller, "President Kennedy had given us a green light to pull together a set of proposals for a 1964 attack on poverty." [24] He believes that two articles by Homer Bigart in *The New York Times* describing distress in eastern Kentucky may have triggered the President's decision; at the least, the articles led Kennedy to initiate a "crash" program to mobilize federal resources to alleviate conditions in that region during the coming winter. Also among the influences bearing upon Kennedy in these months must have been the civil rights movement. "The demonstrations that we are seeing in the streets today are ones fostered by despair and hopelessness," was the way Whitney Young put it some months later.

On November 19, Kennedy gave Heller a flat "yes" to the question whether anti-poverty measures would be in the 1964 legislative program and asked to see the measures themselves in a couple of weeks.

Acting on the October "green light" from the President, Heller began to canvass the government for specific anti-poverty proposals. Heller's memorandum to the departments and agencies identified three approaches: to prevent entry into poverty, to promote exits from poverty, and to alleviate the difficulties of persons who cannot escape from poverty. For the moment, the proposed program was labeled "Widening Participation in Prosperity," a concession to those who thought the word "poverty" had a negative tone and would offend those whom the program was designed to help. Budget Bureau, CEA, and White House staff were in the midst of a review of the departmental responses when they were interrupted by the news from Dallas.

President Johnson lost no time in restoring their momentum. At his first meeting with Heller on November 23, Johnson said, "That's my kind of program . . . Move full speed ahead." [25] There remained, however, the all-important question of what the legislation would contain. The Budget Bureau staff distilled out of the agency suggestions thirty-five major possibilities, some of which were already pending on Capitol Hill in one or another form. But in mid-December, according to one participant, the bureau was still "floundering" in search of a theme and a rationale that would distinguish the new legislation, as dramatically as possible, from all that had gone before: the Area Redevelopment Act, MDTA, Appalachia, the Public Welfare Amendments of 1962, the YCC, the pending proposal for a National Service Corps (the so-called "domestic peace corps" that Kennedy had proposed), and all the rest. What was the new element that would mobilize all of these efforts into the "comprehensive coordinated attack" that Kennedy had been seeking? And how should the funds be concentrated to get the most results?

In November, David Hackett, of the President's Committee on Juvenile Delinquency and Youth Crime, had tossed into CEA's collection of ideas a suggestion that community organizations like those his committee had been assisting be utilized as instruments in the War on Poverty. Hackett and his associate, Richard W. Boone, had subsequently discussed their idea with Heller and his staff. But they were thinking, at that stage, of the kind of cautious experimentation that had characterized the work of the President's committee, with comprehensive studies to be made in a limited number of carefully chosen demonstration areas before legislation was even proposed.

Credit for seeing that in this proposal might lie the rationale and the new idea that the bureau was so frantically seeking is given to William B. Cannon of the Budget Bureau staff. Cannon suggested in a memorandum that ten demonstration areas be selected and that a "development corporation" be formed in each. In these areas, federal funds would be provided for a wide range of programs, with the corporation to plan the programs, expend the funds, and provide the coordinating mechanism. This scheme would solve several problems at once. It would introduce a distinctive and highly visible new element—the development corporation. It would resolve the immediate problem of selecting from among the battery of new programs being advanced by the competing government agencies—the corporations would make the selection. And it would meet a criterion advanced by Assistant Budget Director Charles L. Schultze that poverty funds should, for maximum effectiveness, be concentrated geographically in "pockets of poverty" rather than spread thinly across the country.

In the course of a single week, in mid-December, aid to community organizations was transformed from an incidental idea in the War on Poverty into the entire war. The Budget Bureau staff first assigned for the purpose $100 million of the $500 million that had been set aside in the budget to finance the anti-poverty legislation, but a few days later they had committed the whole amount. Schultze had endorsed the idea to Budget Director Kermit Gordon, with a note that a better name than "development corporation" was needed. The phrase "action program" was found buried in Cannon's original memorandum; somebody put the word "community" in front, and the name was born.

The advocates of community action, uneasy while the matter rested on Gordon's desk, turned to Paul Ylvisaker for reinforcement. Ylvisaker called Gordon and argued from the Ford Foundation experience that, in effect, "this is the way you should spend your money," and he brought the administrators of several of the Ford-sponsored community-action agencies to Washington for a breakfast meeting with the budget staff. At that meeting, the staff's acceptance of community action was clinched; they presently persuaded a skeptical Gordon, and he and Heller in turn convinced President Johnson. So the President, in his State of the Union Message, declared "unconditional war," and the budget contained the original $500 million for community action plus about an equal amount that would be provided in other appropriations but spent through community-action programs. "I propose a program which relies on the traditional time-tested American methods of organized local community action to help individuals, families, and communities to help themselves," he said in his budget message. Locally initiated, comprehensive community-action programs would be developed to "focus" federal, state, and local resources and services (health, housing, welfare, and agricultural services were specifically named) "on the roots of poverty in urban and rural areas."

The report of CEA presented the statistics and economics of poverty and the rationale of the proposed strategy with an eloquence and passion that is surely unmatched in the two decades of economic reports. As a "strategy against poverty," the council enumerated many measures: tax reduction, civil rights legislation, regional development programs, urban and rural rehabilitation, improvement of the federal-state employment service, better educational services, the pending youth-employment act, health measures, adult education and training, and medicare for the aged. But existing and new resources would be marshaled into a "coordinated and comprehensive attack" through community-action programs.

Meanwhile, the Budget Bureau, CEA, and White House staffs were laboring to refine the community-action concept. When they discovered the idea in mid-December—suddenly, fortuitously, and almost too late—they did not know, and had no time to find out, just how community action was in fact working in Manhattan, New Haven, and elsewhere. They were sufficiently aware of a confusion of doctrine, however, to recommend that the program begin on an experimental scale in a limited number of communities. Marris has identified three distinct and conflicting "strategies of reform" that were then being followed.[26] One, exemplified by the Ford projects, sought to work through existing institutions—the local government, the school system, the private social agencies—with the hope that they would be influenced through coordinated planning. Another, of which MFY was the prototype, went behind the "power structure" to organize the poor to assert and defend their own interests, but "as Mobilization for Youth discovered . . . the support of protest can bring a crushing revenge from the institutions upon whose cooperation the programs depend." The third strategy, adopted by the President's Committee on Juvenile Delinquency and Youth Crime, put its faith in the application of knowledge, through comprehensive planning, with the risk that planning might never lead to action. Along these three paths, community action was groping toward a doctrine. Some of the experiments had been set back severely by community controversy. The theory of community action could be described, in late 1963, as filled with promise but by no means either tested or proved. Both Ylvisaker and Hackett were moving with great care, city by city, with months of consultation and review preceding every grant.

The planners of the President's community-action program did not choose among the divergent strategies; insofar as they recognized the divergence, they recognized, also, that no one pattern would fit all communities. An outline of staff thinking as of January 21 specified only that a community should have, preferably, a single organization or official with authority to coordinate public and private efforts. It did not specify how the organization should be created or whom it should represent. It made no mention of organizing the poor for self-assertion. It compromised the issue of planning versus action by requiring a comprehensive plan but permitting initiation, during the planning period, of some action programs. Of the $500 million, it set aside $50 million to finance planning, $275 million to finance grants to communities for new programs, and $175 million to supplement existing federal programs in community-action areas. As for content, the emphasis was on children and youth—where the poverty cycle could best be broken—and on services that would help young people develop their capabilities, particularly improvement of health, education, training, welfare, rehabilitation, and related services.

This entire approach had at least one vigorous dissenter—Labor Secretary W. Willard Wirtz. In a memorandum responding to the January 21 outline, Wirtz said that improvement of health and education services, while desirable, would produce no immediate visible results. Poverty was, by definition, lack of income. Income came from jobs. To have impact among the poor, the War on Poverty must begin with immediate, priority emphasis on employment. Fresh from another battlefront—the war on structural unemployment—Wirtz could find in the community-action program few new jobs apart from summer and part-time employment for students working their way through school.

Throughout December and January, also, the President's staff had been wrestling with a jurisdictional problem: Who would administer the community-action program? Among existing agencies, HEW would be the logical choice, but the other departments responded coldly to the notion of being coordinated by HEW. The alternative of an independent agency headed by a director reporting to the President gained support. Names, including that of Sargent Shriver, brother-in-law of the late President Kennedy and director of the Peace Corps, were put on paper. President Johnson bought the idea of an independent agency—and Shriver.

THE PROGRAM IS REASSEMBLED: THE SHRIVER PHASE

Shriver moved into his new assignment with the same verve and energy he had brought to the Peace Corps. Notified of his appointment on Saturday, February 1, he arranged to be briefed on Sunday by Heller and Gordon and convened for Tuesday an all-day meeting of presidential advisers, departmental representatives, outside experts, and long-time friends on whom he had been accustomed to try out new ideas. Wirtz and Heller were present, as were Gordon and Wilbur Cohen, Ylvisaker and Boone, Michael Harrington, and Adam Yarmolinsky, whom Shriver had already tapped to become his deputy. Some of this group, plus others borrowed from government agencies and from private organizations on a catch-as-catch-can basis, remained for varying periods as members of Shriver's task force.

The community-action idea was explained to the uninitiated at the February 4 shakedown meeting, but it emerged in a form somewhat different from its conception. Gone was the notion of a limited number of demonstration areas; it was simply not compatible with the President's rhetoric to fight an "unconditional war" on a pilot basis. Further watered down for the same reason was the idea that action programs should await the development of comprehensive, coordinated plans. The consensus was that individual-action projects called "building blocks" should go ahead where they would be consistent with the ultimate plan. Secretary Wirtz presented forcefully his plea for job-creating programs.

Shriver quickly joined Wirtz in the view that community action alone was not enough. Its victories would not come quickly; the presidential election was but nine months away, and in a year Shriver would again have to face Congress and render an accounting. Moreover, the President and the press had by this time built up expectations so vast that a one-idea, one-title bill would be a serious letdown. The very idea of a massive, coordinated attack on poverty suggested mobilizing under that banner all, or as many as possible, of the weapons that would be used. Let the community-action organizations coordinate as much as they could, but were there not other things that other organizations—including federal agencies—could be doing also?

Beginning on February 4, Shriver began the march back to the position that the Budget Bureau had left when Cannon wrote his memorandum in December. Not only were the departments and agencies given a chance to resurrect all of the proposals the Budget Bureau had buried then, but Shriver positively encouraged them to do so. Meanwhile, he cast a dragnet out to the business community, to the intellectual world, to state and local governments, and to private organizations of all kinds in the search for additional suggestions. People who might have ideas were brought in for conferences with members of the task force. Among them were Mayor Lee and Mitchell Sviridoff of New Haven, Governor Sanford of North Carolina, Mayor John Houlihan of Oakland, Hilliard of Chicago. In his testimony presenting the EOA Shriver listed 137 persons who had participated in the writing of the act. And if a new idea was presented, the burden of proof was on any listener who said it might not work.

In the ensuing weeks, the one-title bill gained five more titles. Two of them dealt with jobs. One, pressed by the Labor Department, embodied in modified form the youth-employment program that was stalled in the House Rules Committee. YCC was renamed the Job Corps, and the emphasis was placed on large "urban" training and remedial-education centers rather than on conservation camps. The local public-service program was renamed the Neighborhood Youth Corps. A third section, borrowed from a pending education bill, authorized a work program to assist college students to earn their way. The second job title authorized 100 per cent federal financing for a temporary demonstration period of the work and training programs for welfare recipients that had been authorized by the Public Welfare Amendments of 1962 but were moving slowly because of the requirement of state or local financial participation. However, a job-creation proposal reminiscent of the Works Progress Administration of the 1930s, presented at a Cabinet meeting by Shriver, was rejected by the President because it would have added to the budget (a tobacco tax was proposed to finance it) at a time when taxes were being cut.

The Department of Agriculture, arguing that a "rural title" would be tactically wise in an otherwise predominantly urban bill, won acceptance of a small-loan program for marginal farmers and rural businessmen as well as a supplementary grant program and a "land reform" scheme, both later deleted by the Congress. The Small Business Administration worked with the task force in devising an "employment and investment incentives" title. Finally, the proposed National Service Corps, which had passed the Senate by a narrow margin in 1963 but was blocked in the House Education and Labor Committee, was incorporated under a new name, Volunteers for America (subsequently changed to Volunteers in Service to America, or VISTA).[27]

The bill was thus a composite of new ideas, like community action, and long-discussed ideas, like YCC. It had something for children, something for youth, something for the adult poor. It offered something to the urban poor and something to the rural poor. It appealed to altruism, with its bold objective of wiping out poverty, and to conservatism by emphasizing that this would be accomplished not through "handouts" but through opening opportunities for people to escape poverty through their own efforts. It was an Economic *Opportunity* Act, administered by an Office of Economic *Opportunity*. And, by incorporating funds provided elsewhere in the budget, the bill added to the original $500 million another $462.5 million without increasing the budget total that the new President had been taking great pains to portray as frugal. Thus, when Shriver appeared before the House Education and Labor Subcommittee on March 17, he was able to hail his bill as both "new in the sweep of its attack" and "prudently planned" in that "it does not raise the national budget by a single dollar." The plaint of the liberals that a War on Poverty of barely $1 billion was a travesty was ignored.

The bill was deliberately drafted to grant the broadest possible discretion to the administrator. The nature of the community organization, the content of its program, the definition of the community itself, were all left vague. The states were given no role in community action except that the director of the new OEO should "establish procedures which will facilitate effective participation of the states." Nor were the cities assured any role; the community-action agency could be either public or private. The total authorization was not divided among the programs in the act. Formulas for division of funds among states and communities were broadly drawn.

THE CONGRESS AFFIRMS

Whatever history may judge to have been its legislative merits, the political merits of the War on Poverty in 1964 cannot be denied. It gave the new President, whose legislative agenda consisted otherwise of left-over Kennedy proposals, a bold and attention-getting proposal on which he could put his personal stamp. And the issue itself was peculiarly suited to the personality of Lyndon Johnson, who could talk feelingly of his first-hand knowledge of poverty in the Texas hills and recall his experience as the Texas state director of Franklin Roosevelt's National Youth Administration. It gave him the excuse to stand on the same southern courthouse steps on which Roosevelt stood and pledge himself to carry on the war on want that FDR had started.

Moreover, it put the Republicans in a dilemma. As one ruefully put it, " 'War on Poverty' is a terrific slogan, particularly in an election year. It puts doubters under the suspicion of being in favor of poverty." [28] At no point did the Republicans attack the bill head on. They condemned it as being "hastily drafted," as being "rammed through" without adequate consideration, as an "election-year gimmick," as violating the principles of federalism, as duplicating existing programs, as granting too much discretion to a poverty "czar," and so on. Peter H. B. Frelinghuysen of New Jersey, ranking Republican on the House Education and Labor Committee, drafted a substitute providing for a state-run program costing half as much, but it attracted little attention or support—not even from governors, who would have had to pay half the cost by the third year. The frustration of the Republican leaders in trying to find reasons why the Congress should reject a bill whose objectives they were compelled to endorse is evident throughout the five months' record of the congressional debate.

When the vote was tallied in the House, Johnson had held 60 of 100 southern Democrats and added 22 Republicans (20 from the Northeast) to his base of 144 solid northern and western Democratic votes. The margin was wider than expected, 226 to 185. The Frelinghuysen substitute could muster only 117 votes. In the Senate, in which the issue was never in doubt, 10 of 32 Republicans supported the administration bill. The vote was 61 to 34. In the minority was Barry Goldwater, by then the Republican presidential nominee, who underlined his opposition by signing a strongly worded two-man minority report from the Senate committee. The Republican convention adopted a plank critical of the "so-called" War on Poverty. Johnson had his victory, and the War on Poverty was underway. But it was, as it had been when declared, the administration's war, not a national war behind which the country was united.

BUT ALL IS NOT SETTLED

After Congress had acted, its members had little comprehension of what, precisely, they had done—particularly with regard to community action. Rarely has so sweeping a commitment been made to an institution so little tested and so little understood as the community-action agency. And no time was accorded Congress to find out. The contents of the proposed Act were not exposed to public discussion until March 16. The bill was rushed into hearings at once, as the Republican committee members vigorously protested, and enacted within five months. On some of the most important sections of the act, little legislative history was written, or none at all. One can search the hearings and debates in their entirety and find no reference to the controversial language regarding the participation of the poor in community-action programs. The whole novel concept of community action—the definition of the community, the nature of the community-action agency, the content of its program, all of which were to have a profound impact on federal-state-local relations and on the social and governmental structures of participating communities—was left to OEO in an exceptionally broad grant of discretion. Shriver could not have told the committees, in any case, what community action would prove to be; advocates of each of the "divergent strategies" were on his staff and the contest for supremacy was yet to be fought. But when the series of clashes between spokesmen for the poor and "the power structure" erupted in the early months of the program, members of Congress were bound to feel that in the haste of 1964 someone had pulled wool over their eyes.

What was unsettled, essentially, was the issue that had been defined in the hearings on juvenile delinquency in 1960. In the War on Poverty, as in the war on youth crime, was the target the individual or the community? Should poverty be attacked through providing opportunity or resources to the individual within the existing social setting, or was it necessary to alter that setting, as Cloward and Ohlin had argued, to heal Cottrell's "sick community," to shatter and remake Lewis's culture of poverty? If it were the former, then what was called for was community organization for the provision of individual services, a concept acceptable to the power structure of most communities. Even more simply, poverty could be erased by the payment of money to raise incomes—an idea that, in the forms it has since taken, was not seriously advanced at any point as the Act evolved. But if the problem were cultural rather than individual, then the remedies were not so clear nor so simple. If money poverty itself were to disappear, would the other evils associated with the culture of poverty remain—alienation, crime, delinquency, apathy, illiteracy, economic incompetence, family breakdown, and all the rest? If so, how would a community organize to alter the character of a subculture? Some community-action theorists contend that the means must be to organize the poor themselves to mobilize their resources under their own leadership for their own ends. But those ends inevitably involve some degree of challenge to, and confrontation with, the larger community. Can a national government maintain, for long, a program that sets minorities against majorities in communities throughout the land? The vote in the House of Representatives in 1967, which is analyzed by William Selover later in this volume, suggests that the affluent majority will be willing to finance an anti-poverty program only if the organizations of the poor are subject to the effective control of local majorities through their local governments.

Another crucial ambiguity concerns the place of the War on Poverty in the array of the country's national goals, a place that tends to determine the role of OEO in the Federal Government structure and the role of the community-action agency in the community. Did the nation establish an overriding objective to which other objectives—and sometimes long-existing—were to be subordinated or merely adopt one more government program known as "the poverty program," or something in between? President Johnson's message to Congress on March 16, 1964, defined the War on Poverty broadly. The Act was the "foundation," but the President mentioned other proposals—from area redevelopment to medicare to aid to education—and said poverty "cannot be driven from the land by a single attack on a single front." To avert "a series of uncoordinated and unrelated efforts," he was proposing to create OEO in the Executive Office of the President, headed by his "personal chief of staff for the War on Poverty . . . Sargent Shriver."

As the weeks went by, however, the concept underwent a gradual and subtle shift. Less was heard of the War on Poverty and more of the "poverty program." And the latter had a much narrower definition, usually confined to the activities that happened to be authorized in the Act.[29] Then the phrase War on Poverty began to take on the narrower definition. Facing innumerable difficulties in getting under way the three novel and controversial programs OEO itself administered—the Job Corps, community action, and VISTA— Shriver had little opportunity to develop his role as coordinator of the "war" as a whole, whatever its total scope was conceived to be. The centrifugal forces within the government were stronger than the centripetal. OEO became, essentially, one more among many operating agencies of the government and the "poverty program" one more (or three more) in the long series of government programs.

In the communities, similarly, almost every community-action agency had to wage a continuing fight for position against all of the established public and private agencies that it was designed to coordinate. While the pattern varied widely among the communities, the new agency appeared in many areas to have simply divided the field with its competitors, becoming one more among community institutions. The problem of coordination was not only left unsolved, it was intensified through the addition of one more institution—and one by its nature conflict-prone—to the range of those that needed to be coordinated in each community.

The distinctive contribution of the War on Poverty as an idea lay less in what it added to the battery of operating programs than in the unifying theme it provided for the activities of many governmental and private agencies and the coordinating devices that were created—OEO in the executive office of the President and the community-action agency in each community. If the national decision was for such a unified War on Poverty, what resulted has been something less. Under the pressure of program operations, the conception has steadily narrowed from the War on Poverty to the Poverty Program—threatening ultimately to add to the "series of uncoordinated and unrelated efforts" that the President, in his poverty message, had decried.

Finally, the "unconditional war on poverty" declared by the

President has proved to be highly conditional, dependent on limited annual appropriations. When budgets are tight, the hardest-to-reach are not reached. If the rate of expenditures per poor family by the community-action agency in New Haven were projected on a national scale, a sum of $10 to $13 billion annually would be required. If we accept Mitchell Sviridoff's estimate that to reach all of the poor families in New Haven the effort in that city should be tripled, the national figure for community action alone in an *unconditional* war reaches $30 to $40 billion. Appropriations for community action are a tiny fraction of that figure—and, under the pressures of Vietnam spending, are not rising. While the ideal may be unattainable, the question remains whether a War on Poverty that falls so short of the presidential rhetoric that launched it will not, ultimately, add the disillusionment of its supporters to the strength of its opponents.

Notes

1. *Economic Opportunity Act of 1964*, Hearings before the Subcommittee on the War on Poverty Program of the House Education and Labor Committee, 88th Congress, 2nd session (March 17, 1964), p. 99.

2. Quoted by Heller in a speech at Indiana State College, Indiana, Pennsylvania, March 26, 1965.

3. *Poverty and Deprivation in the United States*, Conference on Economic Progress, Washington, D.C. (April 1962).

4. Arthur H. Schlesinger, Jr., *A Thousand Days* (Boston: Houghton Mifflin, 1965), p. 1009.

5. Message of January 31, 1955, *Public Papers of the Presidents of the United States*, 1955, pp. 216–223.

6. *Report on Juvenile Delinquency*, Hearings before a Subcommittee of the House Appropriations Committee (March 10, 1960), p. 94.

7. Quoted by John Edward Moore in his case study of juvenile delinquency legislation, entitled "Controlling Delinquency: Executive, Congressional and Juvenile, 1961–64" in *Cases in Urban Legislation* (Washington, D.C.: Brookings Institution, 1968), p. 127.

8. Quoted in *ibid.*, p. 150.

9. Policy guides issued by the President's Committee on Juvenile Delinquency and Youth Crime (September 1963), p. 3.

10. Gregory Farrell, *A Climate of Change: The New Haven Story*, Urban Studies Center, Rutgers (New Brunswick, N.J.: the State University of New Jersey, 1965), pp. 3–4.

11. Speech before Citizens' Conference on Community Planning, Indianapolis, January 11, 1963.

12. Peter Marris and Martin Rein, *Dilemmas of Social Reform: Poverty and Community Action in the United States* (London: Routledge and Kegan Paul, 1967), trace the early development of the Ford Foundation projects, as well as those of the President's Committee on Juvenile Delinquency.

13. Indianapolis speech, *op. cit.*

14. *The New York Times* article, inserted in *Congressional Record,* July 21, 1961, p. 13053.

15. Charles E. Gilbert, "Policy-Making in Public Welfare: The 1962 Amendments," *Political Science Quarterly,* LXXXI (June 1966), 203.

16. Special Message on Public Welfare Programs, February 1, 1962, *Public Papers of the Presidents of the United States, 1962,* pp. 98–103.

17. *Temporary Unemployment Compensation,* Hearings before the House Ways and Means Committee, February 9, 1962, p. 331. Gilbert Y. Steiner has pointed out that the 1962 amendments actually added little of substance to the language that had been written into the law in 1956. "The great thrust on behalf of prevention and rehabilitation seems more gimmicky than substantive," he writes, adding: "Somehow the 1962 amendments got oversold somewhere along the line." *Social Insecurity: The Politics of Welfare* (Chicago: Rand McNally, 1966), pp. 40–47.

18. Testimony of Franklin D. Schurz, editor and publisher, *South Bend Tribune* and chairman of the St. Joseph County, Ind., Manpower Advisory Committee, in *Manpower Development and Training Act,* Hearings before the select subcommittee on labor of the House Committee on Education and Labor, August 15, 1963, p. 601.

19. Testimony of Ronald W. Haughton, co-director, Institute of Labor and Industrial Relations, Wayne State University, August 1, 1963, in *ibid.,* p. 399.

20. *Ibid.,* p. 15.

21. *Ibid.,* pp. 444–448.

22. Theodore C. Sorensen, *Kennedy* (New York: Harper & Row, 1965), p. 753.

23. Schlesinger, *op. cit.,* p. 1012.

24. Heller speech, *op. cit.*

25. *Ibid.*

26. Peter Marris, "The Strategies of Reform." Paper delivered to the Conference on Community Development, San Juan, Puerto Rico, December 1964.

27. Two more programs were added by the House Committee: A basic adult literacy program taken from a pending education bill and a program to provide services for migratory laborers and their families, taken from a series of Senate-passed bills pending in the Committee.

28. Representative Charles B. Hoeven of Iowa, *Congressional Record,* August 6, 1964, p. 18315.

29. This terminology varied, too. In the entry entitled "poverty" in the *Encyclopedia Americana* of 1965, written by Sargent Shriver, the "War on Poverty" is described as originally embracing "three major parts"—tax reduction, civil rights, and the "poverty program." The "poverty program," however, is defined more broadly than EOA. While the terms are general, the program would clearly include such related activities as Appalachia and MDTA.

Chapter 3

☭ *The Beginnings of OEO*

ADAM YARMOLINSKY

It is always difficult to mark the point at which an idea becomes a program for social change. In the Kennedy-Johnson anti-poverty program, that point may have come on the evening of February 2, 1964, when the authors of the first draft of the legislative proposals for the War against Poverty met across a table in the government-green-painted Peace Corps conference room with the man who would have the responsibility for taking the program to the Congress and putting it into operation. Kermit Gordon, the director of the Bureau of the Budget, and Walter Heller, the chairman of the Council of Economic Advisers (CEA), had been assigned by President Kennedy, some time before his assassination, to develop a program for a comprehensive new approach to the problem of poverty in the United States; $500 million had been set aside in the budget for this purpose. The previous day, President Johnson had persuaded Sargent Shriver, just back from an around-the-world trip as director of the Peace Corps, to take on the added assignment of Special Assistant to the President to handle the Poverty Program, and the President had announced this assignment at a press conference the previous afternoon.

THE TASK FORCE OF THE WAR AGAINST POVERTY

At the beginning of the evening, Charles Schultze, then an assistant director of the Bureau of the Budget, outlined the premises of the Gordon-Heller program:

1. The program should be designated to get at the root causes of poverty, not to ameliorate its consequences. Without explicit statement,

these root causes were taken to be the lack of capacity or opportunity to earn a decent living, rather than the simple lack of money. Emphasis would be on education and improving family environment. Measures to maintain economic prosperity (like a tax cut) were thought to be an essential condition for the program, but not a part of it.

2. Poverty had to be attacked in the neighborhoods where it was concentrated. Existing or proposed additional categorical welfare programs were too diffuse for this purpose.

3. The effort would have to be concentrated in a limited number of subject-matter areas for it to succeed.

4. Existing federal, state, and local programs suffered because they were uncoordinated. Several different agencies might be dealing with the same family. Therefore, coordination was essential both at the federal and the state and local levels.

5. It should be assumed that the primary responsibility for the kinds of services that had to be provided would continue to be state and local.

In the light of these premises, the Gordon-Heller program proposed to use the entire half-billion dollars in a massive community-action program. The program was described as human development rather than area development, emphasizing human resources rather than, as in the Appalachian program, physical infra-structure. It was aimed at the problem of poverty in the midst of plenty, the rehabilitation of people and neighborhoods, rather than the rehabilitation of underdeveloped areas of the country. It was described as a "high risk, high pay-off" program: high risk because it departed from the traditional standards of categorical welfare programs and made great demands on individual initiative; high pay-off because it could be adapted to the specific problems of particular communities.

There was a small but solid body of experience in community action familiar to the participants in the evening's discussion and growing out of the pilot programs developed in seventeen cities by the President's Committee on Juvenile Delinquency and Youth Crime. The Committee had deliberately chosen to move slowly from plan to action, believing that planning itself served to educate the community and mobilize community resources more effectively. It had therefore suffered a certain amount of prodding from at least one articulate and irascible member of Congress. Earlier community-action projects had first been pioneered by the Ford Foundation's Gray Areas Program. Both programs had shared a common philosophy and developed a common body of expertise that was essential to the work of the task force.

The draft program also contemplated, as a separate piece of legislation, a $140-million special education bill to supplement state and local funds for public education in poverty neighborhoods and to be administered through the Federal Office of Education and state education departments on a traditional state-allocation formula. The activities financed under this bill were to be an adjunct of the poverty program, but not incorporated into local community-action programs. It was in a sense a precursor of the Elementary and Secondary Education Act of 1965.

The immediate reaction of Shriver and his associates to this first proposed poverty program was, "It'll never fly." Community action, they agreed, had the positive advantages of emphasizing local control rather than central direction by the federal establishment, self-help rather than handouts, and comprehensive planning rather than overlapping efforts. But a single focus on community action would not be broad enough, they felt, to encompass problems of the many different groups of the poor: urban and rural, children and teenagers, breadwinners and old people. They were particularly concerned that community action would not be able to produce the kind of concrete results in a foreseeable time period that would be required to satisfy the Congress. It would take at least a year, they estimated, on the basis of the previous experience, for a community to develop a workable plan—even longer in rural areas.

Their first effort was to try to find the other pieces that would make up a more comprehensive program and one that could, hopefully, produce enough visible results during its first year of operation to enable it to survive the first round of congressional review, since the legislation would come up for renewal at the end of its first year. A program that cannot accomplish enough to justify a second year's congressional appropriations, they pointed out, will not live to come within sight of its intended goal.

It is equally important to point out the negative premises, explicit and implicit, that were not seriously called into question in Shriver's re-examination of the Heller-Gordon proposals. The separation of area-development programs like the Appalachian Program from the Poverty Program proper was accepted and even emphasized, and the rejection of an income strategy was assumed to be politically unavoidable and only mentioned in speeches explaining that the Poverty Program was not a handout but a hand up. Even by hindsight, there seems little reason to doubt the political wisdom of the judgment—absent a deliberate decision to pursue a politically unattainable goal and then to make an election issue of a legislative defeat. That course was never, to my knowledge, considered, and hindsight makes this alternative no more attractive than the other. If a program has to show results in one year to satisfy the Congress, a fortiori an income strategy could not precede a fair trial for a jobs strategy.

PROGRAM DEVELOPMENT BY THE TASK FORCE

Shriver's search for new ideas to beef up the program began with a kind of brainstorming session two days after that Sunday evening at which he gathered scholars, foundation executives, businessmen, and pundits for a day-long discussion with a small staff he had rapidly assembled from various branches of the government. The session not only introduced into the discussion the concept of maximum feasible participation of the poor but broached the essential ideas of Headstart, Upward Bound, and the rehabilitation of draft rejectees.

Because of the paucity of literature on the problem of poverty in an advanced society and what to do about it (an early bibliography prepared by Robert Lampman of the University of Wisconsin ran less than two pages), the conferees started almost from scratch. There was the pioneering experience with the idea of community action, and there was a text, the chapter on poverty in the Economic Report of CEA, published in the preceding month. The 1964 report, focused for the first time on poverty in the midst of plenty, struck a number of notes that reverberated through the subsequent discussion of the issue.

Its choice of an income definition for poverty—the $3,000 family income as roughly the poverty line—settled that question initially almost without argument. Its emphasis on building earning power as the way out of poverty, through better education and health, training, job placement, and community and area rehabilitation, formed the central theme of the poverty program and gave second place to the provision of more adequate social services for those who could not prepare to support themselves. "Economic Independence Act" was the first tentative title of the proposed legislation, and "Economic Opportunity Act" struck the same note. A number of other ideas in the report became major themes in the development and discussion of the poverty program itself: the alienation of the poor; the hidden character of the problem at that time; the generational nature of poverty, breeding on itself, handed down from parent to child; and the disproportionate impact of poverty on special groups, such as Negroes, and households headed by women (the link between these two groups was not yet underlined) . In many respects, the report was quite optimistic (at least by 1968 standards) , as in its discussion of the expected effects of better formal education; and the Poverty Program reflected the same optimism.

The task force did not lack for exposure, however, to the more radical and less cheerful vein of thought about the problems of poverty. Writers like Michael Harrington and Paul Jacobs took part in the early deliberations of the group, stressing the need for major— but largely unspecified—changes in American society. Their attitudes, however, had remarkably little operational impact on the program, perhaps because they themselves were not inclined to think in operational terms. It may be that the Harringtons and the Jacobses had done their job by calling people's attention to the problem of poverty in America in a way that could not be ignored.

Another source of ideas for the task force was in the proposals, emanating particularly from the Department of Labor, that had not been picked up by the Heller-Gordon team during the fall and early winter. These included the suggestion that the school-leaving age be raised from sixteen to eighteen, that a major public-employment program be undertaken, to be financed by an additional five-cent cigarette tax, and that the annual Defense-appropriations rider prohibiting any differentials in Defense contracts to cover additional costs of placing Defense contracts in depressed areas be removed. None of these ideas survived the initial competition, however. Raising the school-leaving age was thought likely by itself only to increase the number of dropouts; nor was there any readily available federal leverage on this issue of traditionally state and local policy. A massive public-works program, financed by a special tax, was thought politically impossible while the Congress was still debating the administration's proposed tax cut, and its proponents had not really faced up to the issue of matching the new jobs in such a program to the people who needed them. Lastly, the proposed removal of the

Defense-appropriations rider was doubtful economics and impossible politics.

The Shriver task force set about to look for one program that could express the central idea of preparing poor people to do the kind of work for which society would pay them a decent wage. They found it, or thought they had found it, in the idea that was to become the Job Corps—offering school dropouts a chance to live, learn, and work in a completely new environment in which they would be prepared for a productive role in society. The choice of the Job Corps carried with it a number of decisions about priorities. The Poverty Program had to serve a wide variety of groups, but it could not serve them all equally, and priorities had to be assigned.

If a poor person was one who lacked either the capacity or the opportunity to make an adequate contribution to society, so that society could give him an adequate reward for his contribution, then the task force had to decide whether to give priority to providing new opportunities or to improving people's abilities; they had to decide whether the proposed legislation should begin by preparing people for jobs or by preparing jobs for people. They chose to begin by preparing people for jobs, in part because this was thought to be the less difficult task and in part because it was thought that the first increment of new jobs would come from the proposed tax cut, which was part of the same legislative program. As the President's March 16 message, transmitting the proposed Act of 1964, declared: "Our tax cut will create millions of . . . new exits from poverty, but we must also strike down all the barriers which keep many from using those exits." While the jobs created by the tax cut were picking up the first wave of newly trained people, new programs could be developed and launched for the second wave of qualified job applicants who would not be ready for some time.

The task force chose also to focus on young people in the age group between 17 and 21, those who had already dropped out of school but had not yet found their way into the labor market. The decision to concentrate on this age group was triggered not so much by their potential for violence, which had not yet become apparent (the first long hot summer had not begun), but by these young people having clearly identified themselves as needing help; hopefully, they could be saved before they continued the poverty cycle through yet another generation.

But it was not enough to have a priority target. From the outset, the task force concentrated on a number of specific groups within the poverty population. The first congressional presentation, in mid-March, listed six such groups and briefly described them: the children of poverty, those bypassed by industrial change, rural families, minority group members, fatherless families, and the aged. The legislation as originally proposed did not contain provisions specifically addressed to each of these groups, but it did contain provisions for the Job Corps and the Neighborhood Youth Corps (NYC) (its companion program to be administered by the Department of Labor for young people who would not be assembled in resident centers but would continue to live at home). It also contained initial provisions for marginal small farmers and for small entrepreneurs who were below the poverty line (or who undertook to provide additional employment for long-term unemployed or underemployed breadwinners). Within the framework of community action, programs were developed for a variety of groups, notably preschool children. The preschool program became Project Headstart, perhaps the most favored offspring of the entire effort. At the instance of House committee members, a special program was added for migratory workers.

As the task force incorporated new elements into the over-all program, it found opportunities to pick up related administration bills that had been stalled at various stages in the legislative process and, by incorporating them, moved them along again toward enactment. The Job Corps and NYC picked up the essential ideas of the Youth Employment Opportunities Act, which had been stuck in the House Rules Committee, and made them part of the program. The VISTA Volunteer Corps (so called after several name changes left it with the grandfather of all poverty-program acronyms, Volunteers in Service to America) was intended to accomplish essentially the same purposes as the proposed National Service Corps. The National Service Corps itself had been in such bad odor in the Congress that an appropriations rider had forbidden the expenditure of any executive-branch funds to continue preparation of legislative proposals for it. The proposed Special Education Bill was incorporated into the community-action proposal, while the amount allocated for education was cut back substantially to allow for inclusion of other programs (job training, employment, health services). The program operated by the Department of Health, Education and Welfare

(HEW) to provide training and income for fathers of ADC children so that they could re-establish themselves as breadwinners was converted from a temporary to a relatively permanent status by inserting it as a separate title of the bill, initially under the stirring caption of "Family Unity Through Jobs."

By the time the bill went to the Hill in mid-March, the $500 million figure had grown to $962.5 million, without increasing the total of the President's budget, simply by taking over and incorporating other items. The program as presented to the Congress broke down as follows:

		Millions
I.	Youth-opportunity programs	$412.5
	A. Job Corps	(190.0)
	B. Work-training program	(150.0)
	C. Work-study program	(72.5)
II.	Urban and rural community-action programs	315.0
III.	Rural economic-opportunity programs	50.0
IV.	Employment and investment incentives	25.0
	A. Incentives for employment of unemployed	(25.0)
	B. Small-business loans	*
V.	Family unity through jobs	150.0
VI.	Volunteers and administration	10.0
		$962.5

* Utilized existing funding authority.

This division of funds was preserved substantially intact through the authorization process, except that a program of adult basic education, authorized at $25 million on a standard state-allocation formula, was added at the behest of Congressman Perkins; the program of incentives for employment of long-term unemployed was eliminated fom Title IV; and the authorization for rural programs was reduced to $35 million. Special provision was added within the over-all total for help to migrant and seasonally employed farm workers. In the appropriations process, the distribution of funds by program was not affected, although the total was cut by almost 20 per cent (from $947.5 million to $800 million) on the theory that a late start would prevent the agency from spending the full amount authorized in the first year.[1]

While it juggled hundreds of millions in program proposals, the task force struggled with its own internal poverty problem, trying to keep afloat on an operating budget of some $30,000 from the hard-pressed President's contingency fund, supplemented by borrowed people and services from other departments and volunteers from private life. It also experienced its own form of urban renewal. Starting out in three rooms temporarily vacated by traveling Peace Corps staff, the task force moved first to the magnificent old Court of Claims building, but hastily evacuated it when blasting for the foundations of a new building next door began to bring down the thirty-foot ceilings in large chunks, one contingent retreating unharmed to a former city hospital and another to an abandoned hotel.

As the legislation worked its way through the congressional committees, the public image of the program began to take shape. The tone of public pronouncements about the program had been heroic from the outset. In fact, some observers characterized it as grandiloquent. But it did reflect a confident, embattled stance on the part of the poverty warriors, who saw themselves as true soldiers of the Lord. A series of task force memoranda issued in April were headed "We Can Win the War on Poverty," "Why the Poverty Program Is a Low-Cost Program," and "Why the Poverty Program Is Not a Negro Program"—this last devoted primarily to the fact that the poverty problem in Appalachia and the Ozarks was almost entirely a white problem and in the Deep South was a white as well as a Negro problem. The crisis of the northern ghetto was simply not foreseen in anything like its present critical character by the draftsmen of the program. The business community was involved very early, through the formation of a Business Advisory Committee, looking toward the time when business would be called on to provide jobs, particularly for Job Corps graduates. An extraordinarily impressive roster of witnesses, including four Cabinet officers, as well as representatives of business, labor, and civic groups, was mustered in support of the program before the House Committee on Labor and Public Welfare.

MAJOR ISSUES BEFORE THE TASK FORCE

The issues (the majority of them) that occupied most of the time and energy of the task force during this period did not concern the over-all shape of the program; they were quite specific and involved questions more of power than of policy. In putting together the plans for the Job Corps, for example, the principal issues were the relative roles of military and civilian management; the number of corpsmen who would be sent to conservation camps, doing work on the public lands, as contrasted with the number who would be sent to urban training centers; and lastly, the propriety of using profit-making corporations as well as universities and other nonprofit organizations to manage the training centers.

None of these issues went to the substance of the Job Corps program. The original proposal contemplated that the military establishment should manage the mechanical aspects of the corps' operations: housing, feeding, and clothing large numbers of young men in temporary installations and seeing that they were moved back and forth with reasonable efficiency, so that hot meals and blankets were ready for new arrivals. It was not an unreasonable suggestion on the face of it, particularly when coupled with the notion that education and training be conducted by civilians. But it aroused violent emotional reactions in those who had been traumatized by World War II basic training, as well as in the middle echelons of the Department of Labor, which had been the principal sponsor of the proposal to establish camps under the stillborn Youth Employment Opportunities Act.

The division of resources between conservation camps, in which corpsmen would receive basic education and experience in clearing the public lands, and urban training centers, in which they might receive somewhat more advanced (high-school level) education, together with training for specific kinds of jobs at the semi-skilled level, was a proper question for manpower economists to address, although the factual basis for recommendations was limited enough to make it highly speculative. But the issue that arose was primarily between the conservationists, whose primary interest was in preserving natural resources, and the education and manpower training professionals. The issue of profit versus nonprofit management ranged the partisans of business enterprise against the champions of liberal tradition. The relative capacities of the two kinds of enterprises remained to be tested by the event.

Another problem that occupied a significant part of the energies of the draftsmen was provision for women in the Job Corps. Originally, it was assumed that the Job Corps would be limited to young men because it was typically young men rather than young women who were dropping out of school and the labor market. Young men bulked several times as large as young women in statistics of juvenile delinquency, crime, and unemployment. But young women had their feminine partisans in the Congress. With some congressional prodding, plans were quickly revised to include a substantial female contingent in the Job Corps.

Other problems that concerned the legislators and therefore preoccupied the draftsmen between March, when the bill was introduced, and August, when it was passed, included the fear that the Job Corps would act as a magnet to draw young people out of school who might otherwise continue; the possibility that Job Corps youths might be engaged in constructing and maintaining their own barracks and other facilities to the detriment of honest members of the building trades; and lastly, and continuously, the charge that Job Corps training cost more than a Harvard education—a charge that overlooked both the contribution of university endowment and the value of stronger motivation and previous training in reducing the cost of higher education.

A subsidiary issue arose as to which federal agency would conduct recruiting for the Corps—the United States Employment Service (USES), through its instrumentalities in the fifty states, operating as the single chosen instrument, or the USES in competition with other instrumentalities chartered by the new OEO to provide competition and to encourage the old-line state employment agencies to reach out for a new clientele.

In the planning for NYC, the Department of Labor was embattled on the jurisdictional question. The department felt with some conviction that just because the task force had shaken loose the essential elements of the youth-employment bill from the House Rules Committee, it was not entitled to shake loose the administration of the program as well. The conservation camps that were incorporated into the Job Corps would have been operated by Agriculture and Interior anyway, and Labor made no bid for the new resident urban training centers, but the NYC was to have been Labor's own baby, and here it stood firm. There were stormy sessions with the secretary, who began with an understandable concern over the rejection of his program suggestions by the Heller-Gordon group. Further he could not, and would not, retreat. The principal substantive issue was whether NYC should offer only employment, in effect make-work designed simply to provide stopgap income and establish minimal work habits, or employment coupled with basic education, training, and supporting services, to prepare young people for opportunities in the private sector. Again, the issue did not arise in a vacuum; if the Department of Labor were to undertake the program, it would clearly be more effective in finding jobs than in providing training; if the new OEO were to play a major role in managing the program, it might give more emphasis to training and correspondingly less emphasis to absolute numbers of young men and women employed. In the end, the Labor Department won; and jobs took primacy over training.

In developing the Community-Action Program (CAP), the task force soon found that the overarching issue turned on the involvement of parochial-school children in educational programs conducted primarily in the public schools. To what extent this problem may have bulked large because Congressman Delaney of Brooklyn was a key member of the House Rules Committee is a matter for speculation. But it is clear that there was a real issue in providing the benefits of educational programs, which were central to any over-all program of community action, to children enrolled in parochial schools without violating the constitutional prohibition against state aid to church-related institutions. The first formulation proposed by the task force contemplated that parochial-school children would be eligible as individuals to participate in additional services provided by the Poverty Program to public schools. When this formulation proved unacceptable, it was modified to permit "noncurricular" activities, that is, activities that were not part of the regular required curriculum, to be conducted in parochial schools with public funds from the Poverty Program. The amount of energy devoted to working out a solution that would be acceptable to urban congressmen with large parochial-school-parent constituencies, that at the same time would not be offensive to congressmen from fundamentalist constituencies outside the urban areas, was perhaps disproportionate to the philosophical significance of the problem itself, but indicative of the kinds of problems most intransigent in moving from ideas to action. The final formulation, relying on the distinction between curricular and noncurricular activities, may have been somewhat artificial, but it worked.

The play of forces here was characteristic. In the development of the legislation, while the legislative draftsmen felt that they had made the maximum provision for the problems of the cities, the urban congressmen were not slow to characterize the executive-branch draft as a "grits and greens" bill designed primarily to meet the problems of rural poverty in the South.

Lastly, congressmen, particularly from southern constituencies, were troubled with the possibility that community-action grants might go to local organizations newly formed to foment trouble among the downtrodden. Accordingly, they modified the legislation to require grantee organizations either to be public agencies or, if private nonprofit agencies, to have an established record of concern with the problems of the poor, or else a link to such an established record by being created by an established agency. That their elaborate protective devices proved ineffective is irrelevant to the accuracy, if not the wisdom, of their concerns. The last-minute amendment by a Mississippi congressman requiring a non-Communist oath of Job Corpsmen reflected the same motivation.

The principal issue in the proposed program of assistance to marginal small farmers was the provision of grants as well as loans to get these family units back on their feet. Grants, even when limited to a maximum of $1,500, were eventually stricken from the bill since, it was pointed out, grants were not proposed for urban slum dwellers. Broadening the rural loan authority of the Farmers' Home Administration so that it can make loans to nonfarmers and for nonfarm purposes has, however, made its loan programs substantially more effective. The Senate also struck out the task force "domestic land reform" proposal to help finance the purchase of large tracts of land for resale to tenants or sharecroppers.

Another legislative issue involved the VISTA volunteer program. The central issue here was the degree of federal as opposed to local control over the volunteers. The eventual resolution of the problem was to provide for federal recruitment, selection, and training of the volunteers, but after assignment to state and local agencies, public and private, to make them responsible to the organizations for which they were working. They were to continue to receive their subsistence pay from VISTA, but they would take their orders from their local employers. True, some of the volunteers would work on federal installations, as in the case of Job Corps tutor-counselors and teachers on Indian reservations, but the principle of local control would be established.

INTER-AGENCY COORDINATION AND
THE ROLE OF OEO

The last great issue that occupied the task force and its opposite numbers in the poverty-concerned agencies throughout the government was the issue of inter-agency coordination. In his Message to the Congress on Poverty, the President said, "I do not intend that the war against poverty become a series of uncoordinated and unrelated efforts—that it perish for lack of leadership and direction, . . . (The) Director (of the OEO) will be my personal Chief of Staff for the war against poverty." Despite some congressional concern about the creation of a poverty "czar" (Shriver insisted he was only a sergeant and disclaimed any ambition to become a czar—"Look what happened to the czars."), the provision in the draft legislation that read, "Federal agencies which are engaged in administering programs related to the purposes of this Act, . . . shall . . . cooperate with the Director in carrying out his duties and responsibilities under this Act, . . ." was left unchanged through the legislative process.

Effectuating this language, however, was less a matter of legislative draftsmanship than of negotiation among the agencies concerned. Officials from Labor, HEW, Agriculture, the Small Business Administration, and other agencies met with task-force members in prolonged sessions that were characterized by an air of somewhat strained politeness at the upper end of Pennsylvania Avenue in the Federal Triangle, while the bill was being debated at the lower end on Capitol Hill. It was clear that the Job Corps, Community Action, and VISTA volunteers would be funded and managed exclusively by the proposed new OEO. It was clear that NYC, the agricultural-loan program, and the small-business-loan program would be managed by the Labor Department, the Department of Agriculture, and the Small Business Administration, respectively, and that the work experience program would be managed by HEW. But it was not at all clear how large a role OEO, which did not yet even exist, would play in the day-to-day management or in the determination of over-all policies for these programs. Nor was it at all clear what role OEO would play in working out relationships with already-existing programs that were a part of the ongoing War against Poverty.

A comprehensive community-action program, for example, presumably would include employment services, health services, housing and community facilities programs, and job training. In some or all of these areas, OEO funds might finance new activities, but the locally designed, OEO-approved programs might and probably would also include employment services provided by the local branch of the state employment service and financed through USES. They might include health programs financed under a federal formula by HEW. They might include urban renewal and community facilities programs financed by the Department of Housing and Urban Development. And they might include job-training programs financed under the Manpower Development and Training Act (MDTA) by the Department of Labor. All of these programs operated under their own financial stringencies. None was designed specifically to help poor people. How would their scarce resources be allocated between the demands of community-action programs and all the other demands pouring in on them? And what authority or influence would the new OEO have through its coordinating powers to assure that the poor received their fair share?

None of these questions was resolved in this period, but they were raised and discussed both within the task force and with other agency representatives. Again, however, the discussion went primarily to issues of the relative distribution of power within the executive branch of the government rather than to the policy principles on which decisions should rest.

ISSUES THAT DID NOT ARISE

These were the issues that occupied most of the time and energy of the task force during the period between March and September. It may be worth noting also some of the issues that did not arise during this period—the dogs that did not bark. A number of problems that occupied the forefront of concern after September were scarcely thought of before that date. The first of these was the issue of maximum feasible participation of the poor, which was indeed brought up at the very first brainstorming session in connection with community action when one of the participants, Richard Boone, who had been active in the Ford Foundation programs and in the programs of the President's Committee on Juvenile Delinquency and Youth Crime, noted the danger that a local plan for community action "might just be a plan among organizations," and might not "involve" the poor.[2] The requirement of "maximum feasible participation" was incorporated into the language of the bill from its very first draft; but it was thought of simply as the process of encouraging the residents of poverty areas to take part in the work of community-action programs and to perform a number of jobs that might otherwise be performed by professional social workers. This author recalls hearing from an official of the Ford-financed Washington, D.C., CAP about a woman who had been visited in the wee hours of the morning by a welfare investigator to see if she had a man in the house. She called her indigenous neighborhood worker—paid by the local community-action board—who came by, took the investigator's name, and later filed a report on the incident, with an eye to avoiding future recurrences. This incident seemed a model demonstration of how maximum feasible participation of the poor should work.

The possibility of major conflict between the organized poor and the politicians in city hall was simply not one that anybody worried about during this period, although Shriver and his associates did see the possibility of conflicts between city hall and the poverty community on one side and the organized social work hierarchy on the other side.

In fact, the whole problem of the northern ghetto was still not seen in anything like its full depth and complexity, despite the experience of the Ford Foundation and the President's Committee. Negro poverty was thought about and talked about largely in the geographical context of the Deep South, and Black Power had not even been heard of. While we see the poverty problem today as almost coal black, in the spring and summer of 1964, it was at most light gray. There was a good deal of concern that the program might be accused of offering handouts to the poor, and indeed such accusations were made on the Hill and in the press, but it was hard to find any basis for them in fact. There was no visible concern at the time that the program might be accused of financing revolt and insurrection in the ghetto.

Lastly, the burning sociological issue as to whether there is in fact a culture of poverty was briefly discussed in some of the early sessions with advisers like Harrington and Jacobs. It did not, however, enter into the construction of legislation except to the extent that the idea of community action implied a comprehensive attack on all of the interrelated causes of poverty.

EVALUATION

The Poverty Program then, as developed by the task force, and nego-tiated by the House and Senate committees, was both pragmatic and eclectic. With the rejection of the incomes strategy as politically un-feasible and the deliberate postponement of the job-creation strategy because of the anticipated effects of the impending tax cut, the pro-gram consisted of a variety of tools designed to increase the capacity of poor people to get and hold decent jobs, particularly at the outset of their working careers. Primary, but by no means exclusive, empha-sis was on the Job Corps, as a striking, if relatively expensive, method of qualifying for the labor force young people who had dropped out of school and were about to drop out of society. The program's reach substantially exceeded its grasp in some areas, particularly in Job Corps and VISTA volunteer enrollments. But in other areas, notably community action, it underestimated local response. Rather than having too little to show the Congress at the end of the first year, OEO found that it had created activities and expectations in more communities than it was able to persuade the Congress to finance during succeeding years, so that incipient programs were not funded and existing programs sometimes cut back.

This apparent underestimate of popular response may account, at least in part, for the impression that the Poverty Program has exacerbated tensions between the poor and the rest of American society. The impression is, I believe, false. If the Poverty Program has had to break some promises, it has by and large achieved an extraor-dinary record of rising to o'erleaping expectations, expectations created not primarily by the Poverty Program itself but by the image of affluent America as portrayed on the omnipresent box in the dark-ened living-room of the still darker ghetto.

But there is an irony in the failure of the original task force— this author included—to anticipate the violent reaction of poor peo-ple and poor neighborhoods to the opportunity to affect their own lives through community-action programs. In a community as sensi-tive to the problems of the distribution and transmission of power as Washington, the power potential—constructive and destructive—of the poor themselves was largely overlooked.

Notes

1. There was also a set-aside of not more than $8,800,000 to cover a totally unrelated legislative rider providing indemnity payments to dairy farmers "who have been directed since January 1, 1964, to remove their milk from commercial markets because it contained residues of chemicals registered and approved for use by the Federal Government at the time of such use."

2. At one point during the February 4 brainstorming session, when Boone had used the phrase "maximum feasible participation" several times, this writer recalls saying to him, "You have used that phrase four or five times now." "Yes, I know," he replied. "How many more times do I have to use it before it becomes part of the program?" "Oh, a couple of times more," was the response. He did, and it did.

Chapter 4

☞ *The Community Action Program— Past, Present, and Its Future?*

SANFORD KRAVITZ

The Community Action Program (CAP) of the Economic Opportunity Act of 1964 was believed by many of its proponents to be a radical new invention for dealing with the problem of poverty at the local community level. In fact, the strain for innovation was so great that most advocates of community action would have objected to any references to the CAP as merely a stage in the evolutionary development of community programs. CAP, despite its trials and tribulations, currently functions as an important anchor, a mangement base, for a number of major federal programs. The task of this chapter is to try to set the history and present tasks of community action in some perspective and to offer speculations as to the future of the program.

HISTORICAL ANTECEDENTS

The idea of coordinated community action to relieve human distress and poverty has been present in American towns and cities for almost 100 years.[1] Various forms of local-community-coordinating structures began to take shape in the first decade of the century as social-service organizations struggled with the requirements for coordination of the services that large-scale immigration and industrialization had brought.

Two parallel efforts for relief of the distress of the poor, the

Charity Organization Society movement and the Settlement movement, both of which had roots in England, had taken firm root in
American communities during the last two decades of the nineteenth
century. These parallel streams, which had attracted the interest of
the philanthropic public, were engaged in an ideological struggle
over the same issue that still divides present efforts to attack poverty.
The Charity Organization Societies saw the answers to poverty in
retraining of the indigent, improving his moral standards, removing
him from the influences of depraved family life, and subjecting him
to the knowledge and counseling skill of an experienced worker or
skilled upper-class volunteer. The Settlement movement was primarily concerned with environment and the effects of the social structure; it thus concentrated its efforts on reconstructing neighborhood
life, on improving facilities and resources in a single geographical
area, and on the stimulation of one program participant by another
through group effort. It was the Settlement movement that led the
fight for shorter working hours for women and for child-labor laws.

Pressure for increased resources from the philanthropic public,
the growth in the number of service agencies, increased interest in
improved management as well as rationalizing the array of programs
for the poor, encouraged the spread of a new coordinating-agency
form, the council of social agencies. The "council" movement was
entirely voluntary, reflecting the nature of practically all of the welfare services of the first and second decades of this century. By the
early 1920s, federated fund raising, the Community Chest idea, had
begun to spread rapidly through the country. The community chest,
however, needed procedures by which it could evaluate the budgets
of agencies that were presented to it for funding and required planning if it was to speak on the priorities of competing community
needs. Increasingly, across the country, community planning was
wedded with voluntary federated fund raising.

The councils were made up of representatives of the member
social agencies that benefited from the chest. Their task was to influence the decisions to be made in the allocation of the Community
Chest's funds and to be alert to new and emerging community needs.
The capacity to meet new needs was governed by the availability of
resources after distribution to existing approved services.

The rapid growth of governmental services after 1930 placed
increased pressures on welfare councils to become more inclusive in
their membership and to widen their concern with social problems.

However, until the 1960s, the councils appeared to be unable to make any major breaks from the form and function that had governed their early beginnings. Some large councils struggled to find scientific means to determine community needs and priorities. Others attempted to cooperate with public agencies and to plan for public services, but councils had only modest funds for planning. Their research efforts were largely statistics on utilization of services that would be helpful to the Community Chest in its campaign. Discussions went on among the professionals from the councils as to their role in generating social action, but fear of jeopardizing tax-exempt status generally put a damper on most council efforts to enter the public arena. The main concern of councils for most of this forty-year period was the balancing of community needs with the capacity of the Community Chest to raise money in the community.

Councils had little or no influence on the allocation of public health and welfare resources. Their impact on public programs was minimal. The coordinating-structure model of organization and the reliance on the business and social elite for key leadership gave the council a stance that was directed toward the refinement of social services rather than social problems and their causes. Social planning or welfare councils, the major community vehicle in American communities for collective attention to social problems, were mainly concerned with coordination and efficiency, not with innovation or structural deficiencies in the community's human-service institutions. Thus, there was no major community mechanism fully prepared to engage the critical problems of poverty in urban America.

THE EMERGENCE OF NEW FORMS

American communities appear to have passed through the 1950s with only mild awareness of the growing number of problems that were to face them in the decade ahead. Urban-renewal agencies had sprung up across the country following the passage of the Housing Act of 1949. Urban renewal brought physical change to the center of the city, but was either unable or more often generally disinterested in coping with the social problems of the poor that large-scale clearance activities both uncovered and generated. The welfare councils turned their attention to the growing problems of suburbia. Little or no attention was given by any community agency to the alarming rise in unemployment. In 1953, unemployment stood at 3.5 per cent; it rose to 3.8 per cent in 1956 and to 5.5 per cent in 1959. In 1940, Negro unemployment was 20 per cent higher than that of whites. By 1953, it had risen to 71 per cent higher than white and by 1963, to 112 per cent.[2] During the 1950s, 1,400,000 Negroes left the South and migrated North and West to urban and industrial centers, replacing the two million whites who had fled to the suburbs. The planning agencies, such as the councils, the physical planners, and the political scientists, turned their attention to suburbia or talked about either regional problems or metropolitan government.

The lack of action or direction in local communities was mirrored in the inaction of a conservative administration in Washington. The grand promises of decent housing for all, of the Housing Act of 1949, were converted to tokenism by the Congress. The amendments to the Social Security Act of 1956 authorized social services to families on welfare, but Congress once again failed to appropriate funds. The Civil Rights Acts of 1957 and 1960 were dismal disappointments.

The elementary- and secondary-education systems of the nation were beset by the Sputnik challenge, with demands for improved education of the talented, and with a concern for academic excellence. But most school systems, and their critics and supporters, seemed unaware of the growing crisis in the inner-city schools.

Although public-welfare programs for the very poor had expanded greatly since the passage of the Social Security Act, they operated in a hostile public climate that reflected the notion that the poor make their own poverty. It was the period when sensationalist newspapers would headline stories of mink-coated welfare recipients. The public had no knowledge of the extent of poverty in the nation and appeared to care even less.

The first substantial departure from the drift of the 1950s and the conservatism of the previous decades came in 1961 with the development of the Ford Foundation Gray Areas Program and the work of the President's Committee on Juvenile Delinquency and Youth Crime, which were described in an earlier chapter of this volume. In the case of the Gray Areas program, substantial foundation grants were to be used to organize a new community agency to develop and coordinate programs in areas such as youth employment, education, and expanded community services. In the case of the President's Committee, a similar focus emerged, except that it was tied to the problem of delinquency. The Juvenile Delinquency and Youth Offenses Control Act of 1961 was sufficiently general in its stated purposes to provide the staff with a broad mandate to attack the social antecedents of juvenile crime, that is, youth employment, poor housing, and alienation in lower-class communities. Although the statute placed administrative responsibility for this program in the Department of Health, Education and Welfare (HEW), because of the special relationship of the Attorney General to the President, his interest in the problem of delinquency, and his confidence in David Hackett, the Executive Director of the President's Committee, the program was in fact managed by Hackett.

The interagency team from HEW, Labor, and Justice all understood that Hackett was really in charge. He had developed the concept of the program with Lloyd Ohlin, based on the Cloward and Ohlin opportunity theory.[3] The staff was small and tightly knit for a government operation and intensely loyal to both Hackett and Ohlin.

At that time, I served as Program Coordinator for the President's Committee. We believed that the answers to lower-class delinquency and poverty lay in a massive reform of institutional practices in schools, social-welfare agencies, and employment services. We believed with fervor that a combination of refined intellectual understanding of problems, mixed with political "clout" and new funds, would be the magic ingredients in the war on delinquency. This same belief in rationality and money was later to be carried into the War on Poverty.

As a basic set of principles for awarding planning grants to communities, we developed the following check list:

1. The stated recognition of the strong interrelationship of social problems.
2. The willingness to focus on remedies that would bring change in the opportunity structure rather than in the behavior of an individual or redirection of personality.
3. The willingness by the community to undertake a rational analysis of its social problems and propose solutions consistent with the problem definition. The solutions were assumed to be capable of integration.
4. The recognition in the community of the necessity for substantial

participation of public agencies and the political-executive arm of government in the efforts to be undertaken.

On the basis of what was believed to be general understanding of these principles, we selected seventeen demonstration projects in sixteen cities. One received action funds almost immediately: Mobilization for Youth in New York City, where the planning phase had been completed under an earlier grant from the National Institute of Mental Health. The remaining sixteen received funds to undertake the planning of the programs. In most cases, the planning grant was for one year.

Although we were aware that there were insufficient funds for all the communities, we strongly believed that as a result of the competition bold new designs of program would emerge. The attitude was not unlike that currently prevailing with regard to Model Cities competition.

THE IMPACT OF THESE PROGRAMS

These new programs, despite their relatively small size and their focus on a distinct target area within a community, very quickly jolted the communities in which they were seeded. They brought new and large amounts of money for planning and they involved a new mix of activities, that is, education, employment, and housing. They were often very critical of welfare councils and other agencies that were openly bitter at being bypassed by this new money. In only one community did we select a welfare council as the grant recipient—Minneapolis. In this case it was due to the confidence of the mayor in the organization and particularly in the executive director. Welfare-council executives saw the handwriting on the wall in the advent of public programs with planning money that would bypass them and were disturbed and publicly hostile.

These new programs emerged, almost coincidentally, at a critical moment in American social history. The civil rights revolution was erupting. There was increasing recognition of the problems of youth unemployment and automation and its impact on the unskilled worker. The new structures highlighted the failures of the existing planning mechanisms, pointing up the fragmentation of effort that characterized local-community approaches to solving these complex interrelated social problems.

They made much of their emphasis on the study of problems rather than of existing organizational structures. They were prepared to cross agency boundaries, to design new systems, to be critical of the status quo. The staff openly acknowledged its awareness of the need for support for change from professional politicians, and in most of the communities that received grants, the support of political leadership was sought before a grant was considered. The critical element that made the difference was the presence of a new federal voice and of a national foundation pointing a finger at the inner city and the poor and calling for a new recognition of public responsibility to do something about these problems.

Both the Ford Gray Areas and President's Committee programs aroused strong feelings among professionals in welfare and in the related human service fields such as education and employment. To those who were dissatisfied with the status quo of programs and of organizations, they became shining symbols of a new leadership. On the other hand, to a broad group who disagreed with assumptions made about "opportunity theory," about the role of political power, about the importance of a focus on the poor, about linkages between institutions, they represented a monstrous compound of evil, waste, and disrespect for experience.

Some of the planning projects were outright failures, others had mixed success, but the total experience threw a strong national spotlight on the following problems:

1. Many voluntary "welfare" programs were not reaching the poor.
2. If they were reaching the poor, the services offered were often inappropriate.
3. Services aimed at meeting the needs of disadvantaged people were typically fragmented and unrelated.
4. Realistic understanding by professionals and community leaders of the problems faced by the poor was limited.
5. Each specialty field was typically working in encapsulated fashion on a particular kind of problem, without awareness of the other fields or of efforts toward interlock.
6. There was little political leadership involvement in the decision-making processes of voluntary social welfare.
7. There was little or no serious participation of program benefi-

ciaries in programs being planned and implemented by professionals and elite community leadership.

The program contribution in the communities of these two demonstration efforts was mixed, but the fact of their development—and even the criticism and attacks they sustained—escalated long-festering problems into wide public view as critical national issues that could no longer be evaded. The two programs had prepared the ground, through the discussions they stimulated and the questions they raised, for CAP, a major plank in the Act of 1964.

DEVELOPMENT OF THE CONCEPT OF COMMUNITY ACTION

Any set of proposed solutions to the central program of poverty must deal with the problems that are faced by the poor in their own communities, problems that are beyond the reach of direct financial assistance or employment through the usual market mechanism. The Social Security measures of the 1930s and subsequent amendments were relatively effective in dealing with a large sector of the problem of poverty, but a significant gap remained in both the local and national capacity to reach the poor effectively. The problem confronting the planners of the War on Poverty in the winter and spring of 1964 was something like this: Poverty is a complex social and economic issue; it is rooted in an extensive array of social and individual causes. What kind of program can be developed that provides a counterattack across the total spectrum of need at the local-community level?

The earlier Ford and President's Committee programs had focused specifically on institutional change at the local-community level. We felt strongly that the remedies lay in effectively diagnosing the problem, coordinating the attacks, and having sufficient funds or a program of sufficient scope to make a difference. In effect, we were saying that education, manpower programs, and social services could change the lives of the poor only if they educated them properly, provided job training and placement, and made available to them the "right" array of social services.

The community-action concept was first sketched out in great detail in an unpublished document developed for the President's task force on the War against Poverty by a team on urban community action.[4] The team, headed by Frederick O'Reilly Hayes and myself, consisted of a group of federal employees, loaned by their agencies for the planning effort, and a small group of outside consultants. This first report on urban community action was accompanied by similar reports on "community action" for Indians, rural areas, Appalachia, and migrants. All of these reports accepted the basic concept that a local group—a city, a county, several counties, or a tribe—had the capacity for coherent, rational, cooperative action in a War on Poverty. In retrospect, this report minimized organizational problems and accepted, rather naïvely, the belief that new large sums of money would reform existing institutions or force the creation of new ones that could carry the responsibility. Our focus on the local community as the locus for action was in part due to our strong urban bias. We felt strongly that the state governments were anti-urban. Our attitudes also reflected the growing pattern of federal aid to cities.

Our model of how the community-action program would work went something like this: A community would carefully study its poverty problems, locate the most severe pockets of need, and identify them as target areas slated for intensive effort. It would plan a program for these areas that would affect all relevant institutions, that is, the schools, social services, job opportunities. It would enhance its ability to implement its program objectives by inclusion of political leadership. It would "remain honest" to its purposes by inclusion of voices representing the poor, residents of the target neighborhoods.

Thus, the model implied a central local authority to exert influence on and make decisions about the local poverty program, presumed the capacity to engage the major community-service-delivery institutions in a coordinated effort, and above all, assumed the power of persuasion necessary to allocate resources to carry on the program.

There was a gnawing question about the capacity of a structure based on "consensus" to work effectively for broad social change, but none of us, in our euphoria over the opportunity to mount the program at a nationwide level, were really prepared to raise openly that question. We had already found from our experience in the President's Committee that the year-long planning efforts had not, in general, been well accepted. The waiting for a group of professionals

to study the problems for a year and then to generate action programs had evoked great impatience in most communities. Certain
congressmen reflected this impatience and opposed the proposed
"planning period" in Title II of the poverty legislation.

To counter this concern, we relabeled planning as "program
development" and formulated a new idea, the "building block" approach. By this we meant the slow building up of the relevant pieces
of a program as ideas were developed and funds became available.
This meant that without waiting for a fully developed "conceptual
framework" for its anti-poverty effort, the community could begin
immediately to implement a program, provided it could justify its
relevance to the problem of poverty. The "building block" approach
also proved to be a realistic way to utilize the modest funds that were
to be appropriated for the War on Poverty.

The image of the earlier juvenile-delinquency programs had
been one in which the new agency had to be prepared to do combat
with major institutions on behalf of its clientele. It cared about
support from political leadership and wanted neighborhood support.
Whether it was also supported by the service institutions or elite
leadership was not deemed to be of importance. The new community-
action program was designed as a consensus structure in which the
relevant actors were (1) the political structure, (2) the social agencies and civic organizations, and (3) the residents of the areas to be
served.

The community-action-program concept was politically ideal in
many ways for a national war on poverty. It met what could be
anticipated as objections to a large new national welfare program by
placing responsibility at the local-community level; it forced no community to participate. It also provided means for a local-community
focus for other titles to EOA. Neighborhood Youth Corps (NYC)
would be locally operated, and recruitment and post-training placement for the Job Corps could be handled by the local-community-
action agency. VISTA volunteers would be assigned to work on local
projects.

The planning sessions reported above provided a basis for the
belief that the model, which was essentially urban and sophisticated,
could be tailored to other settings. For example, the necessity for a
substantial population base in rural areas, to mount certain programs, was covered by the development of the idea of a "multi-
county" community-action program. The model fitted the Indian

situation, since a reservation could be the locus for a program and the Indians themselves would run the program. This was seen as an added plus since there was a general lack of sympathy among the program planners for the Bureau of Indian Affairs.

The open-ended nature of the community-action concept, the lack of specification of fine details of organization, the emphasis on local initiative and local program development, provided a framework within which a wide range of activities could be rationalized. The community-action program could serve all ages and could provide an umbrella for education, manpower, health, economic development, housing, and social-service programs, rural or urban. Thus, it became an all-purpose program.

One of the outstanding innovations, with import beyond the expectations of the bill's drafters, was the requirement for the participation of the program beneficiaries in policy development, planning, and implementation. During the short span of three years, Title II-A, in its development of a new array of actions (or at least a rearrangement), in its focus on problems, and in its precise emphasis on the poor, has wrought some changes in the interests, the power alignments, the leadership, and the social-welfare programs of most communities that have felt its impact.

There have been several efforts to trace the origins of the concept of "maximum feasible participation," and the full history is not yet written.[5] Adam Yarmolinsky notes in another part of this volume his own incomplete understanding of the full implications of the concept at the time it was written into the bill. Leonard Duhl has traced some of the origins to Leonard Cottrell and his interest in "community competence." Those of us who had also worked for the President's Committee were regularly concerned with participation of target neighborhoods in the delinquency programs, but this was expressed largely within the framework of building "competence."

Much of the emphasis on resident participation during the planning or task-force period for EOA centered around creation of new subprofessional job opportunities. During this period there was clearly a concern for the presence of residents at the neighborhood advisory-board level, but the question of resident control of community-action agencies never arose and was never cited as a basic requirement by those of us who were planning the program. The clear intent was to substantially increase resident participation in program development and in the administration of programs at the neighborhood level.

Other writers tracing the development of the maximum-feasible-participation issue cite its congruence with the civil rights issue. David Grossman has said

. . . the Civil Rights Act . . . opened up opportunities for Negroes and other minorities to claim long overdue rights. The Economic Opportunity Act had the potential effect of making . . . exercise of these rights more than a theoretical possibility for the vast proportion of the nation's minorities who were trapped in poverty. The civil rights movement carried with it overtones of participatory democracy that had been dormant in much of American life for decades. This legislative combination clearly had much to do with the way the maximum feasible participation phrase was interpreted by Negroes, and to a lesser extent Puerto-Rican, Mexican-American and other minority groups.[6]

The issue of the precise meaning of the phrase "maximum feasible participation" has been with CAP since the first day of the program. It has been extensively discussed at all levels of national life from the neighborhood to the White House. The Office of Economic Opportunity (OEO) has generally insisted on local solutions and local interpretations within reason.[7] "Reason" was defined as an average representation on the governing board of a community-action agency of 30 per cent from target areas to be served. In 1966, the Congress amended the act and mandated that a minimum of 33 per cent of the community-action-agency board be democratically selected from the target areas of the program.

The concept of participation in program operation and decision-making by the residents of target areas, thought by many to be completely unworkable, has become an accomplished fact. Meaningful resident participation has not always been easily achieved. Often more articulate, militant, and forceful residents have pushed the less aggressive into minor roles. Sympathetic and patient staff support has been required to make resident participation really work. In Baltimore, for example, ghetto residents planned, developed, and carried into being an elaborate housing scheme, but only after intensive and creative staff service from a professionally trained planner. The effective process took over a year to accomplish. Even partisans of "resident participation" were often not prepared for the hard work of obtaining real resident involvement.[8]

Prior to this development, social welfare could be accurately characterized as a *noblesse oblige* responsibility of the more fortunate for the less fortunate. During the first three years of CAP, many communities have faced major changes in the leadership and power alignments that affect the coordination and distribution of social services. The democratization of social welfare that has seen a generation of change in thirty-six months is yet to be completed. This change is affecting the elite leadership of social welfare, the social-work professional, educators, and public officials, so there can never again be a retreat to positions held before this program concept was introduced.

In three years, over a thousand communities have been organized for the purpose of providing more effective programs and services for the poor. This might be compared with the 45-year period it took to organize about 500 welfare planning councils. For many of these 1,000 communities, the goal of a truly comprehensive poverty program is not in sight, even if understood. The tasks of ascertaining needs, planning programs, coordinating services, maximizing all relevant resources, are well beyond the present capability of many. For a few communities with skill and competence, the process is well under way. Many are embarked on a handful of critical programs, but their range is limited and their relevance to providing any basic long-term solutions to the problems of poverty is a gnawing question.

THE PROMISE AND THE CRITICISM

In the three years since its inception, CAP has been a critical factor in awakening many communities to the deep-rooted social, economic, and physical problems of poverty. Important new services have been brought to hundreds of thousands of poor people.

By focusing attention on doing things in a new way, by involving poor people in programs as participants rather than solely as program beneficiaries, there has been some narrowing of the gap between the poor and the rest of the community. CAP has proved the catalyst for the development of leadership among those regularly excluded from leadership. Hidden issues, lying dormant for years, have been given visibility. Critics of the program were awaiting problems even before it was launched. The accumulated years of structure and tradition do not shift easily, without trauma. The rapidity with which CAP moved out across the country sparked visions of an ever-accelerating attack on poverty, and local communities were led to expect substantially increased resources in successive years of the program. These expectations were heightened by a campaign of "maximum feasible public relations." The image of a massive War on Poverty has instead become just the "Poverty Program." From the initial grand promise of EOA, funding and organizational problems have led to a series of specific programs aimed at selected areas of the problem but having in almost every instance only a small portion of the funds required to attack the total problem effectively.

The program has been the victim of two enemies. The first has been its own rhetoric, in part created by the desire of all associated with it to believe that it was more than it was, and thus in turn to promise too much. It is not an income-redistribution program. It is not a large-scale public-employment program. It contains only modest program elements to effect a structural reorganization of the American community to serve the poor more effectively. It has only a small part of the responsibility for dealing with an immense problem that crisscrosses federal, state, and local responsibility and bridges both public and voluntary responsibility.

Second, the local programs mirror the problems of the federal effort. The community-action agency is a local agency, locally organized, with varying degrees of power and delegated decision-making capacity from local government, voluntary social agencies, civic organizations, and residents of poverty areas. These subgroups are not and cannot be immune to the shifts and vagaries of local leadership. While this is clearly in keeping with the principles of democratic participation, it does not make for careful adherence to a well-developed master strategy for dealing with a problem like poverty. There is no nationally mandated program, and the relative freedom of local organizations would make a national program difficult to impose and maintain. In addition, the local communities have been beset by serious personnel problems. The rapid expansion of the program gobbled up a leadership already in short supply. While many skilled persons lacking professional credentials have been successfully attracted to these programs, top leadership is still a serious problem.

It is the rare community that has not undergone at least one searing battle over the issue of resident participation. That issue appears to have been resolved in most areas. The ready availability

of large amounts of funds for loosely supervised programs has resulted in a number of instances of program and fiscal mismanagement. A far more serious charge is that of failure to achieve
institutional change. The random program efforts of the community-
action agency have generally had little effect on the large bureaucratic health, welfare, education, and employment structures that
receive the bulk of their resources independently of OEO.

The community-action agency has within it (as most institutions
do) certain bureaucratic tendencies that have already been demonstrated in a number of cities. There is a tendency for an "inversion of
purpose" as a growing organization becomes preoccupied with its
organizational maintenance functions and forms alliances that help
maintain itself and opposes initiative or imagination or independence of groups that are critical of its efforts.

The concept of community action ignores the first set of problems and assumes the second is resolved through a combination of
good will, recognition of the rightness or goodness of the mission of
the Community Action Agency, and the skillful use of federal
dollars.

WHAT OF THE FUTURE FOR COMMUNITY ACTION?

The fate of CAP has hung in balance through each session of
Congress. Surprisingly, as if unable to recognize the fraternal relationship, the Congress has sanctioned a new version of community
action called "Model Cities" under the Department of Housing and
Urban Development (HUD). This new HUD program has built into
it a longer planning period and has tied social development to the
physical renewal of a model neighborhood. An additional difference
is the lack of ambiguity about its control by local political authority.
It is the mayor's program if he wants it.

I should like to argue that these changes will make only a minor
difference in the experience of the Model Cities as compared with
CAP, because the new programs lack the backstopping effect of a
major national commitment to eradicate poverty and eliminate the
ghetto. Programs such as CAP and Model Cities can only function in
a piecemeal and fragmented fashion, inadequately funded as they

are, unless a floor of service programs is developed to undergird these local-community efforts.

The first element in such a program is some form of national-income redistribution based on right rather than on a means test. Without such a program, community-action programs inevitably appear as if they might be such programs. The financial relief provided by such a program would remove from the purview of CAP all the poor who are perfectly able to cope with life except for the absence of money.

The second is a large scale public-employment program that would be locally administered and that would assure a decent wage for all those willing and capable of working. It would allow the community-action agency to work closely with other community resources, particularly the private sector, on programs of job upgrading and career development.

The third national program must be housing for low-income families. It has been recognized that the nation requires five million new low-income dwelling units as soon as it can get them if it is to meet the current housing needs of the poor. Such a program must be nationally organized even though it can be effectively administered locally. Major efforts in this direction would remove the presence of the most ubiquitous environmental hazard that the poor face, the place they live in. Every person needs a livable physical environment if he is to thrive and be productive. This program also has substantial employment potential. To attempt to conduct a community-action program or to enter the Model Cities game without a substantial commitment to tearing down slums is a cruel and hopeless task.

If such national efforts as I have proposed are undertaken, the concept of concerted community action has a chance of surviving and of making a significant contribution toward the reduction of poverty and poverty-producing conditions. Even with the national efforts described above, additional conditions will be required:

1. The community-action agency must have a strong planning and diagnostic capability. It must understand thoroughly the array of problems faced by the poor in the community and then be able to produce or cause to be produced a program to meet the need. This may imply more cause-effect knowledge than we currently

possess, but it is essential that community-action agencies improve their program capability.

2. The community-action agency must gain increased control over the allocation of resources in all the areas relevant to its program. As a step short of this, it must begin to utilize some of the more promising findings of cost-benefit analysis in this field as they emerge. The agency would be better off than at present if it even knew how much was being spent, and by whom, for services.

3. To assure the vitality of the community-action agency and its responsiveness to need, it must begin, whenever appropriate, to decentralize responsibility to smaller community units. The community-action agency must contribute to the production of responsible leadership for meaningful community programs by developing the competence of residents of poverty neighborhoods to manage their own programs. This is vital because of the absolute necessity for finding new ways to combat the increasing alienation of poverty-area residents as they encounter the service bureaucracies.

Under these conditions, there is a possibility that the high purpose of CAP may be fully realized. It could perform the following very vital tasks in a real war on poverty:

1. It could link low-income people to critical resources, for example, education, manpower training, counseling, housing, and health.

2. It could increase the accessibility of available critical services that the poor still often find beyond their reach or blocked off by the manner in which their need has been defined.

3. It could create competent communities by developing in the poor the capacity for leadership, problem-solving, and participation in the decision-making councils that affect their lives.

4. It could restructure community-service institutions to assure flexibility, responsiveness, respect, and true relatedness to the problems faced by the poor.

Poverty has many causes. So, too, the relatively simple concept of community action has had many limitations as a major element in the War on Poverty. As I have noted, the problems have been financial (there was never enough money to do what could be done), organizational (the organizational scheme could not carry the load intended, particularly in bringing about institutional change), and conceptual (the problems of poverty go well beyond the capacities of a locally based, service-oriented program). None of these defects has yet proved fatal, but unless they are attacked, community action and its fraternal twin have little chance of surviving.

Notes

1. For a more complete review of the origins of community-wide coordination and planning effort, see Frank J. Bruno, *Trends in Social Work* (New York: Columbia University Press, 1957); Ralph E. Pumphrey and Muriel W. Pumphrey (Eds.), *The Heritage of American Social Work* (New York: Columbia University Press, 1961).

2. Peter Marris and Martin Rein, *Dilemmas of Social Reform* (New York: Atherton Press, 1967), p. 11.

3. Richard A. Cloward and Lloyd E. Ohlin, *Delinquency and Opportunity* (Glencoe, Ill.: The Free Press, 1960). "Opportunity theory" may be described briefly as follows: Services to delinquent individuals or groups cannot prevent the rise of delinquency among others. Delinquency is not a property of individuals; it is a property of the social systems in which the individuals or groups are enmeshed. Pressures that produce delinquency originate in these structures. Thus the target for preventive action is the social setting that gives rise to delinquency. Those who wish to eliminate delinquency should direct their efforts toward the reorganization of slum communities.

4. David Grossman, *The Community Action Program: Innovation in Local Government,* 1966 (mimeo), p. 16.

5. Leonard Duhl, "Some Origins of the Poverty Program," unpublished paper and private communication.

6. Grossman, *op. cit.,* p. 18.

7. The general model outlined for community action could accept this because of the high value placed on local initiative and local decision making.

8. For a thoughtful, descriptive, and sympathetic account of the issues encountered in planning and program development with residents of target areas, see Ferne K. Kolodner, "Observations on the Process of Planning with the Poor," paper presented at the National Conference on Social Welfare, Dallas, Texas, 1967 (mimeo).

Chapter 5

The Politics of Local Responsibility: Administration of the Community Action Program—1964–1966

JOHN G. WOFFORD

In the Community Action Program (CAP), poverty was to be defined, its causes were to be specified, and solutions were to be proposed not by the Federal Government but by local communities throughout the nation.

To be sure, the Office of Economic Opportunity (OEO) published a suggested definition of poverty (chiefly based on income level adjusted for size of family); it had some notions that poverty arose out of a complex relationship between the opportunity structure (jobs, schooling, welfare, the bureaucracy) and those who should have been seizing the opportunities (their aspirations, their abilities, and their assumptions about what the opportunity structure was like); and it believed that the solution lay in changing both that structure and those aspirations, abilities, and assumptions.

But these federal definitions, notions, and beliefs did not amount to a program. The program was to be designed by each community to meet its own needs.

This chapter will attempt to set forth the reasons behind conceiving CAP in this way, the early administrative decisions that tried to carry out this basic concept, and the slow erosion of local programmatic responsibility that led, by 1967, to a transformation of CAP from what was to have been the keystone of the federal anti-poverty program into a less central but politically embarrassing force on both the local and national scenes.

These elements will be described from an admittedly limited and personal vantage point: the writer became a part of the staff of the President's Task Force on the War Against Poverty in July 1964, after the task force's essential work had been completed and just before the Congress in August 1964 passed the Economic Opportunity Act. From then until June 1966, the writer was staff assistant to the director of operations (and later the deputy director) of CAP, an office that had major responsibility for designing and carrying out the administrative policies and procedures that attempted to create out of CAP a significant exercise in local responsibility.

AN "OPPORTUNITY" PROGRAM

Little thought, if any, was given by those of us who helped administer CAP to a distinction between poverty (a lack of money) and the "culture of poverty" (the life style that goes with poverty). If we had been forced to say which of these concepts was a more central target of CAP, we probably would have responded that the emphasis (and it was only a matter of emphasis) was on attempting to deal with the life style of the poor, but primarily through qualities in the environment—particularly institutions—that affect that life style. Still, as soon as one emphasizes changing institutions and removing environmental barriers to opportunity, one is necessarily talking about attacking both poverty and the culture that goes with it.

The language of the Act itself supports an approach that aims at both poverty and the culture of poverty. The Preamble to the Act states:

It is . . . the policy of the United States to eliminate the paradox of poverty in the midst of plenty in this Nation by opening to everyone the opportunity for education and training, the opportunity to work, and the opportunity to live in decency and dignity. It is the purpose of this Act to strengthen, supplement and coordinate efforts in furtherance of that policy. (Sec. 2)

And the definition of a community-action program makes it clear that the Act did not attempt to prescribe whether the main focus of a local attack on poverty should be providing jobs and job training (an "employment" strategy) ; or assisting the poor to gain enough confidence in their own power to set about making their way in the environment and even, occasionally, attempting to change that environment (a "community organization" strategy) ; or improving educational, medical, legal, and other social services (a "delivery of services" strategy). A "community action program," the Act declared,

> means a program . . . which provides services, assistance, and other activities of sufficient scope and size to give promise of progress toward elimination of poverty or a cause or causes of poverty through developing employment opportunities, improving human performance, motivation, and productivity, or bettering the conditions under which people live, learn, and work . . . . (Sec. 202 (a) (2))

"Developing employment opportunities," "improving human performance, motivation, and productivity," and "bettering the conditions under which people live, learn, and work"—Congress gave pretty clear signals that communities were to be permitted, and indeed encouraged, to choose and blend strategies into a program tailored to community needs.

Nor did the Act define "poverty." The preamble merely makes the following finding:

> Although the economic well-being and prosperity of the United States have progressed to a level surpassing any achieved in world history, and although these benefits are widely shared throughout the Nation, poverty continues to be the lot of a substantial number of our people. (Sec. 2)

And in the part dealing with community-action programs, the Act said that in determining whether to make a community-action grant, the director of OEO must consider, along with other relevant factors, ". . . the incidence of poverty within the community and within the area or groups to be affected by the specific program or programs . . ." (Sec. 205 (c)) In determining the "incidence of poverty," the director was required to

> consider information available with respect to such factors as: the concentration of low-income families, particularly those with children; the extent of persistent unemployment and underemployment; the number and proportion of persons receiving cash or other assistance on a needs basis from public agencies or private organizations; the number of migrant or transient low-income families; school dropout rates, military service rejection rates, and other evidences of low educational attainment; the incidence of disease, disability, and infant mortality; housing conditions; adequacy of community facilities and services; and the incidence of crime and juvenile delinquency. (Sec. 205 (c))

The theory of poverty that the above section implies is complex but familiar: Persistent unemployment and underemployment contribute to the debilitation of an individual both economically and psychologically, and when added to the system of rewards offered by the welfare system, tend to lead to the disintegration of stable family life. This in turn contributes to low educational achievement in the young that, when combined with inadequate community services such as housing and medical care, adds to the difficulties of finding a job. Without a job and without the ability to train oneself for a job, the poor man becomes a drifter at best or a delinquent at worst, and the poor woman produces more children to grow up in an ever-worsening environment. In simplified form, this is the "vicious cycle of poverty" that CAP assumed existed.

What was CAP supposed to do about this cycle of poverty? The program's role was necessarily a limited one. Notes that I used in briefing groups who wanted information about the program suggest some of the limitations:

The Community Action Program is not a job creation program. We have to assume that the economy, spurred by the tax reduction, will create the jobs and that it is our task, or rather yours out in the communities, to help train the poor so that they can find a job and keep it.

The Community Action Program is not an economic development program. Although rational economic development, usually on a regional basis, is essential to combat poverty in many areas of the country, this is not our job.

The Community Action Program is not social work. We are not financing programs which will primarily do things *for* poor people. Rather, we are concerned to enlist the support of the poor in the solution of their own problems—by hiring them to do neighborhood surveys, by including their representatives on boards which will plan programs which meet their own needs as they perceive them, and by helping to carry out those programs in jobs which have usually been reserved for professionals but which have aspects which can be performed effectively by the poor themselves.

The Community Action Program is not a dole. The Act does not contemplate giving sums of money to the poor for doing nothing. Instead, we are trying to help communities improve the capacities of poor people so that those people can make their own way in the world. Of course, some of the poor are going to continue to need welfare and other public assistance, and ways need to be found to provide such assistance consistently with economic incentive (to earn a living) and with human dignity (to have a private life uninvaded by midnight raids and other forms of investigation). Some kind of guaranteed income for those who cannot earn a living may be a solution to this problem, but that is something not presently available and certainly not within the scope of the Community Action Program or any other parts of the Economic Opportunity Act.

In short, instead of a job creation program, or an economic development program, or improved social work, or a better dole, the Community Action Program is designed to assist communities to mobilize their own local resources to improve the capacities of the poor in their midst. This is an opportunity program to assist the poor to begin to pull themselves up by their own bootstraps.

If my notes are an indication of what others in the program were thinking and saying—and I believe they are—then the emphasis was squarely on improving the capacities of the poor, and the capacities of the community structure surrounding the poor, so that the poor could have a better chance of escaping both from poverty and from the culture of poverty. In this emphasis, we were supported by what seems to me to be compelling statutory language. In making community-action grants, Congress required the director to

give special consideration to programs which give promise of effecting *a permanent increase in the capacity of individuals, groups, and communities* to deal with their problems without further assistance. (Sec. 205 (d) —redesignated subsection (e) in 1965, and subsection (f) in 1966.)

LOCAL RESPONSIBILITY AND LOCAL CONSENSUS

The responsibility for developing the programs that were to bring about this "permanent increase in the capacity of individuals, groups, and communities to deal with their problems without further assistance" rested with the communities themselves. OEO viewed its role as a limited one, although its basic approaches to local planning and local administration had far-reaching consequences.

One of the earliest pamphlets produced by CAP was entitled "A Hometown Fight." Designed to encourage communities to apply for community-action grants, this little brochure set forth the central role that local action was to have in the War Against Poverty:

Local community action programs are central to the war on poverty. These programs are designed to fight poverty in the community through local initiative. The individual community decides how best to attack poverty in its midst. Initiative and direction must come from the community itself. The decision to participate in the War on Poverty becomes a local responsibility.

The Community Action Program reflects confidence in the ability of individual communities to organize and carry out anti-poverty programs tailored to local needs and priorities. In developing its program, the local community is asked to:

1. Mobilize its own public and private resources for this attack.
2. Develop programs of sufficient scope and size to give promise of eliminating causes of poverty.
3. Involve the poor themselves in developing and operating the anti-poverty programs.
4. Administer and coordinate the programs through public or private nonprofit agencies, or a combination of these.

Local community action programs should be broadly based, involving representatives of the chief elected officials of the community, key public and private agencies and representatives of the poor themselves.

Community action programs should see that existing local, state and federal programs are linked in a concentrated drive against poverty. They should fuse older programs which have proved effective with new attacks against the varied problems confronting the poor.

In a community with limited resources, local leaders can begin a community action program in stages. For example, with the "building block" approach a community might start with a child development program including health services. This should be followed by other specific programs all linked to each other in a coordinated campaign.

The major goal of community action programs is to help individuals help themselves. Inherent in this approach is the conviction that the poor should play an active part in helping to develop, manage and work in community action programs.

Some assumptions contained in the above quotation are worth noting, partly because of the pitfalls that they were designed to avoid.

First, the emphasis on local initiative and control assumes certain things about the appropriate role of the federal government. There was to be no federal blueprint, no magic formula worked out in Washington that would be imposed on local problems. Federal standards were to be held to the minimum required under the Act, so that local communities would be free to devise their own solutions to their own problems. Problems of decaying mining towns in Kentucky, of Indian reservations, of rural Mississippi, and of urban slums were seen as too different to permit meaningful detailed federal direction. And even if the federal government could have promulgated certain permissible alternative models for local action, the fear of federal domination over local affairs was so strong in Congress and in city halls that the problem of designing programs to meet local needs was left squarely with the localities.

There was an added reason for leaving the designing of programs to people at the community level: Planning itself was seen as a form of action. The very process of getting communities to think about their own problems was viewed as an essential means of mobilizing local resources, most of which had been either unused or diffused in the past. In communities throughout the country, at the time of the enactment of the anti-poverty legislation, most programs dealing with local poverty were "single-tracked." School boards, city halls, departments of welfare, juvenile courts, settlement houses, were going their separate ways without significant contact with each other. The person who suffered from this programmatic insularity was, of course, the poor person himself; his problems were segmented into traditional molds, and he was rarely, if ever, viewed as one human being with connected crises, needs, and styles of life. Thus "linkage" of programs at the local level became an important goal, and the local planning needed to develop these linkages was conceived as the first and one of the most important forms of community action.

Although planning was viewed as one kind of community action, its purpose was the ultimate action itself—the initiation of programs that would directly and quickly benefit the poor. A long period of community planning could not be tolerated unless it was accompanied by some action.

Thus we placed great reliance on the so-called "building-block" approach. We would tell communities when they inquired about how to get an anti-poverty program started that they were eligible for a "program development" grant (under section 204 of the act) for community surveys, conferences, and the hiring of a small planning and organizing staff; but we would also emphasize that if there were some programs, even one, that the community already knew were needed, such programs could be started immediately. Thus, one of the pitfalls of some other federal programs, such as Urban Renewal, was to be avoided: Communities were urged not to have a long planning period before beginning some action programs. Some false starts, we thought, could be more easily tolerated than a delayed start, or no start at all.

THE COMMUNITY ACTION AGENCY:
A "THREE-LEGGED STOOL"

One of the central building blocks that a community needed to develop was the administrative structure that would operate, either directly or through subcontracts with other community organizations (called "delegate agencies" in the statute), whatever program was devised to combat local poverty.

Jack Conway, the first director of CAP and later the deputy director of OEO, was fond of describing a local community-action program as a "three-legged stool." By that he meant that the local community-action agency should derive its support from three main sources: participation by the public officials of the community, both elected and appointed; participation by private agencies that had been fighting poverty long before OEO came along; and participation by representatives of the poor. Local programs were not to be the "tools" of "city hall"—but without effective support from city hall or the county commission, the program would be doomed. Nor were local programs to be mere extensions of health and welfare councils or the Red Cross or settlement houses—but without effective support from such groups, a large and influential part of the community would be alienated and valuable experience would be lost. Nor were local programs to be controlled by the poor—but without an important role for the poor the program would be scorned by the very people it was designed to assist. As Sargent Shriver put the same point on a number of occasions: Community action was not federal action; it was not state action; it was not city-hall action; it was not health-and-welfare-council action; it was not action by business or labor; it was not action by the poor—it was none of these alone, but it was all of these together; in short—community action.

The earliest draft of community-action guidelines, prepared in July 1964, before the bill was enacted, reflected a proposed statutory provision that would have required the community-action agency to be a broadly based organization drawing on all portions of the community concerned with poverty. This provision was struck out of the bill by an amendment offered by Congresswoman Edith Green (D., Ore.), who was concerned lest communities be forced into a long planning period when an existing agency, say the school system, was ready to move quickly and independently.[1] Thus, OEO had no power to *require* communities to establish a broadly based agency, although the logic of the rest of the statute led OEO to express a strong preference for a broadly based coordinated approach. As the eventual guidelines expressed the point:

The existence of a broadly-based community action agency is a prerequisite to the granting of Federal assistance. However, applicants for programs of limited scope from communities where a broadly-based agency has been or is being created are required to provide adequate evidence why they are unable to combine their efforts with those of the broadly-based agency. If there is a broadly-based agency in the community, but operating within it is not possible, a single-purpose agency must provide evidence that it has made every reasonable effort to coordinate its activities with those of the broadly-based agency. Applicants from communities where there is no broadly-based agency shall provide evidence as to why it is not possible to develop such an agency, as a preliminary step in applying for aid to a program of limited scope.[2]

This provision turned out to have unexpected and extremely important application in the South. OEO's policy from the beginning, in accord with its preference for a broadly based community-wide agency, was to encourage the establishment of bi-racial committees throughout the South. In some places, as in most of Georgia, including the rural areas, this proved feasible. In other areas, as in most of Mississippi, this proved to be impossible to achieve, at least in the early months. In places in which a Negro group was prepared to develop and carry out a community-action program and the whites were adamant in their noncooperation, OEO gave the green light—and a grant—to the Negro group.

This was the justification for funding a large-scale Headstart program in the summer of 1965 through the Child Development Group of Mississippi (CDGM), which operated through local grass-roots organizations that were almost wholly Negro. When, after an extremely successful first summer, the white community sought to get involved (and some would say to take over the program), OEO was faced with a political dilemma of major proportions. The theory of community action suggested moving toward a community-wide agency, including whites, but the fact of an existing and exciting grass-roots program suggested strengthening what had been developed rather than scrapping it in favor of a belated bi-racialism. After pressure from all sides, OEO eventually decided to do both for an interim period while moving in the end toward a less activist bi-racialism.

The difficulties that OEO had in coping with the CDGM problem suggest that community action was northern and urban in origin. The concept did not fit easily into those parts of the South that were predominantly rural and resistant. As is indicated in the chapters in this volume that trace the intellectual forerunners of CAP, I think this was, in fact, the case.

Of course, community action did not fit *easily* anywhere, for community action was really seeking community consensus. And consensus, at least in dealing with poverty, was difficult to build. Community action was supposed to be a way in which all important segments of the community would mobilize all available resources to deal with local poverty. Such a conception of community action obviously thrust the program into the midst of local politics. If politics is basically the struggle of groups over policy and power, and control over funds and programs is a form of power, then—for better or worse—poverty and politics were inextricably bound together.

The character of local politics, we assumed, would in many instances be heated, with different groups pressing for different kinds of coordinating agencies, different program priorities, and different mechanisms to achieve maximum feasible participation of the poor. We tried not to tell communities how to resolve these differences. Instead, we basically said that these were issues for each community to work out. Through what was frequently a painful, headline-making process, most communities moved toward a local consensus.

"MAXIMUM FEASIBLE PARTICIPATION"

The intensity of this form of politics took us somewhat by surprise. The evolution of the administrative handling of the requirement that there be "maximum feasible participation of residents of the areas and members of the groups served" is the best illustration. What this phrase meant to those who drafted the legislation is discussed in Adam Yarmolinsky's paper in this volume; to those of us involved in carrying out that legislation, it represented, at a minimum, an attempt to deal with the condition of "powerlessness" that characterized the poor. Our assumption was that many of the poor felt little power to affect their own environment; the important decisions were made for them by remote authorities beyond their influence: their absentee landlord, the owner of the supermarket, distant city agencies, foremen on construction crews, judges, the police. To the extent feasible in the local community, this sense of powerlessness was to be changed by giving representatives of the poor some real power in the development and conduct of programs designed to assist themselves. For the first few months of the program, from August to November 1964, when only a handful of communities were preparing draft applications, the small Washington staff would sit down with community representatives—usually sent because the mayor had put together a small group of influential local leaders—and ask them, among other questions, whether representatives of the poor had participated in developing the proposed program to the "maximum feasible" extent. Usually the answer was, "Well, not very much, but about as much as was feasible. We needed to move fast." For a short while, this answer satisfied us, and we would admonish the delegation to expand its committee as soon as possible once the program was underway.

But then, about November 1964, an avalanche of telegrams of protest began. They would arrive, often on the day a grant was to be signed, addressed to Mr. Shriver, to the congressman for the district, to senators, to the President, protesting the alleged failure of the "mayor's committee" to consult the residents of the area.

In the early days, such allegations usually meant that the local branch of the Urban League or the NAACP or the American G.I. Forum (of the Mexican-American community) had not been consulted. It is easy to forget that as late as 1964 many communities in this country thought that community-wide programs affecting the poor could be designed without substantial involvement of even the most moderate local civil rights leadership—let alone the militants. The telegrams of protest indicated that members of the civil rights movement had seen in the War Against Poverty a way to begin to alleviate some of the social conditions that led to discrimination and a way to establish some local bases of real power. With the statutory mandate of "maximum feasible participation," Washington forced communities to accept these organizations as partners in the community-action process.

But protests by moderate, established civil rights groups were only the beginning. The next step in the local community-action game was often for more militant spokesmen—usually sparked by white and Negro clergy with churches in the ghetto—to organize in opposition to "the establishment-oriented" mayor's committee. Then there would arise the "Central City Committee for a More Effective Community Action Program." We would urge the mayor's committee to sit down with the new organization to try to work things out, usually by expanding the size of the committee. A fascinating and not surprising pattern often emerged: After weeks and sometimes several months of negotiations, the mayor's committee would usually offer not only a place on the governing committee but one of the top staff jobs—frequently the staff directorship—to the head of the protesting committee. And then, if he decided to "come aboard," the former protester would be accused by some (although not all) of his followers of having "sold out to the establishment." Frequently, a new committee then would appear: a "Committee for an Even More Effective Community Action Program." We learned that at a certain point we had to end the negotiating period and fund the local program despite local protests. It was impossible to satisfy everyone.

By this painful and prolonged process (sometimes running into many months), a kind of local consensus would in most cases be achieved. In the meantime, the local headlines denounced the "mess" at home and the "delays" from Washington. Mayors and congressmen were surprised, puzzled, and angered. Why did this negotiating period result in such public criticism? Partly, I think, because the press and the Congress naturally became part of the negotiating process: If a local group did not get what it wanted, it took its problems to the newspaper or to its congressman. In addition, though, there was not enough straight talk either from OEO or from local officials to make it clear that some controversy was inevitable and, in most cases, healthy.

The administrators of the program took an experimental, case-by-case attitude toward developing a local consensus. Sometimes the chief problem was to persuade the local health and welfare council to cooperate with the mayor; sometimes it was to reach an accommodation between the mayor on the one side and the county supervisors on the other; sometimes it was to persuade the school system to cooperate, or to get heads of public city agencies such as welfare to agree to participate in innovative programs.

Most often, however, controversy centered around the proper local application of those very ambiguous statutory words: "maximum feasible participation of residents of the area and members of the groups served." As a matter of policy, CAP administrators took care not to specify any fixed percentage of representatives of the poor on local governing boards of community-action agencies, leaving this instead to be worked out as part of the local consensus. (The activities of OEO "field representatives" in helping to shape this local consensus will be discussed in the next section.) There were great variations from community to community, with national averages running about 27 per cent at the end of the first year and about 30 per cent at the end of the second. In the 1966 amendments, Congress put a floor under this numbers game, requiring from and after March 1, 1967, that at least one-third of the members of the governing boards of local community-action agencies represent the poor.

The notion that one-third of the members of the governing board of a community-action agency should represent the poor probably derived in part from the conception of a community-action agency as a "three-legged stool." But OEO had never said that each of the major supports for a local program must have equal representation. The closest we came was to say the following:

We have purposely refrained from establishing specific percentage requirements for representation. It is probably true that the more representatives a group has the greater its chances for effective representation. It is also obvious that representation in a quantitative sense does not guarantee quality. With this reservation in mind we are proposing as a guide that representatives of the poor be approximately one-third of the membership of a CAP governing body. Where something less is proposed it should be noted and discussed in the highlight memo. [From memo to CAP regional teams, October 20, 1965.]

In other words, by October 1965, the one-third principle had at least become a yardstick: Any lower percentage needed special discussion and justification. But many lower percentages were, in fact, approved.

An important, but little understood, principle that OEO administrators emphasized repeatedly was that it was the validity of the representation that was important: The representative himself need not be poor. In a memo to CAP regional teams dated July 7, 1965, the principle was clearly set forth:

The requirement for resident participation in a community action program —as stated in the Act and in the CAP Guide—refers to "residents of the areas and members of the groups" to be served. This requirement is met— in part—by including on the governing body or policy advisory committee of the CAA at least one representative selected from each of the neighborhoods or areas in which the CAP will be concentrated . . . In discussing this requirement, or in correspondence, be sure that you do not equate our requirements for resident participation in policy-making with the fact that one or more poor persons may be placed on the governing body or policy advisory committee. In determining whether the requirement for *representation* has been met, it is not the incomes of the representatives that we are concerned with; it is the degree to which they truly represent the persons to be served by the community action program. We do *not* require that such representatives themselves meet an income test.

Mr. Shriver emphasized the same point by stating many times that representatives of the poor did not necessarily have to wear "patches on their pockets."

Devising a system of representation that would assure effective participation by the poor was difficult, at best. Philadelphia and Los Angeles tried the election approach, and the results in terms of voter turnout were so pitiful that Mr. Shriver nearly forbade use of federal funds to finance any future "poverty elections." New York City tried the community-convention approach, with delegates to the neighborhood conventions representing any existing organization—churches, schools, settlement houses, protest groups, etc. The conventions then elected representatives to sit on a community council and on the city-wide anti-poverty board. Selection by the mayor was used in some cities. Others developed a series of neighborhood corporations. Techniques that seemed to work in some places did not work in others.

In 1965 and 1966, OEO was criticized by some (such as the U.S. Conference of Mayors [3]) for paying too much attention to the structure of local community-action agencies and not enough to the content of local programs. Content, of course, needed more careful scrutiny than it received. But structure was essential, too. Only by focusing on local structure, we believed, would communities significantly change local institutions so that the community could itself cope with its poverty.

One risk involved in encouraging the establishment of these new community-action agencies was that they would become monopolies unresponsive to the varying needs of the community. How to keep community-action agencies both responsible and responsive is an unsolved problem. The amendments requiring stricter personnel and accounting procedures are steps toward assuring proper accountability, although the $15,000 limitation on salaries (paid from federal or matching sources) may keep communities with limited resources from obtaining the caliber of people needed. Perhaps the requirement that OEO put at least 5 per cent of its unrestricted community-action funds into the hands of "independently funded" programs—that is, independent of the local community-action agency—is another appropriate step, although it tends to undercut the coordinating function of the local community-action agency. There also exists an "appeals procedure" by which a local organization whose proposed program has been turned down by the local community-action agency can appeal to the OEO regional office for review of the decision and for funding either under the community-action-agency umbrella or independently, although only a handful of such appeals has been made.

There are presently about 1,000 community-action agencies in the country. Are they a new bureaucracy that will either remain as a stifling monopoly or be superseded by some new agency? Or do they have the continuing capacity to mobilize community resources in innovative anti-poverty programs? Do they have the support of the poor? of city hall? of the private agencies? And will they survive the opposition of many congressmen who feel that CAP has stirred up a hornet's nest of local political pressures and counterpressures?

Some of these questions will be addressed below; most have to be answered by citing facts and figures of a particular local situation. With local responsibility and local consensus as the major pattern in the community-action design, the effectiveness of local structures and local programs must be evaluated for the most part on a local basis. Part of the pattern was unraveled, as will be seen in the next section; but enough of it remained so that community action should be viewed and evaluated from a local point of view.

FEDERAL SUPPORT FOR THE LOCAL AGENCY

Three important administrative principles were adopted in Washington in support of the strategy that placed key responsibility in the hands of the local community-action agency. These principles were:

1. Equity of distribution of federal funds.
2. Simplicity of federal procedures.
3. Flexibility of program priorities.

If a grant-in-aid program is to have any continuing part in combating poverty, the lessons learned in the course of trying—for the most part unsuccessfully—to apply these principles in practice will be worth some study.

EQUITY OF DISTRIBUTION OF FEDERAL FUNDS

The Act set certain minimum requirements designed to achieve an equitable distribution of assistance under CAP. Section 203 prescribed a formula for the allotment of funds among the fifty states, in proportion to each state's percentage of all public-assistance recipients, all unemployed, and all children under eighteen years of age living in families with incomes of less that $1,000. And Section 210 required the director of OEO to achieve an equitable distribution within the states between urban and rural areas by establishing criteria based, at least in part, on six specified poverty indicators. Within these prescriptions, however, there was great administrative flexibility in deciding where the funds should go. Section 203 itself, of course, authorized the director to reallot from time to time during the year the portion of any state's allotment that the director determined would not be required by that state. The reallotment was to be made to the rest of the states—using, again, the specified formula.

Administratively, we went beyond these statutory requirements. We took the six poverty criteria set forth in Section 210, translated them into categories of statistics available in the 1960 Census, weighted each category equally, and did a "run" for every county in the country, on a state-by-state basis. This, in principle, gave us the percentage of state poverty that existed in each county. Dividing the available funds (based on the state allocation formula prescribed in Section 203 (b)) in proportion to these county percentages, we produced a "guideline" allocation. In other words, on the assumption that an approvable application for a community-action grant would be submitted to cover every county in the country, we knew how much could be used in each county. Of course, we realized that there would not be applications—and certainly not approvable ones—from every county, so for planning purposes we assumed that one-third of the counties would not have approvable applications. This meant that the others could count on funds 50 per cent above their "guideline" figure. We called 150 per cent of guideline the "expanded guideline." It was a rough estimate of the amount of community-action funds that should be expended in each county covered by an approvable community-action application.

There were some obvious problems with applying the "guidelines," even in "expanded" form. In the first place, the geographical scope of a particular poverty program was more frequently either a city or several counties than it was a single county. Second, because of substantial experience and able personnel, some applicants had a greater capacity to expend the funds in a worthwhile manner than did others. And third, some concentration of programs was desirable in order for there to be some meaningful impact on the causes of poverty. Our general solution to these problems was to break down further the county guidelines to estimate the funds available to a particular city within the county; to provide a greater amount to a city that had demonstrated the capacity to put together a good program (while urging the states to provide technical assistance to those areas that did not have this capability) ; and to urge cities to adopt a "target area" approach, so that there would be a meaningful concentration of funds within the worst poverty areas of each city. The result of these various considerations was that urban areas received far more funds than rural areas.

Why did we even make the assumption that the funds should be spread all over the country? Why did we not opt for the kind of formula used in the Area Redevelopment Act, in which only the poorest one-third of the counties were eligible even to apply for assistance?

Part of our reasoning was based on a view that the legislative history pointed us in this direction: This was to be a program that every congressman expected would operate within his district. In addition, we believed that the assumed distinction between urban and rural areas was a fuzzy one, that most counties with a rural economy were in fact partly urban and partly rural, and that effective local community action would attempt to link the two in a single program. There was also a deliberate political intent to proliferate community-action agencies across the nation to help build a base of support for the program. More fundamentally, we knew that every county in the country had pockets of poverty—even Westchester County in New York and Montgomery County in Maryland. It was precisely the lingering pockets of poverty, both urban and rural, that the Act was designed to eliminate. Further, we did not want a county (or other unit) to feel singled out as a "poor" area in order to be eligible for funds to deal with poverty in its midst. We therefore concluded that every area of the country was eligible for a community-action grant; the guidelines would be used not as a rigid ceiling but as a yardstick: Any departure from the guidelines needed special justification.

Having decided that every county in the country was eligible for assistance under CAP, we knew we would have to deal with the problem of counties in which there was a substantial amount of poverty but in which there was not the minimum local capability even to apply for a grant. In this effort, Washington relied chiefly on the states, which were authorized to receive "technical assistance" grants under Section 209 (b). Under these grants, state agencies—frequently replicas of the federal OEO—were supposed to assist communities in the state in developing and carrying out community-action programs. Like the cities and counties in their midst, of course, the states also had varying capabilities in the technical-assistance field. Those, like New Jersey, that could assemble a capable staff with administrative resources got results. Those, like Texas, that for political or administrative reasons were slow to get off the ground provided little assistance, either technical or any other kind, to their communities.

Two important problems emerged, resulting in part from the original administrative decision to make community-action funds available for use in every county, city, or hamlet in the country. One problem was implicit in the difficulties encountered by the state technical-assistance program: The very poorest areas needed local individuals with enough programmatic and administrative abilities to put together a workable program, yet the very poverty of the area usually meant that such talent was not present. The areas with the greatest capability to begin with tended to receive proportionately more community-action funds. Such areas, primarily the major metropolitan centers, needed the funds, of course, but one of the questions we never really answered was how to provide effective outside assistance (without undue outside interference) to the less capable areas.

The second and more critical problem resulting from making poverty assistance available throughout the country was that expectations were raised—expectations that could be fulfilled only by continually accelerating amounts appropriated by the Congress for CAP.

Although in the first fiscal year it was difficult to expend all available community-action funds, by the second year funds were extremely tight. And the lower rate of acceleration resulting from a critical Congress and other demands on the federal budget—particularly Vietnam—meant that city after city, and county after county, were forced to put a ceiling on local anti-poverty efforts. CAP, without a rapidly increasing budget, was spread exceedingly thin, with amounts available at the local level adequate to fund coordinating structures and some programs, but not enough to make much dent in local poverty. This problem derives, however, not from the early decision to make funds available in every area of the country but from the subsequent lowering of anticipated total CAP budgets.

SIMPLICITY OF FEDERAL PROCEDURES

Anyone who has experienced the red tape involved in obtaining a community-action grant might be surprised to learn that one of the early objectives was to make the federal procedures so simple that no more than 60, and preferably less than 30, days would elapse between the receipt of an application by OEO and the dispatch of funds to the grantee through a letter of credit to a local bank. Yet it is a fact that speed was one of our objectives—for the most part unattained.

Why did we believe that simple procedures were essential? Because we knew that we had to get the funds out fast; that the anti-poverty program had to "prove itself" quickly in the eyes of Congress, the White House, and the country at large; that the procedures had to be within the capabilities of local communities to follow; and that bureaucratic slowness could not be tolerated. This was supposed to be a "war."

Two administrative decisions were essential to our strategy for making the community-action staff of the new OEO responsive to the need for speed and efficiency. First, we rejected review of applications by specialists in favor of review by generalists. And second, we decided to move toward decentralization through the establishment of regional offices as soon as possible.

Specialists and generalists: the "field representative." Specialist review is one of the chief causes of bureaucratic slowness in processing applications for federal grants-in-aid. There are several forms of specialist review. One is to convene a "panel" of outside "experts" to review applications. Typically, as in the case of the President's Committee on Juvenile Delinquency, the panel comes together several times a year, discusses the applications, and depending on the powers of the panel, either advises the agency or approves or rejects applications. Review by such panels would have been unworkable in a program the size of CAP, and it would have been slow. Another form of specialist review is to have a full-time staff that represents different areas of expertise, with each such area required to approve an application before a grant is made. Under this procedure, applications generally move from the desk of one expert to another. Sometimes there is concurrent review; more frequently, an application does not move from one desk to another until the first desk has "signed off" on the application. "Sign off" implies that any problems have been worked out to the satisfaction of the particular expert; the problems that seem important to the next expert are not uncovered until the application reaches his desk. Under this procedure, the applicant may have to go through several revisions (a different revision for each expert) before the application is approved.

Instead of using either of the above patterns, we decided to put the essential review into the hands of "field representatives" who would be assigned to particular geographic areas. A small team of such field representatives, each team having a variety of levels of experience, from the recent college graduate to the seasoned bureaucrat, would work with the communities in an area, come to know the people who were preparing the application, raise obvious points of deficiency as soon as possible, work with the community on revising the application, and make a recommendation that OEO would (in 90 per cent of the cases) accept without further questioning. These generalists would be supported by experts (in the central office) in such fields as health, education, housing, and manpower who would give their advice when asked. The application forms were designed to require the least possible quantity of information about the proposed program, with the statement of budget the most important document submitted. Within reasonable limits, in short, we set out to "wholesale" community-action funds.

It was partly because of the significant responsibility of the position of the field representative that the community-action program was able to recruit an outstanding staff. We were looking for bright generalists with an ability to negotiate, to review budgets, to know their own limitations, and to ask the right questions. We found them

in many places, but we had to sift over 15,000 applications and interview about 2,000 job applicants for several hundred positions. They
were former high-school principals and teachers, foreign-service officers, lawyers, community-development workers who had been with
AID in Vietnam and elsewhere, civil rights leaders, social workers,
government bureaucrats, returned Peace Corps volunteers, labor ne-
gotiators, businessmen, and administrators of existing local anti-
poverty programs, to name just a few. They ranged in age from their
twenties to their sixties, with the average age about thirty-three. (A
high percentage of them, varying from about 25 to 35 per cent between 1964 and 1966, were either Negro, Puerto Rican, or Mexican-
American. It was probably the ablest and largest group of minority-
group *professionals* ever assembled in one government program.)

Regrettably, but perhaps inevitably, our hopes for this staff and
our conception of what the field representative could accomplish
—did not materialize soon enough. On the one hand, the nature of
the field representative's task at the community level became an increasingly "political" one. And on the other hand, the importance of
his recommendations in the Washington office became increasingly
diluted by unanticipated specialist review.

As indicated above, it was clear from conception that CAP, in
attempting to create a local consensus behind a local anti-poverty
program, would be in the middle of local politics. What was not clear
at first, however, was the crucial role that CAP field representatives
would play in the local political pulling and hauling.

The essential power of the field representative (and of OEO
itself) was to say no—that is, to refuse to approve a local proposal.
Sometimes this refusal would reflect the field representative's independent judgment of the merits of a program; at other times, it
would reflect the fact that a local consensus had not been created,
that a significant group had been left out or had been given too small
a role.

It is at this point that the power to say no blended with the
power to make positive recommendations, and the power to make
recommendations appeared to the local people as the power to command. For example, when a proposal would state that representatives
of the poor would have, say, 20 per cent of the seats on the governing
body of a local community-action agency, the field representative
would be called on to give his opinion as to whether this was sufficient. Usually there would be a group pushing for a higher percent-

age. The field representative had no clear guidelines to answer this question since the statute merely said that there should be "maximum feasible participation," and administrative policy was not to specify a fixed percentage but rather to let this vary with local conditions and wishes. He was thus forced to rely on his own sense of what was required in order to obtain local agreement, since that was always his objective. As an outsider, he presumably had the advantage of some objectivity, although to the extent that he had become thoroughly familiar with the local participants, he undoubtedly had come to trust the judgment and the objectives of some more than others. Objectivity was thus hard to preserve in the face of detailed knowledge of the local scene; but without such knowledge, an appearance of objectivity was simply a form of arbitrariness.

In short, the field representative frequently became both judge and participant, a negotiator whose negotiations were often the subject of large headlines in local newspapers and who was almost always labeled as a partisan of one side or another at some stage in the grant-making process. (Frequently, the field representative found it convenient—and properly so—to blame final judgments on his regional director or on Washington.) In short, OEO faced a dilemma in administering CAP: It wanted to give the major role in shaping the local program to the local community itself, without detailed federal specifications; but the very absence of such federal specifications propelled the federal field representative as a personality into the center of the local political stage.

Meanwhile, at the central office of OEO, the field representative's power was being subjected to pressures of a very different sort. Specialist review crept back into the picture, often for very good reasons; and with it came incredible bureaucratic red tape. First, the director insisted that his lawyers (the Office of General Counsel) review every grant before he approved it. Second, because of the Act's prohibition against "general aid to education" and its specific endorsement of "special remedial and other noncurricular educational assistance," a staff of educational experts (some of them from the Office of Education) had to review and approve every application to fund an educational program. Third, because of the increasingly controversial nature of the Act's requirement for "maximum feasible participation of the residents of the areas and members of the groups served" in the development, conduct, and administration of local programs, OEO's Office of Inspection became responsible, in the eyes of the director, for satisfying him that this requirement had been met. And finally, because of the concern that local community-action agencies have adequate representation of minority groups on local governing boards, one of the director's special assistants was given the task of reviewing applications for compliance with this requirement.

Thus there were at least three, and frequently four, "sign offs" on every application: "legal," "inspection," "civil rights," and "education." For many months—roughly from January to August 1965—the director resolved disputes at "sign-off" sessions. With Mr. Shriver presiding, the field representative (or, in his absence in the field, a representative of the central community-action staff) would be called on to defend a proposed grant against the criticisms of the lawyers, the inspectors, and the civil rights staff. After about August 1965, proposed grants were brought to Mr. Shriver's desk, with a sign-off sheet appropriately initialed or with memoranda of objections. Whether oral or written, however, the result of the minute attention given by the specialist staffs to each particular proposed grant was, as someone inside OEO put it, certainly not "wholesaling," and not even "retailing," but was more like "woodcarving."

Let it be said in Mr. Shriver's favor that the result of this vigorous questioning was frequently a more effective program. Let it also be said in his favor that in every instance I know of in which the community-action staff decided to fight the lawyers or the inspectors or the civil rights staff on the merits of a proposed grant, he supported the community-action staff. In addition, the sign-off sessions were an important way for Mr. Shriver to make his presence at the head of the agency directly felt down the line. Finally, Mr. Shriver's sensitive political antennae—his awareness that at any minute his phone might ring, with some congressman or senator or mayor or county commissioner or civil rights leader complaining about a particular program—corrected many deficiencies that might have been embarrassing later.

Nevertheless, the cost was great. My guess is that Mr. Shriver's phone rang more often about delays in approval of applications than about funded grants with problems. Given specialist review, delay was inevitable. Proposals were far from perfect when received from the communities. The field representatives and the central community-action staff therefore faced a dilemma: Either they must batten down every hatch and submit only perfect grants, in which case the job became too big for them as they were swamped by large numbers of vastly inadequate applications; or they must submit an imperfect proposal and let the specialists correct the deficiencies. Usually, of course, both occurred: the community-action staff did the best job it could, *and* the specialists gave the proposals further minute attention. Instead of sixty days, it took more like six months to get most community-action grants through OEO. This was true at least until early 1966, when a large amount of authority was given to regional offices. The importance of regional offices will be discussed in the next section; suffice it to say here that central-office specialist review, when combined with a director who imposed a rigorous standard of excellence on every grant he signed, meant that speed was sacrificed. Individualized administration thus took its toll in a reputation for bureaucratic bungling at its worst—a reputation that was hard to change even after efficiency improved.

Decentralization to OEO Regional Offices. The other major procedure designed to provide administrative speed, efficiency, and responsiveness fared a little better than the decision to have review by generalists instead of by experts. In form, at least, decentralization was begun early. We established regional desks by December 1964, after the first two groups of community-action grants had been signed. In those early days, field representatives worked out of Washington, but they frequently traveled to the region for which they were responsible. By March 1965, temporary offices had been opened in Atlanta (for the Southeast), New York City (for the Northeast), Chicago (for the Great Lakes region), and San Francisco (for the Pacific region). The beginnings of a regional office opened in Washington to handle the Middle Atlantic states. By summer, the last two offices were opened: in Austin, Texas (for the Southwest), and in Kansas City (for the central region).

But we could not call them "regional offices" because regional directors had not yet been appointed and would not be appointed until Mr. Shriver had recruited his directors, had "cleared" them with all important state and congressional interests, and had persuaded the Bureau of the Budget and the Civil Service Commission to establish the pay level at the top of the regular Civil Service pyramid: GS-18 (about $25,000 at the time). This latter was no mean achievement since regional directors for most federal departments were at the GS-16 level (a few were at the GS-17 level). It took Mr. Shriver at least a year to win this victory, a victory that was somewhat diluted by the long, painful period when the community-action staff wanted to decentralize fast but met resistance at the top and when communities seeking speedy assistance from OEO became disgruntled with an unanticipated and inefficient centralism.

When appointed, regional directors were to have authority (in varying degrees) over CAP, the Job Corps, and VISTA, the three programs created by the Act that were administered directly by OEO. But until the regional director was appointed, which did not happen until the summer and fall of 1965, we had to call the offices "temporary office space" for our community-action field representatives.

Regional offices without authority were empty vessels. It was not until December 1965 that the director delegated to the regional directors the authority to approve community-action grants up to $500,000. Proposed grants over that amount were sent from the regions to Washington for review by central community-action staff and sign off by the specialists. In January 1967, complete authority was given to the regional directors without financial limit. Review by lawyers, inspectors, and civil rights staff became less important as their review functions were either decentralized or abandoned under prodding from the regional director. (Review by educational specialists was abandoned partly because of the passage of the Elementary and Secondary Education Act of 1965, which absorbed many of the educational programs funded the year before under the poverty Act, and partly because the lawyers had been at least as wary as the educationists of anything looking like "general aid" to education.)

The delay in the establishment of full-scale regional offices convinced most large cities and many smaller communities that Washington was the place to get their problems solved. It was hard to convince the person on the other end of the phone or the delegation in the corridor that he really should be talking to the regional office staff, particularly if the regional staff had already indicated that the delegation would not get exactly what it wanted. The presence of the Congress in Washington added to the importance of the central office; congressmen do not like to be told to call a regional office to find out why a pending application has not been approved, so the central office had to keep up to date on the status of every pending application in every region.

Uneasily and somewhat equivocally, regional offices grew in power and responsibility. Increasingly, they have become the focal points for community contact and, to a lesser degree, for federal coordination. Working relationships have been developed between OEO regional offices and those of the Department of Labor and the Department of Health, Education and Welfare (HEW), so there is some hope that meaningful attempts will be made to coordinate federal progams as they affect particular communities in a region. One should not be too sanguine about the prospects, however, partly because the regional boundaries and headquarter cities established by the three departments do not coincide (HEW, for instance, has a regional office in Boston; OEO does not), partly because the responsibility of the various regional offices varies from program to program, and partly because independent programmatic interests tend always to win out over interagency coordination. Nevertheless, by now, most communities have gotten the idea that they should begin negotiating with OEO at the regional level; a few of the big cities have not learned, probably never will, and politically at least, perhaps never should.

Both review by generalists and the early establishment of regional offices were designed to make CAP responsive to the needs of local communities. This was not to be a program run by experts out of Washington; it was to be run from nearby federal offices by people who talked the language of the generalists running the local programs. Early and perhaps inevitable compromises were made with both principles. The administration of community action came to appear as a peculiar blend of bureaucratic remoteness and active interference. Federal procedures turned out to be neither simple nor speedy. In short, what was thought to be an important ingredient in eventual success was missing in the crucial period when congressmen and mayors and the White House were forming their impressions of community action as a technique in federal anti-poverty strategy.

FLEXIBILITY OF PROGRAM PRIORITIES

The Act specifies no particular program priorities, authorizing, instead, community-action programs

including, but not limited to, employment, job training and counseling, health, vocational rehabilitation, housing, home management, welfare, and special remedial and other noncurricular educational assistance for the benefit of low-income individuals and families.

There was probably no more important early administrative decision than the one to leave these program priorities flexible—in the hands of local communities that would have to establish their own priorities in allocating scarce federal funds. This decision, like others just discussed above, was soon eroded from both the local and federal levels.

It was thought important to maintain flexibility of priorities because conditions differed so much from community to community and because there was such distrust of a federal blueprint to solve local problems. Indeed, the very articulation of local priorities was thought to be an essential part of community action, one of those instructive exercises that a community had to do for itself.

Many communities took the easy way out: They set no priorities at all. Instead, local bureaucracies with a capacity to spend federal funds, such as school systems that needed more remedial teachers, obtained unduly large amounts of money. Most community-action proposals were little more than a number of separate "component programs" put together in one binder. It was the rare community that developed those linkages among programs that community action was supposed to facilitate.

While most communities paid little attention to priorities, Washington began to provide some priorities of its own by making available funds that for certain purposes and under certain conditions could be obtained "over and above guidelines." While these "national emphasis programs"—beginning with Project Headstart and expanding to include legal-service programs, manpower programs, and health programs—resulted in some excellent programs that otherwise might not have been started, they nevertheless tended to cut the heart out of community action. For example, in the 1966–1967 fiscal year, Congress earmarked for the extremely popular Project Headstart *more* funds ($352 million) than it made available for unrestricted use by communities in *all* other community-action fields ($323 million). As of July 1, 1967, there was not enough unrestricted community-action money left even to refund all existing community-action projects.

There has been much talk that some of these national emphasis programs might be "spun off" and administered by other federal agencies, such as the Office of Education in the case of Headstart, the Department of Justice in the case of legal services, and the Labor Department in the case of manpower programs. If this were done, these programs would then take their place among other federal grant-in-aid programs. On the merits, local community-action agencies might not object since it is already their responsibility to attempt to coordinate *all* available federal, state, and local programs, tying them together into a meaningful local package. (This was "bottom-up" coordination, which was thought more likely to succeed than top-down coordination from the federal level, although both strategies were tried.) Politically, however, such spinning off of popular programs would appear to be a slap at OEO, would encourage the splintering of local efforts, would leave OEO with only the least popular programs within its direct domain, and would take away from the local community-action agency much of the direct operating responsibility that has turned out to be the life blood for most such agencies.

More basically, spinning off some of these very successful programs might seem to preserve community action as a source of unrestricted and innovative seed money, meeting local needs as the local communities defined those needs. But it is not at all clear that local community-action agencies really are innovative. Particularly under the pressures of the restricted community-action budget, local community-action agencies have tended to think mainly about how they can continue to fund and in some cases expand programs that they have already begun. Little thought has been given to the development of new programs. In this setting, priorities have tended to reflect the strength of particular local bureaucracies fighting for particular programs rather than any independent community-wide assessment of the comparative value of the programs themselves.

The objective of maintaining administrative flexibility in establishing program priorities so that the local communities can do it for themselves has resulted, for the most part, in the absence of any priorities at all. And community action without community priorities is almost a contradiction in terms.

LOCAL POLITICS AND NATIONAL POLITICS

The Act was immersed in national-party politics from its inception. Passed in the summer of 1964, less than three months before the Presidential election, the Act was viewed by most Republicans as a partisan measure. And Democratic congressmen, senators, and a Democratic President undoubtedly expected to reap at least some harvests from the distribution of substantial amounts of federal money to local programs. This is not to suggest that partisan concerns were predominant, simply that they were present.

It may seem surprising, therefore, that traditional party politics in fact played little role in the administration of CAP. For reasons that have been described in previous sections, it was local politics, not national politics, that concerned us. Yet, one of the lessons of the first four years of the program is that local politics turned out to be of acute interest and impact at the national level. The controversies that erupted in community after community in building a consensus behind a local program found their way quickly to the national stage, antagonizing Republicans and Democrats alike. It was a very bipartisan antipathy that, in 1966, came close to scuttling the program.

The White House was an important receiver of complaints from governors, mayors, congressmen, and senators, and before a year of operation was barely over, it had become embroiled in controversy. By the summer of 1965, big city mayors had complained directly to the Vice-President about the problems that CAP was creating in their local bailiwicks. Democrats on Capitol Hill and in state houses had gone directly to the President. Presumably in response to these pressures, in the fall of that year, second-echelon officials of the Bureau of the Budget gave "instructions" to second-echelon CAP officials to downgrade the importance of "maximum feasible participation" and to use the poor primarily in carrying out local programs rather than in designing them. Within a week of these instructions having been issued, Mr. Shriver publicly refused to make any change in policy, saying:

The Bureau of the Budget has a statutory duty to advise and consult with all agencies of the U.S. Government. And the Bureau's help in the War against Poverty has been extraordinarily useful from the earliest days to the present. In this case, the Bureau of the Budget may well believe that we have stressed the statutory requirement too strongly. But the poor don't think so. Many Congressmen don't think so . . . it is a serious misunderstanding of fact and policy to conclude that there has been or will be a decreased emphasis on maximum feasible participation of the poor. There will be no retreat from our earlier policies and no slackening in our effort to press for vigorous and creative compliance with that requirement.[4]

Mr. Shriver's stand was essential to the encouragement of local consensus-building, which was then in its most intense period, as many communities sought to put their local structures into final or nearly final shape. For Mr. Shriver to have taken any other stand might have been good national politics, but it would have been bad local politics, and thus bad for community action.

After Mr. Shriver had taken and preserved his position, one might have supposed that he would have received overwhelming support from the poor. For after all, if the Poverty Program did not have the poor for constituent support, whom could it count on? By late 1965, consensus politics, far from succeeding in making everyone happy because they had a part in the action, had alienated nearly every potential supporter. Every mayor had a gripe; congressmen were plagued by visiting delegations from two, three, or four local factions; governors were irritated at mayors; social workers and many other professionals resented intrusions both from the politicians and from the poor; liberals who wanted local programs to shake up the established politicians were upset at the amount of accommodation OEO required; and established politicians wished they could run their own anti-poverty programs, with their own trusted friends among the poor, rather than negotiating compromises with more vocal and militant local groups and individuals. In short, by dangling a difficult consensus in front of every major element in each community, the program appeared less like a golden egg of opportunity than a golden apple of discord.

In fact, even the poor could not be counted on for support. In April 1966, five months after Mr. Shriver took his stand, he was booed out of the hall at the first national gathering of representatives of the poor. A new kind of politics expressed itself at that meeting. The intensity and unpredictability of that politics can be measured partly by the fact that the representatives of the poor at the same meeting spent their major effort in trying to pass a resolution that would have required that the governing board of the host group be composed of at least 51 per cent of representatives of the poor. The host group was the "Citizens' Crusade Against Poverty" (CCAP), an organization created by liberal labor forces to mobilize the private sector in support of effective community action. The poor were not then in a mood to accept either leadership or support from their customary benefactors, even under the guise of a "citizens' crusade."

Was CAP a cause of this new militancy? I think not. The program's existence and its format may have accelerated movements already underway and may have stimulated "indigenous" leadership that might otherwise have been undiscovered, at least for a while. But basically, the response to "maximum feasible participation" was more a symptom than a cause. It was a symptom of a larger malady that had glimmered in the serious racial disturbances of 1964 and in the "burn, baby, burn" of Watts in the summer of 1965 and that had fanned the flames of the riots of 1966 and 1967. During the same period, "black power" was becoming an important new element on both national and local scenes, and the same slap at liberal whites that was implicit in the CCAP meeting was seen in the virtual expulsion of whites from the more militant civil rights groups in the same period.

Community action, in short, was attempting to reach community consensus at a time when race, politics, and poverty were pulling communities and the nation apart. In retrospect, the consensus that CAP sought to build—and successfully so in many communities—appears both more difficult and more important. Indeed, the pulling and hauling, the alliances and counteralliances developed in the course of creating a local community-action structure may well have served to familiarize one set of leaders with another in a manner that will prove ever more useful as more extreme elements enter the local picture. Those who have struggled over the structure and programmatic content of the local community-action agency may find that they have more in common with each other than with those on the outside who say they want to overthrow the whole system. In this light, it is neither surprising nor insignificant that in the riots of 1967, local community-action workers were prominent among the peacemakers.

Community action thus demonstrated the close connection between local politics and national politics. Local consensus-building was played out on a national stage. In the first two years, community action was an embarrassment at the national level. After 1966, however, it began to play a role that was more constructive, both nationally and locally. This was partly because it had taken time for most communities to work out the basic structural, or political, problems involved in creating and setting the directions of the local agency. It was also partly because times had changed, and what was earlier viewed as divisive was later seen to have important unifying attributes. Local-poverty politics, in the end, may thus provide an essential technique in helping to hold this nation together.

WHAT HAVE WE LEARNED?

What lessons can be learned from nearly four years of experience with community-action programs? Is there a role for community action in a larger anti-poverty strategy?

The first conclusion is that not much can be learned from this particular period. The growth and development of community action was stunted after its first year when, in December 1965, the White House imposed severe and unexpected budgetary limitations on domestic programs for the period beginning July 1, 1966. These limitations were made more severe the next year when Congress earmarked large portions of community-action funds for specific programs. This double deceleration of the central community-action program was particularly painful because of disappointed expectations around the country, right down to the neighborhood level in city after city. The limitations also made it harder to recruit and retain capable local administrators and project directors, whose presence may turn out to be the single most important variable in the success of local programs. In other words, community action has been funded with too little money and for too short a time to determine whether it has been successful, and it probably will not be permitted to survive in a form and at a funding level that can conceivably produce either success or a fair evaluation.

What might success have looked like? An image of neighborhood boards—including the local school principal, the minister, the settlement-house director, the head of the tenants' union, the articulate welfare mother, the bright ex-convict who is a neighborhood leader—conceiving, planning, organizing, and running neighborhood programs comes to mind. The programs would include job centers reaching out to people who wanted jobs to tell them what was available, how they could train to be qualified, and if the job was located in suburbia, how they could get to the job; neighborhood law offices and medical centers; schools being operated at night as community centers and in the mornings as cafeterias; Headstart classes and adult-education classes, with high-school students teaching in both; day-care centers in which children of working mothers are given more than baby-sitting care. One could go on. The point is that localism has an obvious role to play when it is effective and when it is part of a larger strategy.

One trouble with community action, and indeed with the whole War against Poverty, is that it was oversold as *the* answer when in reality it was neither the answer nor part of any larger strategy. CAP was not really part of a "war," and the military language—assuming victory at the end—was misleading.

It was more like a local political game in which the poor were beginning to learn the rules and play their part with others in a community effort to bring about institutional, psychological, and educational change. This is an important objective, but not one that will eradicate poverty if nothing else is done. Clearly some form of public employment is needed beyond those "nonprofessionals" who were hired to work in community-action programs. And, clearly, major changes are needed in our welfare system to provide an adequate income to the majority of poor who cannot work either because of age or disability or the need to care for children.

Assuming that such a larger strategy is developed, however, there is an important role for community-action agencies. In establishing these agencies, communities have been through a political exercise that was both intense and useful. And the structure that emerged is worth preserving and encouraging; if more anti-poverty funds are ever made available at the federal level, a viable entity exists at the local level with a real potential for working, in conjunction with other programs, toward the elimination of local poverty.

The danger is, however, that in saying that community action alone is not sufficient we will be interpreted as suggesting that it is worthy only of the scrap heap and that some new program is the magic solution. We must face the fact that there are no magic solutions to the problems of poverty. A variety of programs are needed to deal with a variety of causes and aspects of poverty. The sooner we learn that we must not overreact to the problems of one program in pursuit of the promise of another, the better for informed dialogue— and for the poor.

Notes

1. *110 United States Congressional Record,* 88th Congress, second session (August 7, 1964), p. 17,997.
2. *Instructions for Applicants,* vol. I, *Community Action Program Guide* (October 1965), p. 18.
3. U.S. Conference of Mayors, *Special Report: The Office of Economic Opportunity and Local Community Action Agencies* (Fall 1965), mimeograph, pp. 5–6.
4. OEO press release, Scottsdale, Ariz., November 5, 1965.

Chapter 6

☞ *Rural Upheaval: Confrontation and Accommodation* ROBERT COLES

The rural South and Appalachia have exerted enormous influence on our nation's political climate, an unjustifiable influence if only the total number of people in both regions is considered. It was in Little Rock and New Orleans that schoolchildren faced mobs, and through television did so before millions of Americans in California, Illinois, and in New York. It was in Montgomery, Alabama, that Rosa Parks said she would not move to the rear of a bus. And it was in that same city that Martin Luther King—a young Negro Baptist minister "out of Atlanta"—came to her side. It was in Greensboro, North Carolina, that four students staged a sit-in; and if they failed to get any of Woolworth's coffee for their effort, they had the eventual satisfaction of seeing a random act of theirs in 1960 become an example to thousands of other nonviolent demonstrators. Freedom rides, marches, state-wide summer projects—the South experienced them all; and so did the rest of the country when newspapers and cameras covered the news that was made.

In 1960 John F. Kennedy went before Appalachia's poor rural Protestant people to ask their help in his quest for the Presidency. They said yes to him, those "hillbillies" did, with their long bodies and craggy faces and their Protestant Anglo-Saxon heritage. The young Catholic aspirant, out of Boston and Harvard, drew them down in large numbers from the hollows. Each one of them seemed at first glance shy and sad, perhaps members of Lincoln's family still in mourning. At first glance, they also seemed impossibly unwilling to commit themselves, content merely to stand and watch, listen and on occasion faintly smile. They nevertheless knew a winner, and they knew that they needed him to be *their* winner. John Kennedy worked hard in West Virginia and never quite knew while there to what avail. From what I have heard these recent years from people in the region, he was the prototypal "community organizer" from the "outside." He came in to offer help and, admittedly, to be helped himself. He was "different," a stranger. He didn't talk the right way: in every promise of assistance, a prickly, oversensitive ear could detect an implied criticism. Still, the mountain people were in trouble, and this man from "over there in Massachusetts" offered help. Despite any misgivings the Appalachian people may have had and any mistakes in their dealings with a "special subculture" made by John Kennedy and his aides, an alliance was forged. To this day, I find the former President's picture on the walls of cabins that lie in the remotest hollows imaginable.

It is possible, then, for isolated rural people to reach and be reached; it is possible for them to affect significantly, even momentously, the populous cities and to respond more quickly to urban influences than some observers would seem to think. It can be argued that the South's villages and small towns provided the atmosphere of clear-cut contrast, of total black exile and total white control, that made the civil rights struggle so appealing to the entire nation. (I fear the word "appealing" may be just right in its implication of something that calls for an almost self-serving kind of sympathy rather than active, dedicated, and sacrificial involvement.) Yet, something contagious happened in the South, something that for a while began—and only began—to make a difference elsewhere, in more ambiguous situations. It is possible to see the War on Poverty as a direct aftermath of conflict in the South and of the "new" interest in Appalachia that developed after 1960 (and perhaps culminated so far as the public is concerned in the famous CBS documentary "Christmas in Appalachia").

Nor is it stretching a point to call many of our present urban problems in essence rural ones that have been exported. The sharecroppers and tenant farmers, the migrant farmers and Appalachian people I have studied these past years all have their kin in Chicago, New York, or Detroit. Some of them have gone North and stayed, so that I now am studying not their rural lives but their lives in transition, their lives as immigrants—from two very distant regions that both, perhaps, qualify as nations within a nation. We in the cities are beginning to learn about what life *was* like in the Delta or in the mountain hollows of Kentucky and West Virginia. The presence among "us" of thousands of confused and virtually penniless exiles from "the land" makes the problems of, say, McCormick County, South Carolina, the very real problems of New York City. For example, I am appalled at the poor health I find among ghetto children, and I am also puzzled when a Negro mother I know refuses to avail herself of the medical services of a "city hospital" that was built and is run to provide people like her and her children free medical care. Yet that mother has only recently come to Boston from McCormick County, South Carolina. She is thirty-five and has seven children. Except for the three times she was taken to Augusta, Georgia, to have her baby in a hospital, she has never seen a doctor in her life. (Her other children were born at home.)

Here are the "facts," the raw medical information that might be called the "background" to her current "attitudes" toward doctors and hospitals. (The welfare woman who visits the mother has asked me to look into her client's "fears" and "anxieties," so that four boys and three girls will receive the attention and care they need, the inoculations and vitamin supplements, the corrective surgery and eyeglasses, the dental care.) There are exactly two (white) physicians in McCormick County, South Carolina. When they are called for help, they ask for a fee, and that is known by the mothers and fathers who are farm hands, occasional harvesters, or out of work altogether. In 1961, the infant-mortality rates in McCormick County were as follows: for white children, 208 per 10,000; and for Negro children, 1,073 per 10,000.[1] Those terrible numbers, comparable to what comes forth from government bureaus in New Delhi,[2] have a far wider, greater, and more persistent "meaning" than the most covetous statistician could ever wish or dream. "In McCormick County we learned to do without doctors, because there just wasn't none around," said our welfare worker's troubled Negro mother recently. Then she went on:

Now up here, they tell us they're here, waiting. But I get the shakes every time I think of going near the hospital, and I don't know how to stop them, the shakes. If you're brought up to have them, you can't just stop because you've moved up the road, no matter how far.

Actually, several months later she did go to the Boston City Hospital, and since then she has overcome her childhood inhibitions, perhaps more directly and easily than some of us. I mention her experience not only to make the obvious point that lives in their continuity transcend abstractions like "rural" or "urban" but also in order to introduce her younger brother, whose activities I believe have helped make poor people all over America more bothersome—if that is the word—to the rest of us.

He is twenty-six, Peter, and it is hard to know what to "call" him. There are words, but none of them quite fit. In the early sixties he was "simply" a civil rights worker, a young Negro college student who worked with Dr. Martin Luther King's organization. He worked in rural Georgia, not too far from his home county of McCormick, South Carolina. In 1965, he became a "community organizer" for a brief period. The work was in Washington, D.C., where he hoped to gain some "techniques" and "skills" that he could put to use in what he then called "the rural situation." (He had already learned a good deal of jargon when he arrived in Washington.) He lasted three months in the city, then went "home"—his way of describing the return South. And he went South with a vengeance—to the Mississippi Delta, where he became involved in the now-rather-famous Child Development Group of Mississippi (CDGM). Without enumerating the historical and political details of the group's brief existence,[3] I can say that the "operation" is designed to reach the poorest children of that very poor state and begin to educate them (through Headstart programs) in such a way that they learn not only their "letters and numbers" but something about *themselves*—children of the Delta, poor Negro boys and girls who need better food, a doctor, clothes, and perhaps most of all a sense of what a future can be, one that is not an endless repetition of the past. CDGM was started in 1965 and funded by the Office of Economic Opportunity (OEO). Many of its leaders were white "outsiders," though fairly soon Negroes from Mississippi became not only recipients of the "benefits" of Headstart programs but by design active in planning the organization's purposes and activities. Peter was one of the early "organizers" who helped shape the philosophy of what might be called, with no exaggeration, the nation's most forceful and unusual preschool "program."

"I think of myself when I'm with these kids," he says repeatedly. He even tells the children about his own life and does so in a direct, open way that commands the extraordinary gift of silent attention from five-year-old boys and girls:

I come from nothing, the way white people would call it, and black men, too, the few of us that have got a lot of money and put on airs like the white man. No one in my family ever went to school except a few weeks here and there, you know, when there was no work to do in the fields or around the house. The white people, they didn't care—they didn't even want us to take school too seriously. And our colored teachers, they wanted us all white and starchy, neat and obedient. They knew they couldn't get what they wanted—us to be little angels for them—so they called us all kinds of names, right to our faces, and pushed us around. We felt lousy before them—afraid and no good, no damn good. I recall when I was about five or six I'd hear from them that niggers were no good, most of them, and they were poor because they didn't know how to take care of themselves. So, I'd go home and tell that to my mother, and she got so nervous she didn't know what to say. Sometimes she would shake her head, but agree. Sometimes she would say it wasn't so, but tell me to mind the teachers and try to follow what she says, so that I wouldn't have to work the white man's land. Most of the time, though, she didn't say a word. Nor did my daddy. They were too tired, and maybe too confused. I don't know the truth, even today.

Well, actually, I owe a lot to one teacher. She gave me a test when I was in the third grade, or the fourth—it didn't make any difference, it was just a one-room school. She said I was a genius or something from the results and I must have cheated somehow. (How's that for building up a guy's confidence about himself!) So they sent me over to Columbia, South Carolina, or someplace for another test, and they watched me like hawks and police dogs and everything. And I broke the bank again.

So, they gave me a special plan, they called it. They asked my parents to keep me in school all the time, no matter what, and they said they'd even send me over to Greenwood, South Carolina, for a special class they had for smart little colored children who knew how to behave and had a lot of brains. They even brought in white teachers every once in a while to give us a special talk. As I recall, we'd spend most of *that* hour or so just looking, not listening. If they had asked me what I learned after a white lady's talk I'd have had to tell them nothing, except what she wore, and how she was made up, and how her hair looked, and the way she talked, and the jewelry she had on, and all that. I'd go home and tell my mother about all that, and she'd tell me that "white folks sure can look pretty"—meaning *we* can't. I remember learning that over and over again when I was five or six—how pretty white people are and how useless and hopeless it is for us to try to be pretty or good-looking, or whatever. (It's not the words, it's the feeling, you know. My parents never came out and told us that "white" meant "beautiful," or "black" meant "ugly" or "menial." They made us *feel* all that—and you never forget it that way.)

That's what CDGM is about. We want to help these kids, the poorest kids in America, feel some self-respect, feel that there's a chance for them, on their own, as black kids from the Black Belt, as farm kids, the sons and daughters of sharecroppers. We want them to feel they can stay here, as well as go North to Chicago—and be *men* and *women*, wherever they go, wherever they live. You talk about poverty; you could give a lot of these people here—maybe a lot of Negroes everywhere—a million dollars and they'd still feel so low and scared before the white man that they'd feel poor, even with color television in every room of a 25-room house.

We try to show them that we respect them, as children, as human beings. We aren't forever comparing them to some white face in a white child's book. We show them the strength and value of their *own* words, their own tradition—they are the children of workers, who built this whole state, with their sweat and tears and shortened lives. We tell the kids that, and they listen.[4]

In 1965 I heard him tell children just that, and they did listen, much more attentively than I might have believed had I not seen them do so again and again. He would stand before them and talk, much as he did with me and then show them pictures of white suburban homes near Jackson, of words and illustrations from books used in both the Negro and white schools of Mississippi, of their own homes. He would emphasize the *reality* of their condition, but insist on the possibilities that nevertheless exist: "We have to learn not because the white man is embarrassed if we can't sign our name to prove we owe him everything. We have to learn *who* we are and *where* we're going and *what* we want." He would say it over and over to the children, that last sentence, and I would later hear them reciting their who's, where's, and what's to one another. They would also carry the message home, to the cabins and huts, up the alleys of the small towns, or alongside the cotton fields.

In one home that I had been visiting for years before CDGM came into existence, I heard this from the mother of one of Peter's students:

That teacher must be sent down here from Someone Big, I'll say. If I didn't think all the Disciples were white, I'd begin to wonder. He talks like he knows everything, and isn't one bit scared. He talks different from those civil rights ones, too. They'll tell you not to be afraid to follow them, their lead. He says go be yourself and don't be afraid of that, being who you are. I tell my boy I don't understand it, to be honest, but it sure sounds different, I'll have to admit. Of course, what should we do next, that's what I'd like to know, and that's what I'd like to ask him, Mr. Peter.

Mr. Peter, like all good modern teachers, wants to bring the home into the school, the school into the home. After he had figured out what he was going to say to his young students, how he was going to hold their interest, he did indeed visit their parents and get them to ask him the questions he knew they had in mind anyway:

I try to tell them that we've got to stick together and *do* something. At first a lot of them would give me that blank stare, or the sly look, and some still do; but a lot of them have changed. Especially they pay attention when I remind them that the only way to change things is *acting*—even when it seems hopeless. I must have told the story of Rosa Parks in Montgomery a million times in the past few months. She reaches them, and the story of the Freedom Rides. I tell them that everyone said they were wrong, the Freedom Riders, or they were foolish, or they weren't doing the right thing in the right way at the right time. Even our "friends," I tell them, said we should "take it easy," and not do too much marching, and too much demonstrating, and too much protesting. "You have to pace yourselves," we'd hear from the conservative Negroes, and "not so fast you don't bring along the rest of the country" from the liberal whites.

Then I tell them what *happened*—because we didn't do the "right" thing, the "sensible" thing, the "smart" thing, the "practical" thing. They *know* what happened, but I remind them, about five times each visit. And before I leave I tell them what *they* can do: support us, CDGM; send their children to a Headstart center that means business; go register to vote; tell the "bossman" they want more money. I know the last thing isn't likely to happen—they'll be thrown off the land first. But they're going to be thrown off anyway—and even *they* know there's no point going North now. All that's up there is welfare and rats; and what happens in Watts is what they'll be traveling two thousand miles to see. So, we've got to stay here, and organize here, and make it work down here. It's our state, as much as whitey's, and we'd better let him know it, and let the people in Washington know it. They can invest in dams and conservation and foreign countries; let them invest in us, right in this place, and they'll be helping their cities in the bargain, I'll tell you.

They nod, the people he visits, and I've seen some of them give him an unbelieving smile that I suppose someone like me has to call "hostile." They sometimes escort him to the door as if he were a white insurance salesman; it's an ingratiating "yes" and "yes" and "yes" until he has left—when you know that they will laugh scornfully and bitterly. The mother in the family I knew best put it this way:

I don't see what they're talking about. There's nothing, absolutely nothing, we can do, except be as always—and hope somehow it'll change. He can't fool me, that man Peter, he can't even fool himself. I can tell that he doesn't know what to do any more than I do.

Yet, her children were excited by what they learned, and they were getting the best meals they ever had—and all at government expense. What is more, she and other parents were coming together and talking—about their children, yes, but about other matters, too. From visit to visit I could watch a federal anti-poverty program—a unique one in a uniquely difficult situation—take root in the mind of an individual mother. Coming together with others prompted this observation from her: "I've never done that, sat and talked about anything with people. At first you don't know what there is to say, and then you find you've been thinking about this and that and the other thing, and you start in."

She would come home and talk to her husband and to her neighbors about the meetings. She began to tell her older children that there were other ways to learn, other things to learn, than those provided by the state of Mississippi and their county's board of education. She would also become downcast and have no reply to make when her husband pointed out that good ideas were useless in the face of a sheriff's gun. But she would go to the next meeting and bring up *that* subject for discussion:

My husband says for me to think about the sheriff and the policemen and what they'll do when we start getting more and more ideas in our head, and then talk out loud about them in front of the courthouse. There won't be one of us left here, he says. We won't have a job among us; we won't have a cent in welfare money; we won't have our homes; we'll have to run for our lives, clear out of the state. And my brother tried that, and went up to Cleveland, Ohio. Now he sits all day in a store to keep from the snow, and he hides from the welfare lady, so that his wife Martha can collect her check. He says it's like a real good job down here, being on welfare is, because they gives you enough to pay the rent and eat. But he says there's not a thing for him to do, and he gets tired, and he thinks he's getting sick from sitting around all day. Sometimes he wishes he could just do some chopping and go get the water like in the old days down here—but he'd never want to come back, you can be sure, just to do that. So, if we're going to leave, all of us, then O.K. But if we plan to stay we'd best be careful, that's what my husband says. And isn't he right?

They weren't at all sure her husband was right. One or two mothers nodded their heads, and another one paid her recognition to the length and ardor of the statement she had heard by saying, as if in church, "Yes, you're right." Peter was there as an observer and a teacher. He wanted to know what "others" thought. For a minute and ten seconds there was silence, and the chairs squeaked with shifting bodies. I used the movement in my watch as an excuse to avoid looking around, and all the while I expected *Peter* to come up with something, to break the impasse and send us along a more hopeful road. Suddenly, one of those enormous women I have sometimes seen at such meetings stood up. I had seen her at several earlier gatherings. She always wore large printed dresses full of flowers and bold colors as if she long ago had decided to enjoy her fat. She regularly sat in the rear, on a long bench, for which she seemed grateful. She had a habit of putting her right hand through her hair as if she were looking for something, then inspecting her palm and fingers when she was through, and finally resting the entire arm on the back of the bench—where no one else sat. The fingers would soon be moving again and one could safely bet everything in the world that the hand would soon be raised again, the fingers soon be weaving and scratching their way on the top of her head.

She had immediately commanded everyone's attention by her move. They heard her get up and move two steps forward. She hesitated. She seemed voiceless. She seemed ready to sit down again. Peter stood up, nervous and ready to have his say. Suddenly the woman spoke:

I have two children here in Headstart. I have older ones, and they're not eligible for anything as I see it. I have three of them younger, and God knows if the government up there in Washington will desert us after a while. But I plan to stay here, and if for no other reason just to hear my boy, he's five, and my girl, she's six, come home and talk to me the way they do. They say I'm a fool and I've been a fool all these years putting up with things. I ask them what "things," and they can't answer except to show me that they can fill in the picture books they're given at school—and the pictures show us with our heads looking up and real proud-like.

So I think we should stay right here and keep our poverty program going the way it is, and if the state police come and try to break it up, and scare us to death, then we might as well fight them over this than anything else. To me it don't matter if we vote or not, because we can't seem to win even if we do vote, from what I hear, like up there in the North. But the children, they're learning how to spell right and speak right, and most of all, learning about themselves and us, the colored people and what we've gone through these past ten thousand years (and every year is a century to you and me), and what we've done for the country—build all that's important, I think, if you would ask me.

She opened her left hand and released, for her own use, a small handkerchief. It was a child's. She didn't wipe her brow, but patted it. She moved back to the bench without turning her back on the others; and then she sat down. The impact of her body on the bench could be heard and so could the sound of the wood accommodating to the new weight. Peter looked around, curious about what would happen next. I thought to myself that the woman had succeeded in triggering off a series of similar exhortations that would come one after another for at least an hour. And to myself I made a reassuring analysis: They were nervous, and they felt stymied; there was just so far they could go, and they knew it; they were becoming "organized," but they were also becoming afraid—and aware of their own weakness; they were now "supporting" one another with brave speeches, but they were also ready to run, and they knew it, and Peter knew it.

In point of fact, it was the state of Mississippi that became afraid; eventually, the Federal Government began to look very warily at the workings of CDGM, to investigate it from top to bottom. Its "management" was declared poor by Washington; its purposes and goals obviously offended the Governor's Mansion in Jackson. In 1965, I was asked by officials of OEO to evaluate and help improve the medical program that had to be a significant part of a rural Mississippi Headstart program. My impressions were welcomed and later that year submitted to the Senate as it prepared to finance the War on Poverty for yet another year. In 1966, quite another set of circumstances prevailed. A beleaguered CDGM had to fight what seemed like a hopeless battle; the state of Mississippi was its avowed enemy, and as for the federal agencies—well, I'll let another mother I heard speak out at a meeting make her summary:

The government people up there in Washington, D.C.—they're more afraid than we are. We must have gone through a lot down here when the day comes that the people representing the United States are more scared than we are. It used to be they'd come down here and tell us *we* shouldn't be afraid. "There's *nothing* to be afraid of," I heard one of them government lawyers tell the NAACP man. "This is still America, and if they go too far, we can take them all into *court*." I was standing there on the street, and they were coming out of the Church they burned down that he was referring to, but I came home and said to my mother that it was the biggest joke I'd heard in 37 years of living—as if the white man doesn't own the courts! And my mother is 64, and she said it wasn't so special, that kind of talk. She said they're always doing that, the outsiders: They come here and tell us to stand up and do this and do that, and then they go away. And who's left? Who's here to have "nothing to be afraid of"? It's us, and we have nothing; and with nothing yours, there's a lot to be afraid of. That's the way my mother saw it, truly, and she never went to school a day in her life. That's the truth. But she knows about things, everything there is to know, I believe.

And now it's changing. It must be when I have to go tell my mother that *we're* not scared, but *they* are, in Washington, D.C. I guess they gave up on us a long time ago; so when they gave us the Headstart program they thought it would be a real quiet-like thing. But we have some real good people teaching our children, and they give us food for them, and a woman like me, they've given me a job, not sweeping after Mrs. Charley for five dollars a week and maybe a piece of donut I'd get to share with the dog and the coffee that otherwise would be spilled out, but a *real job* and one that pays me good *to do what's important for me and my family*. I never believed there were jobs like that, where you could get paid a good salary to spend your time helping your own children and your people's children, instead of the white man's kids. (I help serve cookies and juice; and I arrange things, and clean up after the kids, and help them go take a nap and wake up and things like that. They call me an "aide" and pay me, but I'll tell you I'd do it for nothing, the way I feel.)

It didn't take them long to figure out we was up to no good, no good at all. We was being "uppity." And we're scaring the colored as well as the white. "An uppity nigger will get shot sooner or later, and mostly sooner"— that's what I used to hear my granddaddy say. Well, his daddy was a slave, I think, or the son of one, so you could understand his thinking. But here I am, and born only 37 years ago, and I believed the same thing until last year. Now isn't that something! And if you had known me five years ago— well you couldn't, because I'd have been afraid to look you in the eye, or let you get within a mile of our house, for fear of being shot dead talking to a man from Massachusetts who is white.

It was the way they went about doing this that got us feeling drawn to it, I'd say. They made us feel it was *ours*, and we were somebody, and not people they'd throw us something, so that they could go home and feel better. (And I mean the colored as well as the white. Have you ever seen a rich colored man telling his "brothers" how bad off they are, and how he's going to give them five dollars, not one but five United States dollars—if they'll be real good and nice?)

They probably saw that they got us going too fast, and that we'd be real, honest-to-goodness practicing citizens of the U.S.A., and they never have allowed that here, and maybe up in Washington they're not ready for it either.

What has surprised not only me, but even a veteran civil rights activist like Peter, comes across in that woman's words, and even more in the insistent, assertive, defiantly wry quality to the delivery of those words. Peter and I both remember the apathy and fear that one met in Delta Negroes, without exception. Whether the "projects" were limited and conservative in aim, or far-reaching and "radical," they invariably came to a slow, familiar halt when ideas planned in New York or Atlanta or even Jackson had to face the "reality" of a sharecropper's life or a tenant farmer's life in Itta Bena, Louise, or Sidon, Mississippi. No matter how clever and persuasive the "field worker" was, the "people" shunned him or accepted him with fear and open distrust. Nor in many cases was "time" the answer. In time, the outsider—dark-skinned, sincere, earnest, full of ideas and plans—can become familiar and likable. What else can he become, though? Does he bring bread, or enough men and guns, to change things, really change them? Does he bring work or land that he owns and wants worked? Does he bring anything but trouble? And trouble for what? So that I, James, called a "boy" all my fifty-eight years, can go put my "X" by some politician's name—and of all crazy things, go get some coffee in one of those Holiday Inns in Greenwood or someplace like that? Even if he laughs with me about all those *other* organizer types, what has *he* got to offer, really? Well, he's got plenty of talk about how bad every white man is, and we've always known that even if we don't tell the white man so. He's got his idea that we should all be like him and be together, and that would create new power, black power, and change things. But when and how would it change things, down here, where there are a lot of Negroes, a lot, but still more whites, and all of them determined to hold on to what they have? And what about the beginning, the dangerous, terrible, awesome first steps when we're so naked and weak, so exposed to those gruff, stocky, beefy, red-faced sheriffs, with the *two* guns they carry around their waists, and the cars they drive with the lights whirling about on top of them? And what are we supposed to do when the plantation owner or his managers—they do the "dirty-work" and they're often the real mean ones—come around and tell us to "get away," to "move on" real fast—if we want to stay alive, that is? And then there would be the storekeeper who'd be after us for all we owe. What do we tell him—that we're together, the poor black people of Mississippi, and let him try to bother us or let the Mississippi Highway Patrol try?

Those are the questions that aren't asked right away. In a stare, a long silence, a gesture, they can be conveyed to the visitor. It is true: In "time" they are put to words—finally, and, in my experience, eloquently, vividly, pointedly. By then it is perhaps harder for the visitor, the organizer, the "worker" in this or that cause, to reply. Some day, when all the accounts are settled and regions like the South or Appalachia have at last achieved the kind of democracy we assume America is all about, a historian or two will need to know about the despair of "outsiders" like Peter, as it emerged—point, counterpoint—in the face of the apathy felt by the "insider," the isolated, lonely farm hand who knew all too concretely about abstractions like "power" or "class" or the "meaning" of race.[5]

In 1966, more than a year after CDGM had proved it could work, proved it could miraculously fit into and inspire the lives of the most "backward" and "remote" farm people—who still live by the thousands in Mississippi and the millions in the exile of our cities—I heard this look backward spoken by Peter:

I never would have believed we could have done it. The whole thing doesn't make sense according to every idea and slogan we believe in these days. Here was a program devised by white liberals from New York and a few civil rights people. We were looking for the *real* poor, and the ones way out in the countryside as well as in the towns. We were running nursery schools, mind you—of all things to go out to people and offer them. I would have laughed at the idea a few years ago.

But we had money, enough money to give people who need food, need clothes, need all kinds of advice, some real, tangible help. That was one thing that made a difference, and the other was our approach. We wanted them to feel it was theirs, their program to do something with and feel proud of. If they owned nothing else, they could own those Headstart centers. They could see that the books were specially designed for them and their kids, that they were the staff, that the "experts" admitted how much they had to learn and didn't know. We could offer them doctors for their kids and good food. We could bring them together to talk about something real, something that *went on* every weekday morning from 8:30 to noon, or whatever. The checks came to the centers, and poor people who never had seen a check in their lives got them—for working as "aides," for cooking and cleaning and "minding" their *own* children, for a change.

That's what got to them, money and a chance to join in together. But the third thing that glued this operation together, if you ask me, was opposition. We never had it easy, even when the War on Poverty was going strong nationally and they were sending all sorts of visitors down here to see how even Mississippi was in the "war." The state caught on to us right away, even if Washington didn't. They knew we were interested in the families of children, not only in five-year-old children, and they knew we considered the words "health" and "preschool education" to be much broader than a lot of politicians would like. So a federal agency was giving us money, and we were trying to let people know—as many as we could afford to let know—that they were actually a little free, to come together and speak out and have their children taught what mattered to *them* and what *they* thought important and desirable. How subversive could you get?

Now no one in power in this state and no one representing this state in Washington can afford to ignore something like that, a program like that; and they didn't. The more they attacked, the stronger we became with the people. It was beautiful: they couldn't really burn down our centers as if they were churches, and it was like in the old days. We were connected to the federal government, and anyway the state of Mississippi has learned it can't let that kind of thing happen too often any more. They couldn't stop us from functioning either. We had the money, for at least a year we did. Talk about "education," it was the greatest education these parents—apart from their little children—ever had. They saw their own strength, their own power, in daily operation—against the white man's opposition. They never had gone through anything like that before, and I doubt they can ever be the same afterwards.

You should see the letters they sent up to Washington, and the petitions they wrote, and the statements they issued—to one another. And when we thought that we were through, that we had had it, that we were getting no more money—well, they knew about it, and they stuck together. They were fighting for *theirs,* for a pay check, against the bosses—like in the old days of the labor-union movement. From isolated, unorganized people—at the mercy of every sheriff, every plantation owner, every redneck in the state— they became tied together as "members of CDGM," that's what a lot of them called themselves, spontaneously, "members."

You know there were a dozen or more critical moments when the whole thing could have collapsed. From the very beginning Washington and Jackson pushed us here and there. They'd want a compromise on this issue, a little ground given on something else. Sometimes they seemed to want to bribe us to surrender! If we'd only move our headquarters, or fire so-and-so, who is too "radical," or too much an "open civil rights type"—like me! If we'd only stop letting the children and their parents know that just about all other Americans are richer; that is they have more money and don't want to share it with a few million Negroes. If we'd only use those nice, sweet middle-class "farm books" and stop telling it like it is, which is called being "inflammatory." We say to a woman who practically never sees money at all that she is being exploited by the white plantation owner and the white political system that won't let her vote and won't give her the kind of food and medicine and education her kids need; and for that we're accused of turning a pre-school program into a "political" program. We're called agitators. And when they call us agitators in Jackson—when the governor does and *his* representatives in the Congress do—then believe me the bureaucrats in Washington listen, even in the "flexible" agencies, the ones full of imagination, like the OEO.

So we'd go tell the people *that,* as if they didn't know in their own way. During one bad time, when they had inspectors all over the place and they were telling us in Washington we'd have to "slow down," cleanse house, and —really—stop being so successful at organizing poor people and helping them get a beginning of what they want and need, I heard a woman get up at a meeting of Headstart parents and say: "If we do like they want us to, we'll turn into nothing. If we make a fight of it, we'll win even if they cut off the money, because for the first time we'll stick together and stand up to them. And maybe when they see we're doing that, it'll be them who'll back down. They won't know what to do with us behaving that way."

She was right. Even *we* were surprised, the so-called "leaders." Those people were determined to have their kind of Headstart program, and if we wavered because we knew "the facts," they kept on telling us that they knew everything *had* to turn out right, even when the checks stopped coming, and we reminded them about the threats coming down upon us.

Yes, I suppose they were "naïve." But they also were "involved," really so. And I agree—their attitude gave us strength even when we didn't admit it. You can persuade yourself to be "realistic"—in fact, to sell out a good and decent program that is working beautifully—when the people in it are only halfhearted members. It's a little harder to do so with a really emotional and enthusiastic group—who talk a lot about the Bible and God and make you feel like a two-bit Judas for entertaining ideas of being "practical" and "realistic" and giving in to the politicians, and I don't only mean the state ones, but the federal ones, too.

The encounter of rural "innocence" and American *realpolitik* had been stated rather well. It was an encounter that to some extent took place inside him as well as one he watched. Yes, he was for "the people," for CDGM, and against the whole social and political system that keeps those people in their present circumstances; but he was also part of that system, perhaps more than he cared to realize. I was myself awakened and stunned at some of the introspection and self-scrutiny that emerged in those moments of "struggle" with the state and federal governments. We had the same all-night "soul sessions" I had once heard civil rights workers "conduct" [6] or unwittingly slip into—always with a later sense of incredulity. ("Like, man, we've spent the whole night talking and taking ourselves down until there's nothing left, and no one knows how it all got started.") A young man like Peter—of the people, for the people, with the people —had to face his own "distance" from "them." It wasn't only that he had gone to college, or even that he had worked at "community organization" or in a protest movement. It wasn't only his "savvy," his political shrewdness, his canny understanding of what in the news was "really" significant—his "worldliness" it used to be called by cloistered men and women. What separated him, finally, from the ranks of the "poor"—so he began to believe and say—were the assumptions he took for granted and ordinarily never questioned or indeed thought about. When he was literally penniless these past years, he had not been "poor"; and when he was fighting hardest alongside the tenant farmers or the abandoned mothers and their children, he was not struggling the way they were. Even when he tried to forget everything he knew, everything he had ever learned, he could not achieve their ignorance, their vulnerability, their concrete, earthy vision—both idealistic, shattered, pitiful, foolish, and at times enormously, powerfully convincing. "You look at me, at my life, someone like you could, and you'd think I could really 'make it' with these people." So he started one night when we were trying to distinguish between the leader and the led—in a "movement" and in an organization that were both doing their best to blur the distinction, or at the very least be embarrassed by it, and call it a temporary, unavoidable "fact of life" or of the "society," a grim necessity. Then Peter went on:

The truth is that I'm miles from the very people I'm "from" and now working "for." It's not my education, and it certainly isn't my "background." It's hard to put into words, but I think something happens to you, no matter how "radical" you are, when you work to change a political system. Some of the system's values rub off on you—you can't help it—even when you're fighting them. It happens to all of us. In fact, in a way the *more* you fight, the more you become entangled in what you're fighting, and the more it all becomes part of you. I remember when I was in SNCC, I'd go up to Washington—in 1962 or 1963. We'd meet all those government people. I remember the time I went into Bobby Kennedy's office. I thought to myself, here I am Peter Woods, from McCormick County, South Carolina, a southern nigger from the back country if ever there is back country, and I'm standing in the office of the Attorney General of the United States. Of course I said to myself, "watch yourself" or "beware," as my mother used to say it, "beware of evil." Well, you know what the greatest evil is? Maybe you don't. Every little colored boy in McCormick County knows that the sin of pride is the worst of them all, them all. My mother used to tell me it didn't matter what the white man had, the property and cash and everything; he has pride, too—the sinful kind, and so he'll burn while we stand by and watch. Later on, of course, is when he'll burn, the time will be later on, and it won't be here on this earth. Our bones will be lying around, tired as usual, but at least getting a rest; and the white man's will be lying comfortable in a satin coffin. But up there it will get reversed—because of pride and its temptations.

Well, you can only be tempted so many times, and even if you resist it every time, you've tasted it and smelled it and felt it and learned about it.

We'd leave Washington all heady and walking on air. Each of us knew enough not to show how we felt to the other. We'd try to be real suspicious and angry—and we *were* suspicious and angry. I'm not telling you that we "sold out" or were "conned" or "had," nothing like that. It's not even that we were so impressed and excited; if that was all, we'd just be ordinary tourists. The point is that we were fighting something, and we left still fighting it, but we also left just a little more a part of what we were against. *We* began to think about this group and that one, and the pressures here and there, and what might happen if we did one thing or another one. *We* began to worry about what one group would do, or another. *We* began to realize how difficult everything was, and complicated, and involved, and hard to solve. We'd leave Washington telling one another how unmoved we were, how unimpressed we were with all the people there, and the offices they had and the flunkies around them—United States power! Then we'd get home and the next thing you'd hear, when we were talking about *our* strategies, *our* tactics, we'd begin sounding like *them* when we spoke to one another. I remember a guy saying to me "What's got into you?" when I said something to the effect that we had to "think our options through carefully," and "not inflame the rednecks into starting their own kind of movement." Then the guy said: "If we thought like you during the last three years, there wouldn't be *any* movement, not ours and not a hypothetical one of theirs to worry about. We wouldn't have had the sit-ins, or the freedom rides, or the projects in Alabama or Mississippi, certainly not the Mississippi one. We'd have had nothing but a lot of talk, a lot of conferences and meetings and discussions and plans that are so well 'thought out' that they lead you nowhere, which is exactly where they're supposed to lead you." I blew up at him and told him it was easy to demonstrate and much harder to figure out what was happening in the country. But as soon as I said that I knew I was a fool, and I apologized to him. The fact was that we were *making* things happen, and the more we sat around and worried about a lot of "effects" and "potential reactions" or "responses" to what we did— well, the less we would do and the less there would be to worry about, though there are a lot of people who can always find something to keep themselves busy, and "worried" too, I guess.

What I mean is that we were trying to change things, but in this country it's hard to keep your momentum going. You try to change things and the first thing you know you're being wined and dined, and the TV people are hanging around you, listening to your every word, and people write newspaper columns about you, and kids come from every campus in America to "help" you, and a million journalists and political scientists and sociologists and psychologists (cats like you) try to figure us out and study us and write about us—and make their living off us, make money from what we *do*. Pretty soon *we're* making money, too. There's plenty of it around, and people will give it to you. Then *we* become worried about our "image," and *we* become interested in the "larger picture"—until that's about *all* we're doing: trying to "mobilize public opinion" by saying things that "get across" or doing things *because* they'll "get across"; worrying about our telephone

lines, our lines to the "power structure," rather than what's going on between us and the people in the Delta. (And we can always defend ourselves for that "approach" by saying we're doing the people in the Delta the
most good possible this way.)

So, that's it. You're with the people here, a guy like me; but you're somewhere else, too—even if you're Negro, even if you're a poor farm boy yourself. That's all right though, so long as you don't forget the difference, and
so long as you stay here and do what you can. I believe a lot of my friends
have left because they're further removed from life down here than they
can allow themselves to admit. So they find excuses, and they leave. I'm
not criticizing them. I'm not. They're—a lot of them—city boys, black
boys from the ghetto. They want to go back. I may want to leave, too; but
for me to go "back" means McCormick County, South Carolina. So, I'm removed from the scene here because I'm "wise" to a lot of things, but I'm
also close to the scene—out of my life, man. You know?

I think I know, a little. I think that in Appalachia I have seen
the very same struggle take place among those who "work" there with
the poor and among the poor.[7] Peter's struggle comes to my mind
often when I hear an Appalachian Volunteer,[8] a middle-class college
student, talking about his effort to "reach" the "people" in a particular hollow and "do" something for them—teach their children, take
stock of their medical problems, join them in their battle with a
county courthouse or a strip-mining company that wants to devour
their land. In eastern Kentucky, western North Carolina, and West
Virginia I have once again seen myths exploded—only to reveal new
sorts of "problems." Like sharecroppers of the Delta, the people of
Appalachia have been called a lot of discouraging things: backward,
disadvantaged, primitive, deprived, parochial, isolated, unreachable,
a subculture, fundamentally different in their values and goals.[9]
Those who would dare try to live among them and work alongside
them have usually heard all those words and then had to face the
inevitable warnings: Mountain people suspect outsiders, distrust
them, find them of little interest, pay no attention to them, want no
help from them—in fact, have so little in common with them that the
years outsiders put into sharing time and space with "hollow folk"
and into making gestures of conciliatory self-abasement at the feet of
"mountain culture" eventually prove futile.

Yet, the War on Poverty (insofar as it has brought on a number
of skirmishes in the Appalachian mountains during the mid-sixties)
has been remarkably able to "penetrate" all those cultural "resist-
ances" and demonstrate one more time that loyalty to a particular

kind of past can live side by side with a willing and even eager acceptance of new opportunities and possibilities. The terribly private, solitary man of the hollows—so out of the world, so out of the way—feels the lure of bread and medicine, work and money. He does more; he abandons in their wake some of the social and psychological characteristics that people like me take pains to observe, analyze, and fit into one or another "frame of reference." He does so almost unnervingly, but only when the "change" makes real sense for him. Here is a man in Wolfe County, Kentucky, speaking:

I don't know about all these college kids coming in here, wanting to do things, all kinds of things—you wonder how they think up so many ideas at the same time. They tell us they want to be here with us and be our friends, and I wonder what about their friends back home where they come from. Do you think they don't have any there? But I don't care. They say they'll go fix our bridge and help us with the road we've been meaning to lay down for—I'd say ten years, I guess. There's enough of them to go do it, too. They'll hurt themselves a little, I think (some of them don't look too strong to me), but they'll do the work, I can tell. And they're good with the kids. The kids like them. My wife says they tickle my son and my daughters, and they're real nice with them.

They've got some money to bring here, and that's welcome, let me tell you. The kids get a good lunch, and if we put up a volunteer, they pay us out of the government's pocket. The one with us, his name is Richard, and he comes from someplace near New York, I think outside the city there. His mother writes him these letters and tells him to be real careful and not to get sick. You'd think he was someplace over in China. But he's O.K. We've never before met anyone from where he comes, or like him, but he's good to have around. I think he's taken to my wife's food pretty good, and he likes the singing we do. He's a little jittery we notice. He can't sit for too long. He has to be doing something or moving about. I guess that's his way. A while back I never thought we'd see people like him hereabouts—ever. But I've lived to see them. First it was in the army, where you meet all types, and we got sent over there to England and France. Yes, and it's television, too. I've never seen so much in all my life as TV brings into your home. It's the thing that my kids pay most attention to—more than to me or their mother, even. Nowadays they've seen everything before a father has a chance to talk.

Of course Richard is in the flesh, not on a program. My daughter Jeanne, she said he's really cute, and she was sure he was like two or three people she'd seen on TV. He talks like them, and he wears the same kind of clothes. I can't figure why he came all the way down here to be with us, even for a summer. And now I hear him talking about staying here for a while and working with us on a couple projects they have in mind, the AV's.

There's plenty for them to do. They say we can fight the mine-strippers.

I think they'll find out different, but let them go try. I don't mind someone coming in here so long as he tries to do what needs doing and not what *he* wants. You know some of the people who used to come through, back in my daddy's day and way before, too, they'd be a certain kind of minister or a teacher maybe—for a disguise—and they'd want to change *us*, not the things that these kids do. They'd preach at us; but these kids, they don't say a bad word about us, and it's pretty clear that they're trying to be of some help, and they want to do some building or clearing or whatever there is. Now that's a difference. Of course you don't really give yourself over to them. Why should you? Some are a little too one-sided for me. You know what I mean? They're so all-fired serious, and they want to make over the hollow and the county and the whole state of Kentucky, for all I know. I told one the other night to just relax and not lose so much sleep on things, the "poverty" as she keeps calling it. Sure it's bad down here, and elsewhere from what you hear, but these mountains have been here for a long time, and so have we, and you can't just dissolve the world's misery in your own time.

I'm glad they're here, though—on the whole. One or two may be a nuisance to us, but they're workers, and that's what counts. And they have money to bring in here, and that's the scarcest thing around. And they don't hand it out, they ask us for help, for their room and food, and to work with them, so it's not something that's welfare and charity. We have to take *that*, too—but no man like me wants it. If there were jobs around here, I'll tell you, none of us would be sitting around trying to get a handout here and there from anyone he can. Not our people. We want work.

A year later, he and others were more wrought up than I ever thought possible. Those "kids"—some of them were well into their twenties—had done a quiet, respectful, but clear-cut job of bringing together people whom tradition, geography, and a sense of futility had long kept apart. Moreover, the volunteers were increasingly coming from within the region, even from local people who were not students but unemployed men whose sharp, well-articulated sense of what is "wrong" with the Appalachian region often surprises the well-meaning and arrogant outside observer. While "we"—student activists and people like me who "observe" them—have come to accept the "wisdom" that relatively uneducated poor people have, it still comes as a surprise to hear an unemployed former coal miner, or even a "dirt farmer" from one of the Kentucky hills, give a sharp and comprehensive analysis of the social and economic system in the United States.

As a matter of fact the repeated irony has been inescapable: It is not due to the reluctance of the hidebound, the "hillbillies" of the backwoods, that the War on Poverty in Appalachia has been a limited one; rather, the issue has been resources. How much can come into the region, after all, to a people largely willing to take what they can get, what they need, and be grateful? "Yes, we get annoyed at some of these people who come in here," I heard one man from near Beckley, West Virginia, say to a group of "outsiders," some of whom, I knew, did indeed annoy him. "But if they bring the bacon in with them, well that's what counts."

In Kentucky and West Virginia both I have seen virtual mob scenes unheard of in "mountain history." That is, "community organization" has worked. People have come together because they have been led to believe that it pays to do so, that jobs and various "improvements" will result. Even more interesting and potentially significant, once a number of people have "organized" themselves, they are newly sensitive and newly prepared to act when confronted with an insult, a rebuff, an assault of one kind or another. "The best thing that can happen to bring one of these mountain communities *really* together is a strip-miner coming along." The owner of a gas station in a small West Virginia town told me that—as a criticism, actually, of the federal government's community-action program. He went on, though:

People around here are to themselves, mostly; they know their kin, and they don't have much to do with others. Maybe it's that way in the city, too—except you notice it more here. Actually, they're friendly to one another here, but they don't work together. Why should they? In the city, they probably do—one man by the other on the assembly line, I guess. Now all this "community action" they talk about, I don't think it means much. I guess the people down here will go along, of course. They'll go along with practically *anything* if it means more food and money and a new road put in and some water from the hills brought under control. But I have noticed that if a stripper comes along now, they'll be in a better position to fight him, the people in the "action program"; and they do so much talking when they meet that I think they're all primed up and *looking* for trouble, for something to go fight and win, if you ask me. I admit we have plenty of things to fight about down here, but it's not so easy to find who the enemy is. From what I see, if they can't find a mine-stripper, they turn on the school people or the mayor, or on the federal government who's paying to "organize" them in the first place. It all goes round and round from what we can figure out. Now they're talking about marching on the state capital, and Washington, and letting the country know about conditions down here. So, you see, they don't just sit together and talk; they look for trouble and go out and make it when they can't find it, and they won't adjust themselves to the real situation around here, but they have to go find someone to have a duel with.

In his "community" he is rather well-to-do. His gas station is also a grocery store, and he has the local post office in his quarters, too. In other words, he is a shopkeeper, a member of the bourgeoisie if there ever was one. I think he deserves to be credited with assets. He has a keen eye for the principles of "group psychology," though he denies himself and his listeners any "formulation" of what he sees. He knows that Appalachia, *his* Appalachia by virtue of property as well as birth, is not for long going to "stay put." Ironically, the region is "backward"—in the case of the hollows unbelievably so to an outsider—but also plagued with the "post-technological" unemployment that comes with automated (mining) industry. The new roads will bring in outsiders—and for a gas-station owner like him, more money. Television sets have already brought him and his neighbors face to face with the rest of the country. Most unsettling of all, however, are "those VISTA types" and "the people who are always talking about organizing, organizing, organizing." He thinks they are looking for trouble, the organizers, volunteers, and activists of all descriptions. He knows there is trouble to be found. He is afraid they will persist long enough to make more trouble for him and for the order of things he has always taken for granted. He once put the whole issue very clearly:

I believe you have to bend with the wind and give way sometimes. But there's just so much giving you can do and still have something yourself. If they keep on telling us this is wrong, and that, and something else, we'll have to *draw the line,* draw it firm, and say: "What you trying to do, change the whole society on us?"

It would seem that those who give and those who demand, those who accommodate and those who confront, may yet have to find out whether in fact there has to be a line drawn, a decisive struggle waged, or whether in America, somehow, the blurred limits of our enormous, confusingly disparate but nonetheless real "middle class" will be yet again stretched, reluctantly or hospitably. I don't frankly know whether this nation at this particular stage in its history will choose to make the political choices, the social and economic changes, that are needed if a vulnerable and relatively powerless and isolated minority is to be made—in essence—wealthier and stronger. In the thirties, the poor, the downtrodden, were all over—visible victims of a "system" that clearly was in trouble. Today, the country as a whole is prospering, as people in the Delta or in Appalachia know better than we may suppose. Yes, some exceptional and highly publicized atrocity—to a civil rights worker, to mountain land by a strip-mining company—can command a certain sympathy from the rest of us. Is that kind of response enough, though, to get a national legislature to initiate the kind of planned economic investment that will reach our rural areas and make them reasonably self-sufficient and capable of keeping people who don't *want* to go to urban ghettos but feel they *must* go? Right now we seem committed to a patchwork of doles, to commodity food programs that leave children on the brink of serious malnutrition, to "happy pappy" programs that are susceptible to the worst sort of political control and, in addition, are humiliating, to welfare checks that are disgracefully inadequate and given or held back in the most inhumane and arbitrary way.

If I have learned anything from the work I've done with migrant farmers, sharecroppers or tenant farmers, and mountain families, it is that the people "we" consider so distant, removed, backward, illiterate, passive—and whatever—may well be more capable of changing themselves than our nation is of changing itself. Of course, people cower and appear dumb, stony, impassive, inert when they face (in the clutch) gun-wielding sheriffs with implied and covert power. Of course, "outsiders" and their "help" are spurned by people who are shrewd enough to appraise that help, to take stock of it, and in an unnervingly brief time see it for what it is—and isn't. Of course, despair and "hostility" appear regularly among people who are hungry or have no significant work. Yet, given a chance, "they" don't have to be that way. I have seen enough to know *that*. Perhaps one of America's achievements is that its rural "proletariat" is not, in psychological and social fact, a *"lumpen proletariat,"* a truly and fatally disorganized "mass." There is hope in that "observation" or "conclusion," but also the makings of a historical scandal and a great tragedy for a rich and powerful nation. The next few years will probably give us the answer: whether or not this country will be persuaded (and led) to concern itself with people all too easily and conveniently kept out of sight, out of mind, deprived of just about everything the rest of us enjoy, pride ourselves on having, and ask the rest of the world to emulate.

Notes

1. Those were the figures given in a report on rural medical problems to OEO by the Tufts University Department of Medicine in 1966.

2. The infant-mortality rate in India in 1966 was 831 per 10,000 according to The United Nations Demographic Yearbook.

3. Excellent historical accounts of CDGM have been written by Pat Watters, Director of Information at the Southern Regional Council. See "CDGM: Who Really Won," *Dissent* (May–June 1967) and *New South* (Spring 1967). Mr. Watters makes quite clear what the political and economic stakes were (and are) in the struggle between an exceptional Headstart program and the "local authorities" in Mississippi.

4. The quotations in this essay have been taken from a number of tape-recorded interviews. As always, for the sake of clarity and force, I have edited them and, in some instances, drawn fragments from different interviews together.

5. In 1964 I tried to describe some of the weariness and despair felt by youths like Peter in a paper called "Social Struggle and Weariness," *Psychiatry* (November 1964). See also the discussion of the civil rights workers I have known in *Children of Crisis: A Study of Courage and Fear* (Boston: Little, Brown, 1967).

6. See R. Coles and J. Brenner, "American Youth in a Social Struggle: The Mississippi Summer Project," *American Journal of Orthopsychiatry* (October 1965).

7. See R. Coles, "Mountain Thinking," *Appalachian Review* (Summer 1966).

8. For an extended analysis of the work done by The Appalachian Volunteers see R. Coles and J. Brenner, "American Youth in a Social Struggle (II): The Appalachian Volunteers." Presented at the Annual Meeting of the American Orthopsychiatric Association, Washington, D.C., April 1967, and published in *American Journal of Orthopsychiatry* (January 1968).

9. There is an extensive literature on the Appalachian "subculture," much of it discussed and listed in the paper mentioned in the preceding footnote. See also R. Coles, "Childhood in Appalachia," *Appalachian Review* (Summer 1967). In this regard, Harry Caudill's book *Night Comes to the Cumberlands* (Boston: Little, Brown, 1962) is indispensable. Also, see John Fetterman's *Stinking Creek* (New York: Dutton, 1967).

Chapter 7

The View from the City: Community Action in Trenton GREGORY FARRELL

It was November 1964. The official from the Office of Economic Opportunity (OEO) stood behind a long table in one of those large, square rooms that federal officials use to brief large groups of people. Ranged in the folding chairs in front of him were mayors and mayors' representatives from about twenty cities who had come to Washington to learn first-hand about the War on Poverty and what it was supposed to mean. The OEO official turned to a balding, patient-looking man seated next to him and asked him to explain the implications of the program from the local level. The official said:

Ben Zimmerman has been running one of the most successful prototypes of the community action program up in Syracuse, and he can deal with your questions from a local perspective better than any of us, but I want to warn you of one thing: In order to get him down here from Syracuse, I had to promise the president of his board that I would make sure no one tried to steal him . . .

There was an appreciative chuckle from the crowd.

Ben Zimmerman stood up and talked a bit about the things he had learned as director of Crusade for Opportunity in Syracuse, and we in the Trenton contingent (mayor, city councilman, city health, recreation, and welfare director, newspaperman, administrative intern) looked at each other and nodded as he spoke. When he asked for questions, the mayor of Trenton raised his hand and started things off; then a question from someone with a Tennessee twang, then the mayor of Trenton again; then a question from the Trenton city councilman and back around the room to some other city, then back to Trenton. At the end of forty-five minutes of questions, the OEO official stood up, looked around the room, and said, "Are there any more questions—from some city other than Trenton, New Jersey?"

The Trenton contingent had a program and an organizational form ready and drafted. We had been to New Haven to study the Ford Foundation financed prototype of the community-action program there, and we were impressed with its lessons: the private non-profit corporation as an operating instrument that would combine the forces of the public and private sectors; a concentration on employment and education as the keystone of the program; aggressive grantsmanship; a premium on early tangible results.

The trips to New Haven and several months of work by a mayor's task force in anticipation of the Economic Opportunity Act had clearly put Trenton ahead of most other cities. Coming home that night, on the four-hour drive from Washington, the Trenton representatives felt confident and impatient to get going. We knew what we wanted to do, and we were sure we were on the right track.

CASE CITY, U.S.A.

Trenton is an industrial town of 110,000 people, the capital of New Jersey, and the county seat of Mercer County. If you come in by train from the South, you can't miss the neon sign on the railroad bridge across the Delaware that gleams the local motto, "Trenton Makes— the World Takes." And you'll alight in the dingiest railroad station among the major stops on the Pennsylvania run between Washington and New York. Philadelphia is forty-five minutes away by train, New York City an hour.

Trenton is a town, not a city. The neighborhoods are large. Negroes in a ghetto on one side of town know the Negroes in a housing project on the other. Except for public housing, there are no major apartment-house developments, and most people live on narrow streets in row houses.

Like other industrial communities in the Northeast, Trenton is composed of various ethnic groups. As in other cities, the middle class is moving out and the Negro population is spreading around a little, but Trenton is still a town of Italian, Polish, Irish, Hungarian, Negro, and Puerto Rican neighborhoods. Thirty-four per cent of the population, according to 1965 estimates, were Negro, and about 4 per cent Puerto Rican. A statue of Christopher Columbus marks the border of an all-Italian neighborhood known as "Chambersburg," and it is said he is standing there looking across Hamilton Avenue to make sure no Negroes try to move in.

But until Christmas of 1967, when the first of several riots broke out in the public high school, there had been virtually no outbreaks of racial violence in the city. Trenton has had a placid racial history. It had no history of militancy on civil rights issues, no anti-Negro vigilante organizations. Before 1967, Trenton accepted its poverty without violence. Before the mid-fifties, it had accepted poverty and urban decay almost without action of any kind.

In the mid-fifties, Trenton was shocked out of civic lethargy by blows to its pocketbook and its pride. The first blow was a proposal by Governor Meyner to disperse and decentralize state government, an action that would have removed an estimated 20,000 jobs from the city. The second was the publication in an October 1957 issue of *House and Home* magazine of a picture story of "Case City, U.S.A.," an urban carcass, dead, or at least dying, a prototype of the worst of urban America. Though the place was not identified in the article by name, every Trentonian knew where the pictures had been taken.

In vigorous reaction, the city mounted a campaign to persuade the governor to leave the state government in Trenton and formed a citizens' group to spur redevelopment and, eventually, to promote urban renewal. Other reforms followed. A new city charter was adopted in 1961, calling for a strong mayor–weak council form of city government. A young mayor was elected on a reform platform. In 1963, a new school superintendent, with a reputation for innovation, was brought in from out of town. The surge of civic interest didn't arrest the problems of poverty in Trenton, however. By late 1964 when the community-action program began to take shape:

The city's infant mortality rate—at 36.8 per thousand—was second highest in the state, and twice the state average.

Underemployment in low-income areas of the city was close to 20 per cent—in a tight labor market. More than half the residents of the inner city had never spent a day in high school.

The average Trenton student was more than three years behind the national average in reading by the time he hit ninth grade.

More than 1,100 families were living on less than $20 per week.

Seventeen per cent of the city's families were living on less than $3,000 per year.

In center city, 35 per cent of the housing units were substandard and 11 per cent were dilapidated.

In the ghetto, Trenton is known as a "bar town." Bars and churches, it is said, are the only places to meet people, and bars outdraw the churches four to one. There was no talk in Trenton's Negro bars in 1964 of militant civil rights activity, of protest and organization. There was some in an East Trenton Baptist church, but the minister who was talking that way was white, and he soon left for Rochester.

The board of education was experimenting with pilot programs of one sort and another, prekindergarten, core curriculum development, and so on, and talking heatedly about the need for "massive aid to urban schools."

Civic interests were devoting their time largely to physical renewal, and progress was coming with embarrassing slowness. People were beginning to say that the talk of reform and redevelopment was all just talk. Urban renewal had succeeded in uprooting Negro families, but it had brought precious little industry to the city and had created *no* new housing. If you had taken a poll at the time in almost any neighborhood of the city and asked whether people thought the city would improve and any of the new reform measures would work, the answer would have been "no."

UNITED PROGRESS, INC., IS BORN

In this context, Arthur Holland, the reform mayor who was to attract national headlines by moving into a Negro neighborhood several months later, took the initiative in getting the Trenton poverty program off the ground. He began by naming a group of prominent citizens to a Human Renewal Coordinating Committee and charging them with making recommendations to him about what the city should do and how it should organize itself to take advantage of the impending Economic Opportunity Act. He put the effort in the hands of his Health, Recreation, and Welfare director, a bombastic Irishman named William Faherty who was Holland's chief confidant and adviser.

The large coordinating committee quickly formed a small steering committee whose members did virtually all of the initial work. The members of this steering committee included key members of the Holland administration such as Faherty, Gerald Sheehan, the city's welfare director, the mayor's administrative assistant, the superintendent of schools, representatives from Rutgers and Princeton universities, and a newspaperman who was assigned to cover the deliberations of the Human Renewal Coordinating Committee and was absorbed into it. I was the newspaperman.

By mid-August of 1964, the steering committee, operating already under the influence of the New Haven model, had agreed to the form of the local instrument and the qualities it would wish in its director and had determined that there was every reason to begin planning programs even before the form of the organization was finally settled. The following is from the minutes of a meeting of the steering committee held at the Rutgers Urban Studies Center on August 14:

It was generally agreed that a new, community-wide, nonprofit structure would have considerable advantages: (1) It would be relatively free of existing antagonism; (2) it would signify the beginning of a new approach to old problems; (3) it would permit maximum flexibility in the hiring of staff; (4) it could receive funds from private foundations; (5) it could both utilize existing agencies and resources and create new ones where this was necessary. It was agreed that a policy decision would have to be made whether it would contract for services or would develop programs and structures of its own.

It was suggested that a potential executive director of such an agency would have to have some of the following qualifications: (1) The ability to get things done; (2) an awareness of the structure of the community; (3) the ability to get cooperation from organizations and individuals; (4) a strong sense of the purpose of the organization and the program.

The question of timing arose. It was agreed that tentative planning of programs could go on while the final form of the organization was not yet clear. Because of the time lag between the submission of proposals and the granting of funds, it would not be wise to hold off on the development of programs until all other matters had been settled . . .

The themes were innovation, flexibility, coordination, and urgency. There were no formal qualifications for the director, only descriptions of "qualities" he ought to have. And there was an early awareness of the delay that could be expected in applying for funds and an impatience to get some programs underway.

The nonprofit corporation, as defined by the steering committee, was to have

. . . A Board of Directors, drawn from the major sources of power in the broad community—both that kind of power which can be used to get things done, and that which can be used to keep things from getting done if it is not made part of the structure.

The Board should be as small as possible (no more than a dozen), and yet broadly representative. If the objective is quick and effective action, the 50-man board (such as they have in Philadelphia) should be avoided.

The executive director's position should be designed so he can move quickly and effectively. He should be responsible to the Board of Directors, but he needs the power to take action when he sees the need.

The local instrument should be closely related to but not a part of the city government. It requires a non-bureaucratic style of operation, demonstrable results in short order, and freedom from the accounting and hiring practices of local government. But it requires the power and cooperation of local government, without which it would be difficult to get anything going on an enduring basis.

These early documents are an accurate reflection of how we who organized Trenton's United Progress, Inc. (UPI), conceived of ourselves and of the job we had to do. We were "public entrepreneurs." We were social reformers, not social workers. We would coordinate, innovate, and operate; plan and evaluate. We were going to exploit federal resources on behalf of the city. We were going to do what Mike Sviridoff had done in New Haven.

We owed a great deal to New Haven and its Community Progress, Inc. (CPI). Besides the initial vision of what we wanted to do, our programmatic priorities of manpower and education, and the personal help and advice, whenever we called (and we called often), of the CPI staff, we got from them an attitude about ourselves, the limits of our jurisdiction, and our relationship to the federal government, which was perhaps most important of all.

CPI and its programs had, of course, preceded the federal government's Poverty Program. It was not a creature of OEO; things were, in fact, quite the reverse. Although OEO provided resources for CPI to use, its activities were not limited to those that OEO financed or smiled on.

Despite the fact, therefore, that Trenton's UPI drew its first lifeblood from OEO, we thought of ourselves from the beginning as an independent agent. We would use OEO money and any other funds suitable to our purposes. The only limits to our jurisdiction were the limits our good sense and opportunities would pose. We took "local initiative" very seriously indeed. The longer we were in operation, the more seriously we took it.

As a result, it was always emotionally difficult to accept any kind of regulation from OEO, particularly when we felt the regulation didn't make sense. I recall one incident, in particular, when I had journeyed to the regional office to negotiate for the funding of community schools and reading programs and was told by our analyst that they couldn't fund education programs because "education isn't high priority." "The hell it *isn't* high priority," I yelled at the poor girl. "It's high priority in *Trenton*. Who does the OEO think it is to tell us what our priorities are?"

There were lots of differences between the Trenton and New Haven situations that gave us pause in adopting their experience so completely, but the one that bothered me most personally, particularly when I began to think that I might be the director of Trenton's program, was a lack of the clout that goes with experience, sophistication, and close relationship to the seat of power. Sviridoff had been president of the Connecticut Central Labor Council, president of the New Haven Board of Education, and a close confidant of the mayor. I, as the apparent choice of the board of trustees, was a newspaperman who had worked in the city a year. I barely knew the mayor. The night my appointment was announced I met a newspaper friend for a beer at Tony Kall's Bar, the regular hangout for reporters from both city dailies. When I excused myself and went home, Tony, a wise and curious man, leaned across the bar toward my reporter friend and said, "He's the director of the War on Poverty? O.K. But what's he going to do? How's *he* goin' to declare war on poverty?"

The board of directors, in faithful imitation of the New Haven model, was to be a coalition of business, labor, civil rights, civic and governmental forces, and the vehicle through which the city would voluntarily pull itself together for a coordinated attack on poverty. The bylaws, however, again in imitation of New Haven's CPI, specified that each member of the board, though nominated by an outside agency, would serve as an individual. It was pointed out that no action could ever be taken by the board at a meeting if each member carried the responsibility of speaking for the organization that sent him, because the member, before voting, would have to go back and consult his organization.

Further, it was decided to make the board entirely a lay organization (the representative from the board of education, for instance, was not the superintendent of schools, but a school-board member) in order to avoid the situation in which the UPI director would find himself negotiating with the director of another agency during the day and answering to him on his board that night.

The board members, therefore, were not prepared to act as coordinating agents between their organizations and the community-action agency; the "coalition of forces" was primarily a gathering of people drawn from various organizations, and the real working coalition was formed on a project-by-project basis at the staff level.

Gradually, it became apparent that the board's major function was ceremonial rather than substantive. The major decisions—hiring, firing, program priorities, questions of whether to administer directly or delegate—were made by the staff. The board simply voted yes or no to questions and propositions raised by the staff and gave it the stamp of official community approval.

Part of this was inevitable due to the newness and complexity of the program and to the speed with which we set about getting programs operating. At the first meeting of the board, before there was an executive director, the members were asked to read and approve nine proposals that had been put together by a volunteer staff. They were told that the proposals "had to be in" in order to take advantage of available federal funds. They grumbled, but they passed them all.

This is not to say that the board always concurred with staff recommendations. They questioned closely; they vetoed some project proposals; when the "federal deadline" problem recurred, they expressed displeasure at having to act on proposals in too great haste, and voiced the need for "greater understanding" of "what is going on." There were some strong, intelligent, and interested people on the board, and they took their responsibilities seriously. But UPI was run by the staff. In Trenton's conception of community action, action and innovation were the important things, and that meant the staff had to get out in front and *move*. If innovative action and the involvement of the community were conflicting principles, then involvement would have to suffer. People wanted to see some things done.

A group of us went out to Paul Ylvisaker's house in Cranbury one night when UPI was just starting, and he asked us how many years of creativity we thought the poverty program had in it before rigor mortis would set in. "Two years," said somebody who sounded as though he knew, "two years at the outside." Paul, who we were *sure* knew, said he thought that sounded about right. "By then," somebody said, "the lawyers will have taken it over and nobody'll be able to do a damned thing." All of a sudden, the weeks right before us seemed the most precious and important we would ever experience.

150 EMPLOYEES, 25 PROGRAMS

Action seemed to be paying off. As UPI geared up in its first year, the first funds came in and programs were started, and they weren't bad: prekindergarten classes for children; work-training for teenagers, which by providing a little pocket-money for in-school youngsters was supposed to prevent dropouts (nobody asked "prevent them from what?") ; a reading program in the schools. You could take tours of the programs to see "what was going on," and if you did, you came back impressed. The superintendent of schools said that Trenton had the "best anti-poverty program in the country," and the mayor was fond of quoting OEO figures that showed that Trenton had attracted more anti-poverty funds on a per capita basis than any city in the country. The newspapers carried the story that Trenton was the only city in the state in which the welfare rolls had been *reduced* "largely as a result of the highly effective anti-poverty program."

By the time it was a year and a half old, UPI had co-funded, operated, participated in, or stimulated over twenty-five projects with over fifteen different agencies, including the board of education, three universities, four state agencies, several departments of the city government, the Lawrenceville School, the YWCA, and several other United Fund agencies. It had itself brought three and a half million dollars in federal and foundation funds into the city. (The entire Poverty Program could account for four and one-half more.) It was growing very quickly indeed and Board President Leon Levy was a little shocked at the answer when he asked one night at a meeting, "How many staff have we now? *A hundred and fifty?*" he exploded. "*A hundred and fifty?* How could we have a *hundred and fifty?* What in hell do they *do?*"

All of a sudden, UPI was a major institution in the city; the

Poverty Program was a major program. But what *did* they do? The average citizen couldn't fight his way through those acronyms and military metaphors to understand what it was all about. The Trenton *Evening Times* assigned its star reporter, John Kolesar, to take a month to study UPI and the Poverty Program and write a five-part series in an attempt to help the city understand what it was doing. Kolesar wrote:

. . . on a typical day a bird's eye view of Trenton's war on poverty would show:

A staff of 150 people working in UPI's headquarters in the Broad Street Bank Building and three neighborhood centers.

Sixty applicants a day coming into the centers for help.

A hundred students learning trades at the Skills Center . . .

More than 300 high school students and dropouts working on Neighborhood Youth Corps projects.

A hundred pupils attending basic education classes at UPI headquarters.

Some 180 people scattered around the city getting on-the-job training.

About 400 families getting broad-scale help in the John Fitch Way III Urban Renewal Area.

And 270 four-year-olds attending pre-kindergarten classes.

With 400 teachers, aides, and community agents providing extra educational service of all kinds, affecting 6,000 children in the schools.

At any given moment, Trenton's war on poverty may involve:

Teaching a high school dropout how to make tapioca pudding.

Starting divorce proceedings for a woman.

Teaching a boy how to swim with his hands and feet tied.

Giving a set of false teeth to a high school pupil.

Getting a first offender out of jail.

Or feeding milk and cookies to a four-year-old child, finding a job for an unemployed father, teaching a high school graduate his ABC's, sending a girl to summer camp, teaching teenagers to make movies, getting a haircut for a man looking for a job, and all the other little things that add up to a $5 million dollar program touching the lives of one-third of the people of Trenton.

Kolesar spent the month, and more, bird-dogging UPI's neighborhood recruiters, sitting in literacy classes, poring over the accounts, talking to people working at all levels of the program, roaming the low-income neighborhoods of the city.

He got past the bird's-eye view and saw and described the patterns and forces that made up the Trenton effort.

All in all, he gave us high marks—but with a reservation.

"If the War on Poverty succeeds anywhere," he wrote in his concluding column, "it should succeed in Trenton."

There is no guarantee it will succeed anywhere. It may peter out for lack of money. It may prove for once and all the Biblical prediction, "Ye have the poor always with you." It may be that Americans will find affluence is not fun without some poverty around.

But if the idea works, it should work in Trenton, for few cities have done as much to put the idea into operation.

Trenton started its anti-poverty program early, beat its competitors to big chunks of federal money and avoided many of the pitfalls that others fell into.

Instead of the lumpy, aimless mixture of programs set up in some cities, Trenton's anti-poverty organization, United Progress, Inc., tried for a broad, smooth blend of programs.

Instead of playing it safe by riding along with the federal guidelines, UPI risked much by putting its money into some of its own ideas—neighborhood employment centers, instead of social service centers; a cram course in reading and arithmetic to replace learning by osmosis; a try at revamping the high school curriculum.

There has been a minimum of the mutinous scuffling for power over the poor, the race for high salaries and the botched bookkeeping that has plagued the war on poverty around the nation.

This is not to say that Trenton's program has proceeded smoothly to a state of perfection.

UPI is not without some administrative disarray. Some of the programs overlap, a few do not quite fit into the scheme of things.

Operation Head Start seems to work, but mostly for four-year-old girls. Boys get far less out of it. Much of the head start disappears in kindergarten. The anti-poverty programs in the schools are spread so thin it is hard to measure the results, if any. A handful of slum children will be fired up enough to go to college, but only after enormous outlay by the community.

Adult basic education has only a peripheral effect on the older generation. The job training courses seem to work, but in numbers far too few to make any quick reversal in New Jersey's traditional inattention to vocational schooling. And while some of the home-grown experiments look promising, none is a proven success.

Above all, it may never be possible to tell whether the programs produce anything like a dollar's value for a dollar invested.

Counting the cash investment is easy. In Trenton, it has passed $8 million.

Counting the cash return is almost impossible. A few thousand people have been helped in Trenton's war on poverty, but how much each case is worth is unmeasurable. Some people might have done as well without help. On the other hand a teen-ager diverted from a life on the welfare rolls means a $100,000 saving for the taxpayer.

The costs are monumental, at times. It takes more than $3,000 to give a boy the one-year automobile mechanics course at the Multi-Skill Center. That's about what a year at Princeton University costs. Not irrelevantly, it is also about what a year at Jamesburg State Home for Boys or Clinton Reformatory for Women costs.

There are other unmeasurable byproducts of the war on poverty.

In part, it has taken some of the steam from the civil rights drive for new laws. Some of the supply of trained young leadership in the civil rights movement has been absorbed into the drive to improve life in the slums. The poverty program has taken some of its staff members, as well as its clients, off the streets.

The poverty program's innovations may penetrate into middle class education. For instance, Head Start may mean every child will be starting school at 4 in a few years.

How will the poverty war end? In financial withdrawal and defeat? Or in all-out victory, with some last lazy, penniless lout surrendering and reporting for vocational training one Monday morning?

Someday the war will probably run into an inert remnant of mental, physical and moral misfits able to do nothing more than collect and spend their dole checks.

As St. Matthew wrote, we probably will have the poor always with us, and so also with the war on poverty.

The themes in UPI's version of the War on Poverty were employment and education. Employment programming, which was at times to occupy as much as 80 per cent of UPI's budget, was the major theme, education a lesser but important one. The basic ideas behind both were legacies from New Haven and CPI, which had made a kind of philosophy out of concentrating on *opportunity programs* rather than casework. We were later to diversify into other areas, but our strong concentration in employment and education at the outset gave us a rationale, a programmatic backbone, a set of relationships and developed competencies to build on. We were fortunate in the choices we made because we were able to make progress in both areas. And they may even have been the most important areas to work in. But the sheer fact that we chose to *concentrate* on *something* was one of the most important decisions we made.

A CITY-WIDE MANPOWER SYSTEM

Employment, we reasoned, was the most important issue in the ghetto and was the area that could provide the most immediate tangible payoff. It could be defended against critics from both the left and the right. Our vision was not of a series of discrete programs, but of a new, city-wide manpower *system* encompassing recruitment, counseling, screening, basic education, vocational training, work-experience, job-development, placement, and follow up. Not having either guidelines or a very sophisticated understanding of the federal program and its limitations, we applied for funds for all of it—the whole manpower system—in the first Neighborhood Youth Corps (NYC) proposal and were chagrined to find out for the first time what we later began to accept as a fact of life: Federal programs were not designed with systems of service in mind, but with *pieces* of systems; they were not arranged to ease the problems of administration at the local level but at the federal. That was when we discovered that we were going to have to prospect for our system, to piece it together through independent negotiations with independent agencies, each of which was concerned primarily with the primacy, visibility, and success of its own piece.

A year and a half later, doing the federal dance, we got most of the pieces into place, and the manpower system we had dreamed about in the early days actually began to function. Helping people get jobs—effectively, humanely, aggressively—became the programmatic backbone of UPI. It was the central function of the neighborhood centers we began to set up in the first year. It was our hard rock of competence. It made us credible to the neighborhoods, to the other agencies, to the white "establishment," and to ourselves. A year and a half after we formally, officially, began operations, an average of 500 new people a month would come into our three neighborhood centers, and we, in a thankfully tight labor market, would be able to place an average of 200 of them in jobs or training positions that carried stipends. The other 300 were either not looking for employment or were unable, because of a lack of day-care facilities, ill health, etc., to take employment. We could *deliver,* at least in this area, and we knew it.[1]

We had something to offer to the neighborhoods, to employers, and to other agencies. The board of education's new Multi-Skills Center found itself with a new Manpower Development and Training Act (MDTA) requirement that 85 per cent of its students would have to come from low-income families. They couldn't produce them. Neither could the State Employment Service. But we could. Nearly all of their courses demanded an effective reading level of seventh or eighth grade. We were in the literacy business, with nonprofessional teachers and programmed instruction, and could ensure that all the people we referred could meet their standard. As a result, not only was the skill center able to meet its 85 per cent quota, but it had the lowest drop-out rate of any such center in the state.

I have often heard the argument that the operations role is incompatible with that of coordinator-planner. Looking back on three years of attempting to combine the two functions at the local level in Trenton, I think that the argument has more truth in logic than it has in experience. It may be, in government at the federal level, that the two are incompatible. At the local level, at least in our experience, the argument doesn't hold. A new organization has to prove itself, and planning and coordinating are perhaps the toughest possible ways to do it. UPI in Trenton proved itself primarily by putting people—lots of people—in jobs.[2]

Our competence in this area gave us a seat at the bargaining table. We were working with people every day, and doing well at it. We had a base in the reality of the street, and we dealt with that reality directly—through employment. As a result, we had the respect of other agencies. And as a result of our operational competence, not in spite of it, we were able to coordinate and plan for the use of the resources of other agencies, and to make the plans work.

Competence didn't come without a lot of failure, sweat, and anguish. The neighborhood centers and the "center process" were the heart of the manpower system. The idea was that recruiters would go out and find the unemployed client and bring him into the center. There he would meet vocational counselors, placement specialists, and social-service workers who, working as a team, would help him find the answer to his employment problem. We would be responsive, nonbureaucratic, sympathetic, where other agencies were cold, disdainful, or matter of fact. But it didn't work. The "team" in our first neighborhood center wouldn't or couldn't work together. People who came in looking for help with their employment problems were confronted with an endless "process" of referral and counseling that was at once more bureaucratic and self-conscious than anything the employment service had ever thought of and less effective in getting the applicant to his objective—a job. "Indigenous workers," whom we had hired from the neighborhood as counselors on the assumption that they "knew the language" and would "relate" effectively and sympathetically, turned out as often as not to be rigid and punitive in their dealings with clients, treating them, perhaps as they had learned through experience, in a manner they deemed appropriate for "officials" to treat lesser beings. Jean Starks, director of UPI's social-services program, whose workers were to assist clients with personal and social problems that prevented their being employed, sat in on a "disposition" conference of the center team one day and stopped it immediately because, as she told me later, "I felt that what was occurring before my eyes could only be compared to that series of events which takes place when laymen perform abortions on kitchen tables."

This was the low point in UPI's young history. We had put nearly all our effort, most of our resources, much of our talent, into the manpower program, and it wasn't working. And if it wasn't, *we* weren't.

But eventually we figured out how the center should operate. We organized it so that everyone who came in saw the center director immediately after he saw the receptionist. The director, who had the job orders and the authority to command the resources of the center, then could decide whether a person simply needed a job, in which case he simply picked up a phone and tried to place the client on the spot, or more extensive service from the center, in which event he would assign a specialist on the center staff to take over. Thus, the client immediately saw the man in charge, the man who could deliver. Unnecessary delays, unnecessary counseling and processing were cut to a minimum, clients began to move successfully through the centers, the morale of the staff zoomed, and we were on our way.

IMPACT ON EDUCATION

Education was a secondary focus. There was the New Haven legacy again, with examples of functioning, successful prekindergarten, reading, and community-school programs. There was a history of collaboration between the UPI staff and the superintendent of schools and his top people. And I had spent too much time reporting on the shortcomings of the Trenton school system to be able to escape putting a great deal of my personal interest and attention into school reform and educational programs.

From the beginning we had a good, slightly prickly, relationship with the board of education staff. The superintendent of schools had been one of the team that put UPI together. And from the first, we had agreed that there would be a position in UPI's budget called "director of education," whose job was to be continuing liaison and cooperative programming with the superintendent and his staff. This person was to have an office at the board of education, as well as at UPI, and our idea was that by becoming part of the decision-making process at the board's top executive level, he would ensure that the point of view of the community action agency would be reflected in board policies and programs.

There was some friction, but largely because of the personalities and working styles of the people who held this job, the approach worked almost exactly as planned. In the early days, we had money— or access to money—to offer, and so together we designed prekindergarten programs, reading programs, teacher-training programs, and community-school programs. UPI was a partner in the planning and design largely because it was UPI that was expected to provide the federal financing for the programs. It was not long before the UPI education director was called in to work with the superintendent's staff on other matters, to help sort out the priorities for the use of funds under Title I of the Elementary and Secondary Education Act, to choose among candidates for an open principalship, to discuss a change in curriculum for the junior high schools.

Together, we pieced together a group of programs that the Board's Title I coordinator, Dave Tankel, liked to call "Focus On Opportunity." We never used the acronym. By the time OEO funds for education programs were withdrawn, the habit of collaboration had been established, and we no longer needed access to funds in order to have access to the decision-making chambers of the board of education.

In a general sense, what we did was provide support to the innovators within the school system. Together, we launched some twenty more or less radical programs. In addition to prekindergarten, they included a system-wide reading program using volunteers as small-group instructors in elementary-school classrooms; a summer teacher-training program conducted by Princeton University; the creation of three community schools, open after school and evenings for the neighborhood; and a new program for high-school under-achievers that we called the "school within a school," with a curriculum more like an Indian puberty rite than anything else through which we attempted to tap the motivation and raise the sense of self-worth of boys with a history of failure in regular school exercises.

Some of the programs were extraordinarily successful. Headstart youngsters' I.Q.'s went up ten to fifteen points over a six weeks' period, the equivalent of the cognitive gain produced by a year in kindergarten. The community schools attracted 200 people a night and began to have a life of their own. Some schools in the reading program reported astronomical gains in reading levels of third and fourth graders, and eleven of the fifty youngsters in the "school within a school" not only made the switch from the industrial arts "track" to the academic "track" but graduated and went on to college.

And we won some bureaucratic battles as well. Defying state law, the superintendent allowed the reading volunteers to teach reading in the classroom, something they were not supposed to be able to do because they did not have elementary-school teaching certificates. UPI staffers ran the community schools, taught in the "school within a school," and counseled and placed vocational students without the necessary certification. A new careers program was begun, with twenty teacher aides drawn from low-income areas.

We pushed along the cause of reform within the Trenton school system. We provided an alternative to the standard teacher's assumption that poor children and Negro children were stupid, dirty, lazy, immoral, or hopeless. Because there were innovators at the top of the school system's administrative staff, because we worked extremely hard and provided staff support to these people, and because we had access to funds, we were accepted as full partners in the deliberations affecting school policies and programs and were therefore able to bring about reforms that were not limited to the periphery of the school day, but included the curriculum, the selection of professional staff, the training of teachers, and other critical areas. We didn't turn the school system around. But within the limits of the resources we were able to command, UPI had a significant effect.

HEALTH, LEGAL SERVICES, AND HOUSING

With these two programmatic themes as a base, UPI began to diversify its interests and programs about the middle of its second year of operation. We set up a city-wide dental program, badgered city and county welfare offices for fairer and more humane treatment of welfare clients, invaded the police precincts and the county courthouse to set up a release-on-recognizance program, began work on a monumental proposal for a neighborhood health center, set up a legal-services program, and tried our hand at designing and operating a program of concerted social services around three hundred families who were to be relocated out of an urban renewal area. And we wrote an application for the city to the *Look* Magazine All-America City contest (and won), prepared the city's application under the Model Cities program, and began to look into housing.

As we mounted new programs, such as the legal-services effort, we tried to build them into the neighborhood-employment centers and into the center "process" so the new service could support those already existing, and vice versa.

When, after nearly a year of staff work, we finally presented our neighborhood-health-center proposal and the Mercer County Medical Society opposed it as "socialized medicine," a year-long battle was precipitated. During this period, UPI became the acknowledged community health planner and advocate of reform of ambulatory care, both city newspapers became increasingly critical of the medical society, and the mayor, who finally stepped in to try to resolve the issues, became the locus of community-health policy. After a year of wrangling, the medical society reversed itself, and approved the health-center proposal, which went to Washington.

The invasion of the courts and the county jail on behalf of release on recognizance and the elimination of money bail was undertaken almost entirely by gentlewomen. When the lady lawyer who had begun the release-on-recognizance project for us suddenly decided to take a job with the Children's Bureau, I asked Freda Milner, an artist and former art-gallery proprietor then working as a kind of general administrative assistant, to take it over. She is a gentle person, with soft eyes and a soft voice, and she was a little frightened by the assignment, but she took it on. That it is truly possible to catch more flies with honey than vinegar was illustrated when I took a trip with her several months later to meet the warden of the county jail, with whom she had made friends and who was making available to her, for release-on-recognizance purposes, all the records of his prisoners. The warden was no liberal. He didn't believe, he told me, in lining up jobs for prisoners prior to their release. ("Gives 'em too much hope. Makes 'em too anxious to get out.") But he liked Freda and, therefore, the work she was doing. At the end of our talk, he pulled me aside and said he had heard that the Morrow Association, an organization devoted to reforming prison practices, was about to begin a project in Mercer County. The Morrow people, I knew, had been extremely tactful and careful in their dealings with the warden and other county officials in order not to endanger the success of their project. They wanted to counsel prisoners prior to release in order to improve their chances for employment and successful rehabilitation. "Look," the warden said, "there's no reason for those people to come in here. As far as I can see, it's just duplication of effort. If they want to run this kind of project, why can't they handle it through you and Freda?"

Of late, UPI has been most significantly involved in housing and Model Cities planning. It has created a nonprofit housing sponsor called North, East, South Trenton (NEST) to rehabilitate sixty-five units of row housing and is working with the Trenton Coalition of Business to acquire and rehabilitate dozens of others. Model Cities so far has been something of a question mark, but the UPI-prepared application has brought the city a planning grant from the Department of Housing and Urban Development, and the city has hired UPI's director of education to be its Model Cities director.

With the emerging business-based groups (the Mercer County Alliance of Businessmen, the Trenton Coalition of Business), UPI has served as a bridge to the community, a means for getting business-sponsored programs to the people, and a source of sophisticated staff support.

A FAILURE: ORGANIZATION OF THE POOR

Trenton was the first city (despite the publicity that attended Phila-delphia's efforts several months later) to hold open neighborhood elections for neighborhood council officers and "target area" repre-sentatives to the community-action-agency board. It did very well at this, with 15 per cent of the electorate participating in the voting. Extrapolating from the 1960 Census tables, we had delineated three low-income "target areas," East Trenton, North Trenton, and South Trenton, with an aggregate population of some 35,000. The plan was to "organize" them, one by one, and to hold elections that would produce a neighborhood council for each, and from each, a repre-sentative to the UPI board, which, when this process was completed, would total twelve persons.

The neighborhood councils were to be "autonomous" bodies, created through UPI action, but separate from the community-action agency. Our idea was that they would be consulted on proposed programs and could propose and operate programs if they chose. But most important, we thought, they, unlike the community-action agency, would be outside the establishment, freer to make demands on it, to protest, to demonstrate. The neighborhood councils would "put pressure" on the system, and UPI, working within the system, would use this pressure to bring about institutional change. It would be a grand collaboration between the pressure groups outside the establishment and the reformer-technicians within it.

It didn't work. There were several reasons. We didn't realize until too late that the neighborhood councils would require a staff responsible to, and working for, them.[3] The people elected to posi-tions of responsibility within the councils seemed unwilling to pursue specific programmatic demands of their own with the city or the board of education, with employers or other groups. Some of them were frankly opposed to the idea of broad community participation and wanted all neighborhood decisions made only by one or two officers. In addition, there was practically no history of community organization or organized protest in Trenton. The NAACP was made up entirely of middle-class Negroes, many of whom lived in the suburbs, and the local CORE chapter at last count had two members, a man and his wife who served as president and vice-president. And finally, despite some strong advocates of participatory democracy and community organization on the UPI staff, few if any of us knew how to go about the job of community organization or understood the dynamics of neighborhood organization.

The frustrations of the neighborhood councils turned then, after a time, on UPI. In their frustration, and with a UPI top staff that was primarily white and preponderantly from out of town, the major issues became jobs on the UPI staff. Later, it broadened to patronage of other kinds. At one point, a neighborhood leader who "controlled" one of the councils withheld his council's approval of a site (an old department store) for a center that was to serve his neighborhood and thereby held up for several months the institution of a major employment program to serve residents of that neighborhood.

He told me later,

I held up on that neighborhood center because I was sure somebody was gettin' a nice rakeoff on rentin' that old department store, and I figured I might as well get somethin' out of it, too. I figured if I was right, whoever it was'd find out how it was gettin' held up, and they'd call me. But nobody ever called, and I finally decided to let it go through. Now tell me, did I do a stupid thing? Was somebody gettin' a payoff on that deal? Should I have waited a little longer?

It was frustrating and unexpected not to be trusted by the neighborhood-council officers. But most trying of all was to be locked into a system of community participation that gave formal recognition to a few self-seeking persons as the official spokesmen for and representatives of the poor, particularly when the representatives were so clearly bent on feathering their own nests and so clearly uninterested in helping the people they were supposed to represent. "What the hell," moaned one of our neighborhood-center directors, having sat through a complaint session with the neighborhood-council representatives,

What the hell do we have to listen to that crap for? They don't care about the people in the neighborhood, they just want to come and shoot off their mouths, and make sure their friends get jobs. It's disgusting. It's like being up in the front lines poppin' away at the enemy and all of a sudden you find some bastard who's supposed to be on your side is in back of you, shootin' you in the back of the head.

In the past year, the neighborhood councils have dwindled away in importance except as they provide neighborhood representatives to the UPI board. Their functions as protest groups and advocates of particular issues have been assumed by several new, quasi-militant city-wide organizations that operate much as it was originally conceived the neighborhood councils would, in collaboration with UPI.

A SUCCESS: NEW CAREERS FOR THE POOR

If maximum feasible participation via the neighborhood-council route was a failure in Trenton, the employment of neighborhood residents in the program itself was a ringing success. Fully two-fifths of UPI's employees live in the "target areas," and $2 million a year of local program expenditures go directly into the pockets of residents of low-income areas as salaries and stipends.

We made UPI into a "new careers" employer. In our first year of operation, nearly all the top staff was white. By the middle of the second year, it was almost evenly divided, and by the middle of the third, it was made up predominantly of Negroes, most of whom had come up through the UPI ranks. Nearly any male who wanted a job with UPI could get one, on a trial basis, as a recruiter in one of the neighborhood centers. If he did well in that job, at the end of two months he was moved up into permanent status and given a raise. If he continued to do well and showed a desire to learn, he was promoted again within three to six months, this time to literacy instructor, follow-up specialist, social-services worker, legal-aid investigator, or placement counselor. And in another three to six months, if he was doing well, he would be eligible for another promotion, another change of job. Some people held as many as five different jobs within the organization in the course of a year, spiraling up through it to learn the different programs, the different functions, and to prepare themselves for administrative positions. UPI became a major consumer and trainer of local Negro talent.

Our other major source of manpower was young, usually white, out-of-town intellectuals: young lawyers just out of Yale, graduate students from Princeton's Woodrow Wilson School, wives of Princeton professors or graduate students. The UPI salary scale was lower than any other major community-action agency in the state (my salary, first $12,500, then $13,500, was the staff ceiling), which kept away the prospectors for soft and lucrative jobs. It fit in well with our emphasis on youth, and it kept some movement in the more mobile, white members of the staff, who tended after eighteen months or so to go up and out, and hastened the assumption of administrative responsibility by Negroes who had come up through the ranks.

A STRATEGY OF ACTION

UPI's early strategy was to take advantage of the initial, flexible atmosphere of OEO, to capture the initiative and get underway a significant level of program activity so people in Trenton would know immediately that the Poverty Program meant business.

While for most of the OEO's first two years of operation our regional office staff urged and advised community organization and talked of the importance of the process of collaborative community decision-making, the top Washington staff seemed to be conducting a raid on the federal treasury and getting funds out to those who had plans ready. We ignored the advice of the regional office staff, and corraled nearly three times our "guideline" or allocated share of OEO funds, which made it possible to establish a critical mass of program effort in the city and established us in our first year of operation as an important force within the community.

For us, community organization was important, but definitely a secondary matter. Other community-action agencies concentrated their first efforts on organizing the poor. Still others concentrated on neither, but followed the swings of federal policy as best they could and tried to do as much as they could of everything.

For Trenton at that time, the strategy we chose was probably the best one to pursue. Only if federal funds had been guaranteed over a period of years according to a stricter allocation formula could we have taken the time to deliberate and work out programs and projects from the neighborhood up without sacrificing several millions of dollars in program funds to other cities with quicker typewriters and more political clout.

We played to our strength and away from our weakness. Our strongest assets were a set of rather clear ideas of what we wanted to do, drawn largely from the New Haven example, a core of intelligent, literate, and imaginative staff people, good connections with the national "change establishment," and the cooperation of the city administration and other public and private bodies. We did not have in Trenton a history of community organization or protest to build on, or even a high level or public energy, of sophisticated and heated public participation in critical issues. The staff was nearly all white and nearly all from out of town. And though we had fairly good ideas about, and some experience with, manpower and education programs, we knew very little of the business of community organization.

More important than that we chose our particular strategy, however, was that we chose one at all. Most community-action agencies saw themselves, and were seen by others, as local arms of OEO. They felt and were often encouraged by OEO officials to think that they were at the local level what OEO was at that time at the national level. For this reason, very few community-action agencies sought funding from other then OEO sources until congressional cutbacks forced them to, or thought of getting out from under OEO's creeping inflexibility by diversifying their sources of support. Our early decisions about what we were and what we were going to do put OEO— at least in our minds—in its proper place. OEO was a means for accomplishing what we wanted to accomplish, a mechanism for our use, one of several that were available. We found the Washington OEO people fairly receptive to this view, the regional staff not so.

Drawing up the plans for programs, however, was the easy part of the job. Funding them was time-consuming, but in the early days, not so difficult, either. What was hard was making them work once they were funded; harder still was making them work in coordination with other programs.

A community-action agency faces special administrative problems. Administrative organization, for instance, should follow functional lines. But the diversity of funding sources, even of the community-action agency that sticks to OEO sources, tends to encourage an administrative structure that organizes itself by funding source rather than by function.

Congressional emphasis on special "earmarked" programs increased the tendency to internal fragmentation and encouraged community-action agencies not to create an integrated system of services and programs, but a cafeteria of discrete and often unrelated projects under an umbrella that funneled funds but did not coordinate. In a neighboring community-action agency, for example, the director of NYC, an employee of the community-action agency, argued for several months, with some support from the NYC, that he should not report to the community-action-agency director, but directly to the Department of Labor. And despite a large number of effectively operating legal-services programs in the state, only UPI's could be said to have had effective day-to-day coordination with the other services and programs of the community-action agency; of the several Title V Work-Experience programs under way in the state, only two (one of them Trenton's) could be said to have been integrated in effective fashion with any other anti-poverty programs.

When we went outside OEO for funding, we found that the funding agent would generally insist on its "own" director; there was considerable hesitation at the federal level at having staff paid for by one agency working under (or over) staff paid for by another funding agency. It was one of the battles we won, but I came away from each negotiation angry at having to spend so much time fighting the Federal Government for the privilege of putting together a sound local administrative structure.

"THE OEO IS BECOMING THE ENEMY"

On the question of administration and coordination, I do not think it is unfair to say that we got no help and received considerable aggravation from the Federal Government in general (except from our congressman, Frank Thompson) and from OEO in particular.

First there was the ballyhoo problem, or the enormous difference between what the program's federal administrators said we would accomplish, both directly and by implication, and what was possible with the funds that were available. This created great expectation in the ghetto that things were going to change in a hurry, that the local Poverty Program boys had all the dough that was needed to do the job and all you had to do was go down there and get it out of them.

At a subtler level, there was the difference between what a specific program described itself as being designed to do, in its public language, and what it was in fact designed to do. The out-of-school NYC is an example. The program was described as work training for "hardcore" unemployed youth. Its stated purpose was to prepare these youths for entry into the work force by teaching them the habits of the world of work. That those who enrolled were hard core was

ensured by rigorous income and other criteria. But hard-core youngsters read and write at the third- or fourth-grade level. They have an
enormous burden of personal problems. If they are going to be "prepared" for the world of work, if they are going to move on into
private employment, they need help with those problems: literacy
training, medical treatment, counseling. But NYC restricted administrative and supportive costs of the program to 15 per cent of the
total, enough to finance one supervisor or counselor for every fifty
youngsters, but no literacy training, nothing that could truthfully be
called counseling, no extensive medical treatment, no support with
other problems. The out-of-school NYC program was not a training
program, but a means of providing work relief. Hard-core youngsters
were not prepared by it for the world of work. Our response to NYC
was to build enough support into it so it would become what its
language said it already was. It took us a year and a half just to get
the support program funded (from three separate sources) and
several months more to organize it so that NYC functioned as a
training and preparation program for hard-core youth.

Any single program funded from several sources had a timing
problem. Invariably, the element of the program that was needed
first would be funded last. There was never, so far as I could tell, any
implementation of the preference clause. We operated on what were
supposed to be year-to-year budgets. Businessmen will tell you that
no sound planning or administration can take place on that basis. In
fact, at one point, for nearly a year, we operated on month-to-month
budgets and repeatedly had to call the regional office for the magic
telegrams that assured the board of education that the money was
there, somewhere, to allow them to go on with another month of
Headstart.

We learned quickly that asking permission to undertake some
new action was not only unwise but a likely guarantee that we would
not be allowed to go on with it, while if you had a good comptroller,
you could do nearly anything you were not specifically prohibited
from doing, and no one would ask any questions about it because if
your books were clean and you weren't having any "trouble," no one
from OEO ever came to see what you were doing.

The processing of our grant applications after that first glorious
rush of funds was sheer hell. The red tape and the string of broken
deadlines and broken promises, of assurances that a project would
"receive undivided attention," that such-and-such a form "should

have gone out yesterday morning," was incredible. I calculated at one point that I spent nearly 75 per cent of my time dealing with OEO and other federal officials, trying to hasten our proposals through the federal pipeline, while, in addition, three exceptionally able people were occupied full time responding to federal requests for documentation of one thing and a breakdown of another. Our regional office, when I visited it, seemed absolute chaos; it was not difficult to understand why proposals and budgets so often got lost or why so little work seemed to get done on our applications.

OEO itself, of course, never made up its mind whether community-action agencies were to be innovator-coordinators and program operators or organizers of and advocates for the poor. Nor did it make up its mind to let the local organization decide for itself. In our case, what OEO did was to provide a series of field officers and regional administrators to whom we had to go for funds, and these individuals would lean in one direction or another, toward "programs" or "organization," and we would fare well or badly depending on how much they liked our philosophy and how compatible they thought it was with theirs.

For the community-action agency, this meant it was necessary to be both effective programmer and community organizer, or at least to carry the image of both roles. Those who thought of themselves as organizers found out soon that there was very little money for that kind of effort and that they would have to find their financial support in funds provided specifically for the operation of programs, where the criterion for success was not the degree to which the neighborhood had benefited by participating in the program's design but the degree to which it had benefited as a result of the program's effective operation.

Others, like UPI, that wanted to be judged primarily on the effectiveness of their programs, had to adopt the posture of those with the community-organization bias. Both kinds of organizations found themselves trying to go in two directions at once, to play both roles: community organizer-advocate and program innovator-coordinator-operator.

Unreasonable demands were placed on administrators of community-action agencies, as we tried in our organizations to reconcile these often incompatible criteria for success. It made the selection of priorities, a difficult matter at best, nearly impossible. It worked toward weakening the integrity and the effectiveness of both approaches. It permitted community-action agencies to defy evaluation by shifting the ground on which their performance could be judged, and it permitted OEO to render judgments by whatever criteria most suited the agent making the judgment.

I was asked at one point to speak, with two other CAP directors, at a training session for the Northeast Regional Office staff on the subject "What's Happening, Baby?" The training session, a weekend-long affair, was held in a motel in Yonkers, and the two-hour drive up on Saturday gave me time to fight down my first impulse to use the opportunity to vent my frustrations on a captive audience. Instead, I spoke about the different patterns of community-action agency activity, and the legitimacy of each. I proposed that OEO allow us to come in at the beginning of a funding period and state our objectives and strategies, and to negotiate agreement of a funding package on that basis. Then, I said, OEO should leave us alone to carry out our work and audit us on a quarterly or semi-annual basis to make sure we were doing what we had said we would. If we were meeting our objectives to a reasonable degree, then they should refund us and let us pursue our programs with maximum local flexibility. If not, we should be cut off or rigorously controlled. The other two speakers, Ted Velez of the East Harlem Tenants' Council and Don Wendell of the United Community Corporation in Newark, apparently hadn't had the benefit of a soothing two-hour drive. They took their time to do exactly what it had been my first impulse to do: They railed at OEO and its red tape, its CAP memos and regulations, its auditing procedures, its meddlesomeness, its delay in processing proposals. They were angrier and more frustrated than even I had been. "What's happening, baby," I thought to myself, "is the public entrepreneurs are using up their energy and talent just negotiating with OEO, and OEO is becoming the enemy."

SOURCES OF SUPPORT

Things were made a great deal easier for UPI by our having good friends high up in the "change establishment." There is a network of information and support flowing in and through the leading foundations, universities, federal offices, state houses, city halls, and private organizations to which our relationship with men like Ylvisaker and Sviridoff gave us access. It meant being invited to conferences with

Governor Terry Sanford and Jack Conway, benefiting from the ideas of Eli Ginzberg and Herb Sturz, being known to officials at the undersecretarial level in the Federal Government. Being in touch this way with the men who had fathered the Poverty Program and now were thinking through and beyond it kept us at the leading edge of things, gave us the feeling that we were not alone; it had the added advantage of ensuring that anything we might do that was good would be heard about in federal and foundation circles.

After the first year or so, we had a good reputation—partially deserved, partially the result of having good friends, which made it easier to get appointments, negotiate for funding, find staff. When we went to a federal agency, we found to our surprise that they had heard of us! And occasionally, federal-program administrators would call up with funds in hand, inviting us to apply for this project or that or asking what ideas we had that we would like to have funded. On some days, particularly toward the end of the fiscal year, when the federal administrators typically found themselves having to unload in a rush the funds they had carefully hoarded throughout the year, it was really wonderful.

AN EXPLORATORY PROGRAM FOR A REAL WAR ON POVERTY

After more than three years of operation, UPI is still a program-oriented community-action agency. Its posture is slightly more militant than before, its top staff are now mostly Negro rather than white, but it is still pursuing reform from within, still depending for the bulk of its influence on its grantsmanship and its competence and flexibility as a program administrator.

UPI has become an established institution in Trenton. It is recognized as *the* manpower agency to the extent that, at UPI's insistence, the U.S. Department of Labor has tentatively agreed that the Concentrated Employment Program about to be instituted there will be tailored to UPI's manpower and neighborhood-centers system, rather than vice versa. This, as far as I know, has not happened elsewhere.

It has operated as a prod and support for innovative educational activity and a source of creative pressure on the school system. It has put the issue of adequate medical care for the poor at the top of the community agenda and caused the local medical society to move several giant steps to the left in its public posture on the issue of publicly supported medical care for the poor. It has initiated the first privately sponsored housing-rehabilitation efforts in the city. And it has advanced the idea and form of community participation in a whole range of issues.

Many of the old issues are still there. Some say there are still "too many out-of-town whites" on the UPI staff and that the UPI director still has too much power over hiring and firing and UPI policy. There is still talk of "duplication" and the need for "better communication." But the Poverty Program is a real program in Trenton; its fruits are tangible; its results are real.

The creeping rigidity that Paul Ylvisaker warned us would take over the Poverty Program in about two years is evident in the increasing attempts at control from OEO and in a now-discernible tendency to self-conscious bureaucracy within UPI itself. I have on my desk now a copy of a letter from the regional CAP director to the UPI director telling him that the regional office has determined what Trenton's goals for fiscal 1969 will be, and telling him how the versatile funds for fiscal 1969 must be reallocated to conform to those program goals.

But UPI's independence and creativity are still alive, protected in part by its own daring and momentum, in part by the lack of competence and the lack of "adequate time in the field" of federal officials, in part by its diverse funding structure. If there were only two years of creativity in the Poverty Program in its official, governmental structure, there was more than that in some of the programs and organizations that it fostered.

What's past, of course, is prologue. We took the program route in Trenton. I think it was the right route to take at that time, in that place. It brought a sense of movement to the city, a style of administration responsive to the need for change, and a mass of successful exploratory program activity. These now all serve as the foundation for increased efforts toward change and toward community participation. What we started with in 1965, however, wouldn't work in 1968. The issue then was poverty; the enemy, inertia; the answer, effective, immediate action. Now the issue is race and power; the enemy is whitey; and the answer has to deal with participation, black self-sufficiency, and a redistribution of influence.

What we found in Trenton was that competence, imagination,

and effective programs are necessary and important. What we are learning now is that community participation and black power are also necessary. I have very seldom seen the two come together. Putting them together was what those of us who joined the 1965 War on Poverty tried to do. Most of us found we couldn't, so we did one or the other and said we were doing both.

Putting the two together is the job of the 1968 version of the War on Poverty as well. The issues are more sharply drawn. The levels of sophistication and energy and tension are higher. It's a tougher, subtler, and more demanding task than it ever was, and resources are just as short.

But Trenton has a leg up, and the rest of it is coming. As militancy grows in the city, UPI becomes more important, more effective as the instrument of programmatic response. Who knows, by the time the country decides to have a real War on Poverty, perhaps *all* the pieces will be here.

Notes

1. The recruiters who operated out of each neighborhood center would compete with each other to see who could bring in most people off the streets and out of the various hangouts, who could then be placed in jobs or helped with the other services that were offered through the centers. At one point, when the competition between centers had gotten quite fierce, I listened to a news broadcast on my car radio on the way to work about two Philadelphia teenage boys who had run away from home the night before and were thought to be heading in the direction of New York. That morning I mentioned the incident to Don Cogsville, then director of the three neighborhood centers, whose pride and joy was the effectiveness of the employment operation and the productivity of our street-workers, the recruiters. "Well," he said, almost casually, "if they came to Trenton, they'll be in the neighborhood centers by three o'clock this afternoon." Later that day he called me, and in a voice he tried desperately to keep matter of fact, said, "Oh, Greg, those two kids from Philadelphia? They were recruited into the South Trenton Center this morning, and we got them both jobs already. They started work at noon. What do you want to do now?"

2. At one point, Charlie Morris, UPI's deputy director for operations, announced to me with a grin that according to our placement figures and the Labor Department's estimate of the number of unemployed in Trenton, in two months at the rate we were going, we would have placed every poor person in the city and would have to recruit more from outside.

3. We submitted an application for funds to staff the neighborhood councils, but by the time the councils could agree on the proposals, and the regional OEO office had held them for nine months, the OEO had fallen on lean days and the proposals returned with the notation that the OEO was "not funding new programs at this time."

Chapter 8

⊂⊅ *The View from Capitol Hill:*
Harassment and Survival

WILLIAM C. SELOVER

Few federal agencies have ever been subjected to such persistent, widespread harassment by politicians and populace alike as has the ragtag Office of Economic Opportunity (OEO). Ever since the Korean War, dozens of new programs have been added to the federal government. Yet none has proved so controversial as this number-one "Great Society" program. No other program during that time has been so threatened and beleaguered.

The setting for most of that controversy—at least, in its public, visible dimensions—has been the United States Congress. A combination of political factors, especially in the House of Representatives, compounded to make Sargent Shriver's anti-poverty headquarters a political target for legislators who entered battle for a variety of reasons—whether to prove the danger or ineffectiveness of a major federal program or to show that the Great Society was barely reaching beneath the surface in coming to terms with American poverty and blight.

The less visible, and ultimately more important, battlegrounds have been in the White House itself, in the privy chambers of the Budget Bureau, and in the back rooms of city halls in a thousand American cities. Here, the major decisions were made that eventually determined the current outlines of the program. And here, again, the attacks on the program were ruthless and occasionally cynical, with a clear eye to the political survival of the party in power and of the man who espoused and articulated the Great Society.

Why OEO was uniquely subjected to such unprecedented controversy is neither easy to discover nor simple to explain. Most of
those who have been in some way involved in administering or legis-
lating anti-poverty laws have their own ideas. Mr. Shriver believes,
for example, that "a very significant part of the answer" involves the
psychology of the powerful and rich versus the "defenseless" and
poor.[1] "The poor have it hard," he says. "The hardest thing they
have is people who are better off. It is easy to defeat the defenseless.
All this nit-picking comes from that fact."

However there are more immediate and practical ingredients in
the baffling controversy that has surrounded this program. These are
essentially the political and personality factors that so often have
played a major role in the development of national policy.

First, the fact that the legislation was drafted by the administration, handed over to a waiting Congress, and expected to be passed
without major changes was bound to arouse hostility among sensitive
congressmen. "What is the Congressional attitude in the long run
likely to be toward a program which it did not help create," asks
John C. Donovan, "once that program stirs 'controversy'?"[2] This is
the basic question raised by the White House procedure.

Second, President Johnson made it clear from the beginning that
his administration expected sole credit for the framing of the anti-
poverty legislation. "This administration," he told a joint session of
Congress on January 8, 1964, "today here and now declares unconditional war on poverty in America. . . ."[3] He did not say, "this
country," or "this government," but specifically "this administration," and he distinctly did not ask "this Congress" to declare the
war. Nor did he give any share of the credit to the Kennedy administration, whose considerable efforts had set the stage for the Johnson
proposals.

Mr. Johnson was intent on making this program uniquely his—
the cornerstone of his Great Society. He cherished a Rooseveltian
vision of his role and was anxious to fulfill this vision as the redeemer
of the poor and dispossessed. As no recent President could, he empa-
thized with these needs. Yet, when the involvement was so personal
and so exclusive, it could only arouse resentment among others who
sought to share the credit for the nation's "unconditional war on
poverty."

The Republicans, in particular, were alienated from the beginning. They were put in the position of either opposing poor people

in an election year or going along with a clearly Democratic program. They were not even welcome to add their names to any amendments. "Johnson wanted this to be *his* program," explains Representative Albert Quie (R., Minn.) ruefully. "He didn't want any Republican amendments on it." [4] This was the beginning of a strictly partisan approach to the poverty program that was to last for three years.

During 1965 and 1966, of course, the Democrats had the kind of majorities in Congress that made some Republican votes dispensable. But when the political tide turned, in the election of 1966, the lack of bi-partisan support became crucial. By that time, too, other support had been lost. Mayors from all over the country—most of them Democratic—had pelted the White House with protests that the poor were being mobilized into political organizations that threatened all incumbent officeholders—local and national alike. By 1967, the President himself had stopped talking about the program, except on rare occasions.

That was the situation when OEO and the Poverty Program faced their climactic test in the House of Representatives. This is the story of how they reached their low political state—and how they survived.

THE 1964 DEBATE: BORN IN PARTISANSHIP

When President Johnson sent his poverty message to the Congress on the morning of March 16, 1964, he appealed for quick passage of his proposals. "I ask for immediate action on all these programs," [5] he demanded. Mr. Johnson was aware of the obstacles he faced from a proved recalcitrant legislature. This was the same Congress that had failed to be moved by repeated efforts of the Kennedy administration. The Johnson strategy, in face of the odds, was to push hard, to dazzle the Congress, to call for quick action on an omnibus bill that would have his personal imprint on it. His cajoling was relentless.

The Congress, certainly its Democrats, chastened by the crisis of the Kennedy assassination and the Johnson accession, appeared amenable to the heavy presidential demands. But for the Democrats in Congress to assure early passage of the program meant that every Republican effort to delay or obstruct consideration of the economic-opportunity bill had to be resisted.

Predictably, from the very beginning, the Republicans attempted what the Democrats could only regard as delaying tactics. The Democratic response was vigorous, possibly highhanded. It took less than one hour, for example, for the House poverty subcommittee to split on party lines during the first day of the public hearings on the President's proposals. The ranking Republican, Peter Frelinghuysen of New Jersey, in his opening statement, pointed out that "if we are going to come up with constructive legislation, I assume that Congress will have to remain in session for twelve months."

Chairman Adam Clayton Powell (D., N.Y.) made his rebuttal unmistakable. "We meet today," he said, "because the message came yesterday, because we are moving with maximum speed, not deliberate speed, by the way." Mr. Frelinghuysen replied that he hoped "this emphasis on maximum speed does not indicate that the Republicans are not going to be apprised of the plans of the committee, who the witnesses are or what the schedule is." [6]

As it turned out, that was precisely what it meant. Mr. Powell had responded to the President's call on that March 16 morning by immediately setting up the Ad Hoc Subcommittee on the Poverty War Program and scheduling its first meeting for the following morning to hear administration witnesses. Mr. Frelinghuysen was not consulted about the establishment of such a committee or apprised of its procedures. He was asked to designate six Republican members. By March 17, then, the battle lines were drawn. The Powell committee did not spend twelve months on the legislation—as the minority had suggested—or even six months, but twenty-three days in public hearings.

The House committee hearings reflected an obsession with speed and a proclivity for partisanship. The five-minute limit on questioning of witnesses was enforced with a certain bias against the Republicans who fired provocative questions at administration spokesmen. And, at the beginning, Mr. Powell called first on all the Democratic members to question the witnesses, leaving the Republicans until last.

". . . Our committee acted in a very unedifying way in my opinion," Mr. Frelinghuysen told a Senate hearing later.

We were subjected to procedures that eliminated almost any meaningful questioning of any witnesses and prevented any normal bi-partisan consideration in executive session. In every case amendments offered in good faith by members of the minority were summarily rejected by the majority of our committee. Now, this should not be necessary, there should not be a Republican approach to this, and there should not be a Democratic approach to this.[7]

In these early days of House hearings, the Republicans had no particular complaint with Mr. Shriver himself. Only with the committee Democrats. In fact, Republicans congratulated Mr. Shriver and wished him well. At that time, Mr. Shriver even assured Mr. Goodell that he welcomed the constructive amendments from both Republicans and Democrats, and urged a nonpartisan approach. At one point in the hearings, when Mr. Frelinghuysen was limited to five minutes in questioning Mr. Shriver, the then Peace Corps director gallantly offered to make himself "completely available to answer questions not only here but in your office or anybody else's office to the extent that they want to ask questions." Mr. Frelinghuysen called Mr. Shriver's attitude admirable and went on to pay tribute to his "organizing ability," and wished him luck in his "new fight." [8]

It was not long, of course, before Republicans were calling him a "poverty czar" and urging the elimination of OEO provisions from the bill. And in fairness to the committee Democrats, it must be said that Mr. Frelinghuysen had given early warning that the Republicans could not support the legislation in its original draft without considerable alteration. In fact, the House Republicans complained that major parts of the legislation had no business coming before the Education and Labor Committee in the first place.

These attitudes, expressed repeatedly and with a certain earnest eloquence by Mr. Frelinghuysen, did much to convince the Democrats that there was little to be gained by cooperating with the minority—if, in fact, they had ever had such an idea. After the hearings, the Democrats on the committee caucused in closed session for two weeks in an attempt to come up with a bill that the Democrats themselves could all agree on. Their draft, with a few minor changes, incorporated nearly all that the President had requested. At the same time, it ignored every Republican criticism. "We have been boycotted and gagged," Mr. Frelinghuysen complained bitterly.[9]

Even if the administration had wanted a bipartisan approach, the accident of personalities might well have made it impossible. Representative Sam Gibbons (D., Fla.), the program's floor manager in later years, explains that—without considering the merits of the differences between chairman Adam Clayton Powell and the ranking minority member, Peter Frelinghuysen (R., N.J.)—their personalities were irreversibly in conflict over EOA legislation. " 'Petulant Peter,' " says Mr. Gibbons, "was like sandpaper on the gears—even when he was trying to be helpful." [10]

When the full committee tried to work on the bill, he explained,

We got so tied up, we couldn't bring up anything. This came before the election campaign—before it got mixed up in national politics. We had to give up trying to make up a bill by the whole committee. We decided, as Democrats, we might as well caucus and see what we came up with—the bill was so controversial and so broad, and the election was approaching. So we operated as a Democratic caucus.

The Republicans were thus locked out. "For the next three years it operated in a Democratic caucus," said Mr. Gibbons. "It set a precedent." Mr. Gibbons now regards this tactic as a "mistake." He admits: "I'd take as much blame as anyone for this." In any case, on May 26, less than two and one-half months after Mr. Johnson sent his message to the Hill, the House Committee reported out the poverty legislation. It was a strictly partisan vote, with nineteen Democrats voting for and the eleven Republicans opposing.

Senator Pat McNamara (D., Mich.), named head of a select subcommittee of the Labor and Public Welfare Committee, opened the Senate's consideration of the bill on June 17, with the statement, "We do not believe that extensive hearings in the Senate are necessary." [11] In fact, he held four days of hearings. During that time, Mr. McNamara gave Representative Frelinghuysen an opportunity to air his grievance.

In retrospect, it must be said that Mr. Frelinghuysen raised some of the issues that were later to give the program so much trouble. They barely got a moment's hearing, however, during the crucial original House debate. In his Senate testimony, he elaborated in detail, asking, for example, about the role of the local community, and especially of the city governments.

"As the bill is now written there is no role for the local government at all," he told the Senate Committee, and he asked, "How would [Shriver] know whether a program in New York City should get some federal money unless he in some way utilized the mayor or the coordination that had been established in New York City?" [12] Mr. Frelinghuysen further pointed out that the U.S. Conference of Mayors had issued a clear statement on this point. "Any federal legislation," he quoted from that statement, "that is to involve local citizen action in a war on poverty must clearly place the responsibility for program development and execution with responsible local government." Added Mr. Frelinghuysen: "I would personally say 'amen' to that."[13]

This is the issue that tripped up the Poverty Program just when it was making important headway. The issue came to a head in congressional passage of the "Green Amendment" of 1967, which effectively placed local community-action programs under the mayor and his city government. Rebuffed at every turn, Mr. Frelinghuysen, on the last day of the House hearings, finally proposed his own Republican alternative, giving greater power to the states. It reflected Republican attempts to capture southern support. His bill also eliminated the proposed OEO.

This was the first of repeated Republican efforts to offer specific alternative proposals. It was at least a recognition that something should be done and that federal funds were necessary, although the Republican alternative proposal called for about half the federal expenditure asked by the administration's bill. While Mr. Frelinghuysen received active support from Republican members of the Senate Committee, the Senate members remained reasonably bipartisan in reporting out a bill similar to the House version. In fact, the Senate committee was never to have the hopelessly partisan deadlock on poverty that the House Committee had. The Senate Committee vote was 13 to 2, with Republicans Jacob Javits of New York, Winston Prouty of Vermont, and Len Jordan of Idaho voting for it. Barry Goldwater of Arizona, by then the Republican presidential nominee, and John Tower of Texas cast the two dissenting Republican votes.

The final Senate vote on the bill, on July 23, was 61 to 34. Southern Democrats split evenly, with 11 supporting and 11 opposing the bill. Ten GOP senators supported the bill and 22 opposed it.

As passed, the Senate version contained two compromise amendments sponsored by George A. Smathers (D., Fla.). One allowed the governor of a state to veto the placement of Job Corps centers in his state. The other gave the governor a similar veto power over antipoverty projects contracted between the federal government and a private agency. The leadership narrowly defeated a broader "states rights" proposal, supported by a coalition of conservative Republicans and southern Democrats, that would have permitted a governor's veto over any community action project. The amendment, sponsored by Senator Prouty, lost by a single vote, 45 to 46.

Meanwhile, the House bill had been holed up in the Rules Committee for some weeks. Hearings opened June 16, under the wily eye of the old chairman, Judge Howard W. Smith (D., Va.). Phil Landrum, Georgia Democrat who was the bill's floor manager, was cross-examined closely about the Job Corps. Would it be racially integrated? Judge Smith asked. Yes, replied Mr. Landrum. But, he assured Mr. Smith, participation would be voluntary, and integration was a "matter of law over which neither you nor I can prevail." Chairman Smith reminded Mr. Landrum that "white boys in your state or mine have very deep feeling" about living with Negroes.[14] But finally, on July 28, the Rules Committee cleared the bill for debate. The vote was 8 to 7.

During those weeks when the bill was in the Rules Committee, the President publicly urged time and again that the committee not obstruct his legislation. Republicans were resentful at what they felt were the President's implications that the Republicans were delaying the bill. "Whether the minority wanted to delay action on this bill or not," said Mr. Frelinghuysen, annoyed, ". . . there would be no way in which we could appreciably slow down the process." [15] He publicly expressed the wish that he had such powers.

In fact, the Rules Committee delay reflected the President's difficulty in holding together his "great coalition of Northern and Southern Democrats" (as Representative Gibbons likes to call it). But in final House action, August 8, the vote was 226 to 185—a much stronger vote in favor than the administration had expected. Sixty southern Democrats had voted for passage. Forty opposed it. Only 22 Republicans supported it, while 145 opposed it. All 144 northern Democrats who voted favored passage. On August 11, the Senate voted to approve the House version. So the President had his program. It took cajoling and compromising. It took persistent pressure.

"Our committee," complained Representative Frelinghuysen, "was subjected to and yielded to intense political pressure. It favorably reported a bill which in the absence of urgent commands from the highest level of the executive branch would have been laughed out of Congress." [16] That is how the Republicans viewed the new law. That view was only to harden in the weeks and months ahead.

But back in August 1964, it hardly mattered what the Republicans thought. The President was going into the autumn of an election with an impressive new program to boast about. "Today is the first time in all the history of the human race," Mr. Johnson said on signing the bill, "a great nation is able to make and is willing to make a commitment to eradicate poverty among its people." [17] Mr. Johnson was swept back into office in a landslide victory.

THE 1965 DEBATE: MORE OF THE SAME

It is doubtful that the administration was entirely aware that its tactics would invite prolonged antipathy. But antipathy there was, as it remains today. The 1965 Congressional Debate was characterized by more of the same: Democrats maintained their partisan guard over the legislation, and Republicans continued and escalated their barrage of opposition.

This first year after the program commenced was a vulnerable one for OEO; stories of scandals, waste, and mismanagement flooded in from every corner. Those who planned hearings on the program knew it would be almost useless to hold long, elaborate hearings on its accomplishments. At that point, the program was only months old. Headstart, for example, was unheard of when the House Committee opened hearings on April 12—in the absence, it should be noted, of Mr. Frelinghuysen, the Quixote of the House Committee who had by that time left the Committee for other quests.

Mr. Powell took everyone by surprise by opening his hearing with charges that OEO had degenerated in many places into "giant fiestas of political patronage." [18] Here, for the first time, Mr. Powell raised the question of participation of the poor. He claimed that, in many places, the poor were excluded from their rightful role in planning the local projects. This charge was re-echoed in testimony from Cleveland, Chicago, and elsewhere.

At that early stage, Mr. Shriver's response to the political turmoil erupting in local anti-poverty programs was singularly liberal and activist. He conceded that poverty had indeed become popular politics. He explained that the intent of his agency had been to "encourage at the local level the basic democratic processes which have made this country great . . . And that includes arguments, disputes, dissension, and what I like to call 'community action.' " He said his agency was not set up "to create community torpor or community apathy. As a consequence, when we see disputes at the local level, then we think we are getting exactly what Congress asked us to encourage." [19]

The committee's majority report contended that "it is indeed vital that the persons who are the objects of this program be treated less as clients or cases and more as partners." [20]

The muscle of the poor was being felt. It caused a kind of euphoria in Washington, this idea—before the clout from big city management became felt—this hope that the poor would behave like PTA delegates, enlisted into the democratic process without really disturbing anybody.

The Senate Committee consideration, under Senator McNamara, lasted two days—June 28 and 29. Senator Javits was able to get the committee to adopt three amendments, the most important of which was a reaffirmation of OEO policy that allowed neighborhood community-action groups or private nonprofit agencies not participating in city-wide umbrella agencies to apply directly to OEO for funds. It was late that same year, however, that OEO would renounce such a policy under severe local pressures as well as pressures from within the administration.

During this first full year, the GOP resentment of the program, its exclusion from any part in it, crescendoed in intensity. Senator Everett McKinley Dirksen of Illinois, in floor debate, called the program the "greatest boondoggle since bread and circuses in the days of the ancient Roman empire, when the republic fell." He insisted that the program was "the very acme of waste and extravagance and unorganization and disorganization . . . a colossal disgrace, and, in some cases, an absolute fraud upon the taxpayer of this country. We are on a binge," he said, "it can't last." [21]

A Republican task force on economic opportunity headed by Representative Frelinghuysen had earlier held its own hearings on the poverty program because, it was explained, the House Committee hearings had been "inadequate." Concluding his own hearings, Mr. Frelinghuysen said the program was in "administrative shambles," and "in deep trouble in many areas." [22]

A final indication of the political danger inherent in the new program came from the annual meeting of the U.S. Conference of Mayors at the end of May. There, Los Angeles Mayor Samuel W. Yorty and San Francisco Mayor John F. Shelley, both former Democratic congressmen, presented a draft resolution highly critical of OEO. They accused it of "creating tensions" by insisting on greater participation of the poor in planning community-action programs. This policy, they said, failed "to recognize the legal and moral responsibilities of local officials who are accountable to the taxpayer for expenditures of local funds." [23] This resolution was shelved, however, in favor of a meeting between a group of mayors and Vice-President Humphrey. But the message, to be sure, got through to the White House.

The most formidable issue raised during the debate was the one involving the governors' veto. During the year, the veto power was used five times. The administration bill, sent to Congress in April, proposed to retain this power. The House Committee approved an amendment by Representative John Brademas (D., Ind.), to abolish the veto, but following protests from governors from all over the country, the committee restored it in a limited form. The new amendment allowed the OEO director to override the governor's veto on community action and related projects, after reconsidering a project application, and this provision remained in the bill when the House passed it. The governors' absolute veto over Job Corps and VISTA projects was unaffected.

The final House vote was a decisive 245 to 158 majority. Republicans remained opposed by a predictably wide margin, 24 to 110, but Democrats supported the bill, 221 to 48. Southern Democrats split, 45 to 46.

Then the Senate subcommittee on poverty adopted an amendment by Senator Ralph W. Yarborough (D., Tex.) repealing entirely the governors' veto over community action and related projects. During the Senate floor debate, repeated Republican attempts to retain the governors' veto, with strong support from southern Democrats, were narrowly turned back. The Senate version passed 61 to 29, with nine Republicans in favor and 20 against. Eleven southern Democrats voted for passage, and 8 opposed it.

When House-Senate conferees reported out a compromise version on September 14, the governors' veto had been deleted altogether. This was too much for the House. In a heady appeal by Representative William Ayres (R., Ohio), the Republican coalition of southern Democrats was revived. By a 209 to 180 roll-call vote, the House acted to recommit the bill, with instructions that the House conferees insist on the limited veto provisions. On this vote the 127 Republicans, acting unanimously, voting for the Ayres motion, picked up 65 of the 80 southern Democrats' votes. The Senate conferees went along with the House, retaining a limited veto.

Thus, in a small, symbolic way, the Republicans had scored a victory. They had registered their discontent and frustration, and the administration temporarily lost its southern Democrats to a coalition with the Republicans. As it turned out, this was merely a flirtation.

THE 1966 DEBATE: THE CONGRESS FILLS A VACUUM

Whatever initiative the administration held over the direction of the legislation during the first two years was clearly on the wane by 1966. "This is not an administration bill," Representative Sam Gibbons proudly told the House members during the 1966 floor debate. "This is a bill which is the work of Congress and the work of a committee." [24] And when Congress was through with the bill, a significant portion of the administration intent had been altered.

It was in the year 1966 that the administration began to respond in earnest to the pressures of the city governments—the criticism by mayors and city councils that the poverty program was creating in its community-action agencies a federally financed independent power base within the cities, a direct challenge to the established structure, unresponsive to the taxpayer and the voter. Most of the protesting city administrations were Democratic.

The day the first letter of protest arrived at the White House from an aggrieved mayor was the day the administration began its retreat. The President had never intended the program to mobilize the poor and tap its spokesmen for the purpose of opposing either local or federal political organizations, or both. But that is, in fact, what happened.

"In all my talks with the President on the poverty program," says Representative Gibbons, "I have the clear impression that the White House wanted the poverty program to be a sensible program— not revolutionary!" [25] Nonetheless, the administration had, indeed, launched a revolution—and it was launched inadvertently, both on the part of Poverty War planners, as Adam Yarmolinsky's article in this volume makes clear, and on the part of the Congress, which did not even mention "the participation of the poor" in hearings or debate.

The administration retreat in 1966 took the form of silence—a failure to push actively for passage of the legislation. The vacuum created by its reluctance on the issue permitted Congress to claim its lost prerogative over the direction of the War on Poverty.

Mr. Shriver had other problems. A big one was Chairman Powell. The year 1966 marked the final decline and fall of the eleven-term Negro congressman from Harlem. Because Mr. Powell had been a supporter of the program (however erratic) his decline was a reflection on the whole program. Hinting at scandals supposedly waiting to be discovered, Mr. Powell had promised to hold formal hearings on the programs in various cities around the country after Congress adjourned in 1965. Congress authorized $200,000 for this purpose. But, faced with the grueling prospect and preferring the alternative of several weeks at his island retreat at Bimini, Mr. Powell opted easily for the latter. He never reappeared on the Washington scene until Congress had reconvened for its 1966 session.

A few Democratic staff members visited several cities to investigate the programs. And the Republicans, Representatives Goodell, Quie, and others, conducted investigations of their own. Some said that Mr. Powell was pressured by the White House to drop his investigation in view of its potentially damaging effect at the polls in November. In any case, when the House hearings opened in 1966, Mr. Powell had unusual praise for OEO and its operation. "I think all of us will be surprised," he said, "at the splendid accomplishments of this glorious war." [26] Mr. Powell had no report to release on the findings of his investigators—although Republicans had information that the findings were very critical. GOP members thereupon began issuing their own reports based on the minority field investigations and inserting them into the *Congressional Record*.

In their first "Republican poverty memo," issued on March 15,[27] Representative Goodell pointed out a discrepancy between the testimony of Sargent Shriver and Labor Secretary Willard Wirtz. Mr. Shriver had testified that "since last summer fewer than fifty ineligibles have been discovered in the Neighborhood Youth Corps." The next day, said the memo, Mr. Wirtz told the House Committee that some five to six thousand New York City enrollees had been found ineligible and dropped since the summer. Each subsequent memo pointed out administration lapses, local incompetence, and bureaucratic mismanagement. Republicans later claimed that OEO was unable to disprove any of the contentions made in these memos.

These daily exposé sheets, which continued for many weeks, also served as a platform for promoting the Republican "Opportunity Crusade" as a substitute for the Poverty Program. Representatives Quie and Goodell described their substitute as "drastically revamping and redirecting the poverty war." [28] They continued:

It will guarantee true involvement of the poor, bringing the states in as partners in the Opportunity Crusade and giving realistic incentives for employers to develop productive, permanent jobs in private enterprise for the unskilled and the uneducated. This and other proposals from both Democrats and Republicans, deserve more than this quick brush-over given to the war on poverty hearings to date.

But, unknown to the Republicans on the committee (except as a rumor), the hearings, discontinued two days earlier, were not to resume at all during that session. When Republicans learned that the hearings were indeed ended without consultation, they were deeply angered. They called the proceedings "a travesty on the legislative process." "None of the 54 witnesses requested by the Republicans has been called," they complained, "nor had Chairman Adam Clayton Powell deigned to even acknowledge our requests. We've had eight days of hearings and listened to virtually nothing but administration spokesmen and apologists for the poverty program." [29] The Republicans added more to their list of requested witnesses, raising the number to 67. Mr. Powell declined to call any, refusing, he explained, "Because I am chairman." This was, of course, a fateful, overconfident statement, given the events of later months that reduced his power and eventually removed him from Congress altogether.

Following the House hearings, the Democrats again, as in the past, caucused without the Republicans, in an effort to work up "a bill we can defend." The meetings that excluded Republicans were designed to keep them from attempting to gut the bill. But Democrats themselves were far from being in agreement on the final version.

Republicans reacted again in a memo by saying that Mr. Powell "is perpetuating one of the sorriest exhibitions of political partisanship ever witnessed in Congress. . . ." "His actions," they continued, "constitute an open admission that he and the majority of Democrats on his committee regard the poverty program as pure politics and the private preserve of Democratic caucus." [30]

On May 18, the Education and Labor Committee reported a redrafted bill that included a number of restrictive amendments. The most important were a series that earmarked the funds, directing specifically where every penny should be spent. In so doing, the committee had bolstered the popular Headstart and Neighborhood Youth Corps (NYC) program but cut back on the Job Corps and community-action (other than Headstart) programs. Thus, the Community Action Program (CAP), which was really the heart of the program and the only genuinely innovative part of it, was badly gutted.

The Rules Committee reported the bill July 14. With this action, in the only published report issued in the memory of the committee staff, the committee criticized Mr. Powell for failing to appear to defend the bill and expressed deep concern over the disposition of the $200,000 previously given to the committee for its investigation. Even the Rules Committee was unable to get a copy of the investigation's findings.

It was not until September 19 that Mr. Powell issued the report —in the face of an impending committee revolt against his arbitrary exercise of power in delaying the bill and suppressing the report. By that time, the details and findings were wholly out of date and largely irrelevant. The report was general in nature and criticized OEO for "insufficient emphasis on the unemployment problem." Many members felt it was hardly worth the cost. During the House debate, the committee Republicans made their first positive contribution to the legislation, a contribution that was partly political in conception but deeply liberal in application. Representative Albert Quie of Minnesota successfully proposed an amendment on the House floor that required at least one-third of the members of local community-action boards to be representatives of the poor and that these representatives be chosen by residents in the poverty areas. The provision was accepted by the Senate and retained in the final version of the legislation.

The Quie amendment was important in redressing the balance in the program in favor of the poor themselves. The White House, responding to the mayors, had already let it be known through its Budget Bureau that the emphasis on the poor should be played down. And OEO had assented. Congress now made its influence felt in countering the Budget Bureau move. Still, the question was by no means finally resolved. An attempt to substitute the Republicans' "Opportunity Crusade" for the committee bill lost 162 to 203. But, on September 29, the House, on a teller vote, moved to kill the bill—128 to 118. After a frantic scurrying, the move was later rejected on a roll-call vote, 162 to 203, and the bill was passed, 210 to 156.

The Senate, far more sympathetic, passed their version of the bill a few days later, after deleting an amendment added in committee that raised the spending authorization $746 million above the President's request.

OEO had asked the Budget Bureau for $3.4 billion to carry on the program in the 1966–1967 fiscal year. Mr. Shriver had been given reason to expect he would get that much by this time. But the administration's budget, sent to Congress in January 1966, included only $1.75 billion. The final congressional appropriation was $138 million less than that, $1.612 billion.

Mr. Shriver was stunned by this unmistakable sign that support for his program was withering away. Had he ever expected to use his government position to launch a career in elective politics, things were hardly going well for him. And this was not an auspicious time for an exit. When the final appropriation was made in November 1966, Mr. Shriver called a press conference to denounce the cut-backs. The usually embullient and forceful director was muted. He lamented that the impact on the anti-poverty program would be "great and grave."

Implicit in his remarks, of course, was deep displeasure that the White House had failed in its commitment to the program. He was speaking not only of appropriation reductions, but also of Budget Bureau cut-backs and White House indifference. He was at the lowest point in his career. During the year he had been the target for personal vilification and rejection by a convention of representatives of the poor at Washington's International Inn, and his resignation had been demanded not only by Representatives Quie and Goodell but also by Chairman Powell. Nevertheless, even then, OEO was mobilizing support in every sector of the country where poverty money was spent, and the next year's plans were being mapped out. Soon, the positive grass-roots response to the cut-backs was to startle a miserly Congress, and even Mr. Shriver himself.

THE 1967 DEBATE: SURVIVAL

The refusal of the House to seat Chairman Powell at the beginning of the 1967 congressional year marked the start of a new relationship between the majority and minority on the House Education and Labor Committee.

The new chairman, Carl D. Perkins (D., Ky.) brought to his task the easygoing, homespun manner of the Kentucky mountains, which, if nothing else, elicited trust from his colleagues, Republican and Democrat alike. While OEO officials directed veiled criticisms toward Mr. Perkins for the slow, plodding way his hearings were conducted, the Republicans welcomed the fact that, for the first time, they were allowed a role in the bill's mark-up process. And, in an uprecedented move, Mr. Perkins held final mark-up sessions in public —in the glare of public exposure, thus encouraging hard work and more responsible consideration. Also, Mr. Perkins called every witness requested by the Republicans. And minority Representatives were accorded reasonably respectful treatment. In turn, the Republican opposition became more responsible. The "Poverty Memos" did not reappear. The Republican alternative "Opportunity Crusade" was more carefully drawn, incorporating more positive responses to the needs of poverty. And, in the end, for the first time in his career, Representative Quie voted in favor of the bill.

But at the beginning, all was not well for the program, for OEO, or for Mr. Shriver himself. In fact, many believed early in the year that it would be a miracle if any bill emerged from this new Congress at all. The 1966 election had seen a rout of liberal Democrats. Most of the forty-seven new House Republicans had won their seats by defeating Democrats who had been members of the liberal Democratic Study Group and had campaigned partly on their record of support for the poverty program. Mr. Shriver however, professed a certain optimism. He pointed out that many local communities had responded to federal fund cutoffs by dipping into local public and private sources. And he said that many affected programs continued into 1967 with volunteer workers.

Yet, most of the top OEO officials were deeply gloomy about prospects for the program. There appeared to be a growing interest among critics of the program in "spinning off" some of the programs to other departments. While this was a Republican idea, Richard

Boone of the Citizens' Crusade Against Poverty testified in favor of it, and Senator Joseph S. Clark (D., Penn.), who chaired the Senate subcommittee, indicated that this was a desirable eventual goal. Others were interested in the idea.

Then the summer riots paradoxically hardened congressional opinion against continuing support to the ghetto needy. Many voiced fears that anti-poverty funds had, in fact, inspired such riots. And OEO officials candidly admitted in private that it was likely that the anti-poverty investment had probably quickened the impulse among those caught in the poverty cycle to fight their way out, or at least to register an unmistakable protest against those conditions. At the same time, funds for the frustrating fight in Vietnam were being increased steadily, and, in response, legislators were looking toward ways to cut back domestic spending. One main target was OEO.

Representative Ayres considered it likely that Congress would fail to pass the anti-poverty legislation and would have to continue the program by means of a continuing resolution that would hold spending to the previous year's level. On October 11, the House, in voting for increases in federal salaries, specifically knocked out pay raises for OEO employees. To counter this congressional hostility, top OEO officials early sought support for their programs in every sector. In the end, their efforts paid off handsomely. For example, in early 1967, the League of Women Voters were wooed by OEO, and as a result, the league mobilized its national membership down to the grass-roots level. It established a position of support for OEO, and its members brought pressure to bear on local constituents and on congressmen. They pinpointed the programs' successes and spelled out what the local agencies were doing. OEO officials now consider the League to have been among the most effective of all their supporters.

The League was only one of several groups drumming up votes for the program during the year. Quietly, a liaison with the business community was set up at the prompting of OEO, though not with its open support, in an effort to enlist the backing of the business elite. Some of the biggest names in American industry were drafted, and their efforts on behalf of OEO were considered deeply effective, particularly with the borderline Republicans. It is known, for example, that pressure on Representative Quie from Minnesota business leaders had an influence on his ultimate decision to support the bill.

At the same time, Mayor Durley of Providence, encouraged by

OEO, was in constant touch with local officials, explaining OEO's important role in cooling summer riots that year. During the months before the bill was considered, he wrote letters to 2,000 local officials on five separate occasions, enlisting their support. And during the final debate, he twice sent telegrams to these 2,000 local officials asking them to urge their representatives to vote for the bill.

In the course of getting Republican approval for the EOA extension in 1966, Senator Clark had promised a massive series of hearings on the poverty program, the kind of investigation that Mr. Powell had failed to produce. Mr. Clark began this investigation early and conducted 33 days of public hearings in Washington and across the country, heard 401 witnesses in 144 hours of testimony, made 11 inspection trips in the field, and considered 18 staff reports and 15 consultant reports. By September, the amassed information amounted to 26 volumes.

While the Senate subcommittee was doubtlessly sympathetic toward the program, OEO officials, faced with such a penetrating investigation, were understandably uneasy. But they need not have feared the outcome. In fact, the very exhaustiveness of the probe probably strengthened considerably the chances for the bill among the senators. They could hardly fail to be impressed during the floor debate by the stacks of green-bound volumes of hearings, studies, and reports piled high on their desks.

Of the five basic conclusions drawn from the investigation, only one directly reflected disfavor on OEO. This was the charge of "lack of sufficient coordination." [31] But among the other findings was the assurance that the basic OEO programs "are desirable and should be continued" and that OEO itself should "continue in operation." [32] The subcommittee also insisted that OEO programs should not be "spun off."

On September 12, the Senate Committee sent to the floor a bill rewriting much of the basic Act and extending it until 1969. For 1967–1968, the committee voted $2.258 billion—$198 million more than the administration had requested. The committee bill included an additional $2.8 billion for a two-year emergency-job program for the hard-core unemployed in the cities' slums. After ten days of debate, the Senate approved the bill 60 to 21, having deleted the emergency-job program against which the White House had vigorously lobbied. On the final vote, a majority of the Republicans voted for the program.

On the House side, the story was considerably different. When Chairman Perkins opened hearings in June, he was faced with two potentially crippling lines of attack on OEO. First, there was strong sentiment among Republicans for a transfer of at least some of the OEO programs to other departments, and they had an influential ally in Edith Green (D., Ore.) who voiced support for transfer of the Headstart program to the Department of Health, Education and Welfare. Second, Mr. Perkins had in hand some sixty letters from mayors across the country professing bitter antipathy toward the way local CAP programs challenged their authority on the local level.

Mr. Shriver launched into the first objection on the first day of hearings, June 12:

It seems to me that a single basic issue faces the Congress this year in connection with the War against Poverty. It is this: Will the agency you brought into being to serve the poor, to speak for the poor, to marshall America's resources on behalf of the poor, continue to do the job you set for it? [33]

Of course, it was stretching the facts slightly to say that Congress had "brought into being" OEO, and had "set" a job for it to do. But in all their efforts to dismantle OEO, the Republicans failed. Not one of the expert witnesses brought before the House Committee testified in favor of such a course—not even those witnesses called by the minority. And for the southern Democrats, the prospect of the Headstart programs being shifted to the Office of Education headed by Harold Howe II (in their eyes a militant integrationist), was enough to inspire solid southern opposition to such a plan.

It was the other issue that was to give Congress and OEO deeper pause: how to placate the mayors. Early in the year, OEO strategists worked up a plan that would amend the law to require local-community-action program boards to be made up of the poor, local officials, and representatives of private groups in equal one-third proportions, thus codifying what had already been incorporated into the OEO guidelines. It soon became apparent, however, that to satisfy local mayors and critical congressmen, a sharper concession would be necessary. It came in the form of an amendment drafted by many persons but finally sponsored by Representative Green to allow the channeling of CAP funds through the local governments where those governments so elected. At that time, an estimated 20 per cent of the more than 1,000 CAP agencies were administered under local governments; the rest were run by private, nonprofit organizations, with public officials playing only minor roles, if any at all.

OEO officials were not particularly pleased with the Green amendment, but they saw it as the only way to get sufficient support for the bill as a whole from southern Democrats and representatives from the big cities. Even the Democratic study-group chief, Representative James G. O'Hara (D., Mich.) was drumming up support for the amendment before it came to the floor and during the debate. Nevertheless, some liberal Democrats joined the Republicans in opposing what they called the "bosses and boll weevil" amendment.

Mrs. Green explained her amendment by saying that it provides that "those who are helping to pay the bill—and who also live in this same community—shall have a voice through their elected officials on how their money is spent and how programs can be coordinated with other existing programs." [34] Representative Quie retorted that the Green amendment "effectively removes the participation of the poor that has been very difficult to achieve so far." [35] Pressures on congressmen to support the Green amendment were very strong. Mayor Joseph Durley of Providence arranged for a steady stream of mayors to be present in the Capitol building during the debate, and members were called off the floor to consult with them. In the end, all efforts to delete the Green amendment failed, and the House passed the bill on November 15 by 283 to 129. The size of the winning margin surprised everyone. Certainly the Green Amendment had helped. But the pressures from local business leaders and other groups engineered by OEO itself had been powerfully mobilized, and this factor was decisive in many cases.

The Senate-House conference was the battleground for the final defense of the Green Amendment. Ultimately, the Senate conferees agreed to accept the provision—with some safeguards against abuse— while the House conferees agreed to the two-year authorization and the higher spending figures in the Senate bill. The final authorization was $1.773 billion, some $287 million below what the administration had requested and only slightly below the $1.788 billion Mr. Shriver considered the minimum amount necessary to continue the program at the current level. The President signed the bill privately while traveling around the world on his pre-Christmas global jaunt, and the poverty program was renewed until 1969—allowing OEO some needed respite.

The respite, however, was not to be entirely peaceful. During

1968, the General Accounting Office, as directed by the new law, proceeded to conduct a massive, impartial probe of its own into the program to be completed by December 1.

By 1968 the program seemed finally to have passed through its years of fierce partisan controversy. It had, however, attained its new tranquillity only at the expense of concessions that threatened the most innovative elements of the program. The community-action programs were subjected to the control of precisely those political structures that had failed in past generations to appreciably help those who remained trapped on the treadmill of poverty.

THE LOSS OF STATUS, 1964–1968

OEO and its programs had survived the years of controversy, but they paid the cost in a loss of status among government programs that probably can never be regained. In his 1968 State of the Union message to the Congress, the President practically overlooked the poverty program altogether. He made reference to it only incidentally, as a sub-point under "other actions" well past the two-thirds point in his speech. Almost every other domestic and foreign issue— except civil rights—preceded his mention of the poverty program. And when he did mention it, he gave it extremely short shrift. In the twenty-five words devoted to the program, the President merely announced that it would be continued for another year.

Thus it was that by 1968 the President himself had relegated this original Great Society program to a low point on the list of White House priorities. It would be a gross oversimplification to say that the de-escalation of the poverty war resulted directly from the escalation of the Vietnam war. It is more accurate to say only that these phenomena coincided.

Mr. Johnson had long since given up on the poverty program as the vote-getter it had once been. It had served its purpose well in 1964. But from that time forward, it had meant only trouble for the White House. Because Mr. Johnson had taken such pains to accept credit for the original idea, he was the first to be blamed when it went sour. And when the problems came, when the controversies erupted, they did not come singly, they came in scores. First, the Republicans protested. Then the mayors. Then the liberals, the civil rights activists, and the poor. Then the black militants. And, of course, through it all, white southerners grumbled their dissent. Anyone who had a gripe could hang it on the poverty program and the White House. This was obviously not Mr. Johnson's ideal immortalization.

Thus, in his 1968 State of the Union address, delivered to a glum audience on that cold Wednesday night in January, Mr. Johnson's major proposal was a vast increase in training jobless slum-dwellers. He proposed to place 500,000 hard-core unemployed into jobs in three years. To this end, he called for increasing the manpower budget for fiscal 1969 by $442 million to $2.1 billion—only a small fraction of which was to be spent by OEO. One major program expanded to handle this increase was the Manpower Development and Training Act (MDTA) program, administered by the Department of Labor. It was profoundly ironic that, by this time, the White House retreat from OEO was so complete that, in the anti-poverty area, the President was addressing his primary attention to warmed-over proposals of pre-Great Society vintage.

OEO officials were disappointed, but not surprised. They were still recuperating from Mr. Johnson's painful silence on the program throughout the 1967 congressional debate. One Shriver assistant confided that "the White House did nothing to help us during the grueling months when the program looked as if it was being retired." This source complained that the President did not even mention the program in public from the time the poverty message was sent to Congress until the bill was passed. Another OEO official, who coordinated legislative efforts with the White House, confided that the only contribution the President made to the passage of the poverty program was to instruct the other Cabinet chiefs not to lobby for OEO "spin offs."

The roots of White House disenchantment went back many months—to the period just after the 1964 elections—and the development of that disenchantment is worth retracing as a case study in politics and administration. It was during OEO's tooling-up period in the early months of 1965 that the agency, in its zeal, made real efforts to carry out the terms of the legislation by promoting the involvement of the poor in the direction of local poverty programs.

To clarify the "maximum feasible participation" clause written into the law earlier by the poverty task force, the CAP guide, issued by OEO in February 1965, stated, "A vital feature of every community action program is the involvement of the poor themselves—

the residents of the areas and members of the groups to be served—in planning, policy-making and operation of the program." OEO officials further advised local communities that the poor were to have a place "either on the governing body or on a policy advisory committee." During those early months, OEO took these guidelines seriously. Mr. Shriver and his aides moved quickly to make clear that participation of the poor was a condition for funding. They took some courageous stands—and made some formidable enemies.

Mayor Samuel W. Yorty of Los Angeles refused to include the poor on his city's poverty board. In response, as an effort to force the issue, OEO withheld funds. Soon thereafter, the Watts riot erupted. Only then did Mayor Yorty agree to include seven representatives of the poor on the board. They were, however, hand-picked by the mayor.

In Chicago, the story was similar. OEO held up funds to force Mayor Richard Daley to include some poor people on the seventy-five-member Committee on Urban Opportunity. Mayor Daley finally hand-picked some poor people to sit on his local CAP board.

By June of 1965 the U.S. Conference of Mayors had become a focal point for the growing dissidence. Mayors Shelley and Yorty proposed a resolution accusing Mr. Shriver of "fostering class struggle." At the same meeting, the executive committee approved a resolution calling on OEO to channel its community-action projects through city-hall-approved local agencies. Mayor Daley became chairman of a new anti-poverty committee of the Mayors' Conference.

Mr. Daley soon conferred with the Vice-President to express his concern over the direction of the program and the potential challenge it presented to city governments. Mr. Humphrey assured the mayors he would work closely with them and be their advocate, and when Mr. Humphrey addressed the National League of Cities in August, he declared: "I can tell you now that your important role is assured in this program," he said. "I'm your built-in Special Agent to make sure that you are represented in this program twenty-four hours a day, 365 days a year. I've been hired for you." When the Vice-President of the United States became the twenty-four-hour-a-day advocate, there was little doubt what the outcome would be.

Early in November, the one man in the Budget Bureau who probably knew as much about what went into the poverty program as anyone, William B. Cannon, reportedly called in some top CAP officials for a private conference about the poor and their role.[36] Apparently speaking for the White House, Mr. Cannon let it be known that less emphasis should be placed on giving poor people actual positions on local CAP boards. He suggested greater emphasis on hiring the poor for anti-poverty jobs in local communities.

An informal memo detailing the Budget Bureau position, put together by an OEO aide, reached the press and was soon stirring up a sticky controversy. Mr. Shriver, who was in Arizona at the time, denied that any change of policy was contemplated. "Frankly," said Mr. Shriver, "no such change in OEO's policy has been directed or ordered by anyone in the Administration. Our policy is today and will remain exactly what it has been from the very beginning." [37]

That was Mr. Shriver's reaction then. But as the facts filtered in, when he came to grasp the realities, the message apparently got through to him. Soon thereafter, at a conference on the War on Poverty in Chicago, Mr. Shriver, in the presence of Mayor Daley, urged cooperation with the establishment, the local political power structures. He added: "Let none of us be so presumptuous as to say City Hall is wrong and the poor are always right." He then used an analogy that he repeated several times in defining the role of the poor in the program—an analogy that signaled a significant change from the zeal of earlier days.

The poor are like clients, he said, who ask architects to design a building. The client tells the architect the kind of house he wants, but he does not design it. The architect designs it, and the client participates in the design. This partial abandonment of the poor brought its reaction from the Republicans in the form of the Quie amendment, writing into the law the requirement that one-third of the members of the local boards should be representatives of the poor. Thus, the mayors were further harassed and the White House piqued.

The mayors had still more to worry about than poor people on their local anti-poverty boards. Throughout most of 1965, OEO funded many local community-action programs, to which local public agencies (usually city governments) contributed the 10 per cent local cost, mostly in facilities, classrooms, and teachers, rather than in actual cash. These were referred to as "umbrella-type" community-action programs because they covered the whole community with one board and one director to oversee a variety of programs. Since the city hall contributed 10 per cent of the costs, the mayor usually had some voice, whether formal or not, in the direction of the program, in staffing it, and in influencing its hiring practices.

At the same time, there were also a few so-called "non-umbrella-type" programs set up for special projects, funded directly by OEO, with the 10 per cent local matching costs made up privately, by foundations and universities, or (in the case of demonstration projects) with no matching at all. These non-umbrella efforts were very troublesome for the mayors in cities where they were funded—especially where there was also an umbrella agency in the city.

One such notable program was sponsored by Syracuse University—a project designed to study ways to involve the poor in anti-poverty efforts. One way chosen by the Syracuse Community Development Association (the non-umbrella group) was to sponsor demonstration marches against the city government and to use poverty funds to provide bail for those arrested in the demonstration. Syracuse Mayor William F. Walsh was enraged. When he protested to OEO, anti-poverty officials said the funds could legally be spent that way.

Mr. Walsh was not alone in his concern. This incident was behind the 1965 resolution of the mayors calling on OEO to recognize the "umbrella-type" CAP agencies as the proper ones for funding local projects. Certainly, the issue was discussed when Mayor Daley, representing the Mayors' Conference, met later with Mr. Humphrey and CAP Director Theodore Berry. Mr. Shriver was soon to insist that these private groups apply for funds through the local umbrella agencies—in order to avoid "a gigantic increase in the amount of paperwork and applications"—and in December, he specifically told the independent Syracuse group to apply for funds through the local umbrella agency. He gave similar instructions to a Cleveland group that had been engaged in city-hall protests. At one point, members of that group had piled rats and trash on city-hall steps to dramatize the conditions under which slum dwellers were forced to live. Thus, Mr. Shriver retreated in the face of pressure from the mayors and the White House.

Senator Javits made a futile attempt to amend the anti-poverty legislation to require OEO to fund the "non-umbrella" type groups. Cynics point out that only Republicans stood to gain from such a move since the independent groups were largely protesting against Democratic mayors. Still, the most famous of the controversies—the one in Syracuse—was revolving around a Republican mayor.

The real question that came out of this struggle was stated best by a Students for a Democratic Society grass-roots organizer in Newark, Thomas Hayden, in a statement before the Powell committee. The basic issue, he said, was "how money can be allocated by government to organize groups which may cause a political disturbance for the same government that gave the funds. Will men with established power take this risk?" [38]

By the end of 1965, the answer to that question was clearly in the negative—from the White House, through the Budget Bureau, on down to every city hall in the country. But the mayors were not satisfied yet. The Green Amendment of 1967 was their ultimate triumph. When Mr. Perkins saw the letters of concern coming in from mayors during the summer—some reportedly unprintable—a strategic concession had to be found. Mr. Perkins, with Representatives Gibbons and O'Hara, began to draft the terms of what later became the Green Amendment. OEO's top legislative officer, George McCarthy, was also in on the drafting sessions. The White House gave its go-ahead. It took some talking to convince Mr. Shriver of the necessity for such an amendment; meeting with newsmen later, he endeavored to minimize its importance.

The Senate conferees had been able to strengthen the bypass provisions of the bill. But the effect was unmistakable. The mayors would have control wherever they wanted it.

Some OEO officials saw a dark White House conspiracy to force OEO to accept the terms of the Green Amendment. In fact, the White House was paying very little attention to OEO. It simply went along with what congressmen and OEO's McCarthy felt was the only strategy acceptable for getting the bill passed. Presidential assistant Barefoot Sanders had, during the legislative year, only two meetings with supporters of the legislation. Those meetings were held at Mr. McCarthy's urging to convince congressmen and private groups such as Leagues of Women Voters and the Citizens' Crusade Against Poverty that the White House was really interested in the poverty program.

The strategy did, in fact, work, and congressmen and OEO officials congratulated themselves. But since the victory margin was so great, there was a residue of doubt among many OEO officials that such a concession had been necessary. Many regarded it as a final sellout to the mayors. Representative Quie's fear that this would diminish even further the role of the poor was echoed by many—even those at OEO. So when OEO officials came to drawing up guidelines for the administration of the Green Amendment, they made considerable efforts to water down its potentially harsh effects—advised, incidentally, by Senate staff members who had helped their principals oppose the provision in the Senate-House Conference. But immediately protests poured in from mayors. And Mrs. Green herself demanded an accounting.

The hassle over the control of the program continued as 1968 moved on. But Mr. Johnson was far from the fracas—his mind preoccupied with Vietnam and his advisers working out new employment schemes under MDTA.

THE SEARCH FOR NEW DEPARTURES

Probably the most remarkable fact about the poverty program is that it survived four years of sniping, buffeting, and high-level indifference. Doubtless, its problems would have been minimized had its functions not impinged so heavily on the fiefdoms of local politicians. More diplomacy and less haste might have helped. And, possibly, it would have been better to have given Congress an early vested interest in the design of the effort. But these refinements were not the special preoccupation of those early planners who saw the blight of poverty eating up the hopes of youngsters and wasting the lives of families, generation after generation.

Few would have dared predict on that mid-day in January 1964 when a new President declared "unconditional war on poverty in America," saying that the objective was "total victory," that in the months ahead the presidential resolve would diminish and withdraw, not all at once, but in numerous, painful, almost measureless ways. But to those who were watching closely, the future soon became ominously clear. There were some who could early see what was happening. William Haddad was one; he left OEO early. The same was true for Jack Conway and Richard Boone.

What became clearer to these men, as problems beset the new endeavor, was that the Federal Government could not get away with providing taxpayers' money to vigorously promote the kind of basic changes needed in local political structures that for years had taken poverty for granted. Richard Boone became director of the Citizens' Crusade Against Poverty (CCAP), set up to serve as the "conscience" of the poverty program and as a clearing house for complaints against it. This he did with funds from private sources—not taxpayers' money. CCAP has been free to protest for changes, to defend Head-start in Mississippi, to focus attention on hunger and starvation in this country. Many had hoped OEO would remain a lobby for the poor. But what is needed to support a lobby—money and power— poor people do not have, obviously. CCAP is an attempt to take this role. But the needs are enormous. And the vigorous little group, operating out of a basement just off Washington's Dupont Circle, is hardly adequate.

Parts of the poverty program will probably be around for a long time. A federal bureaucracy is very difficult to kill. But it can be ignored. And being ignored by the White House is deadly in Washington. Some of OEO's programs will doubtless be spun off. During 1967, the President ordered a moratorium on Cabinet sniping for these plums. But it will, no doubt, resume. OEO may eventually be reduced to an idea-production function—retaining few program responsibilities, if any at all. In any event, OEO's importance in the post-Shriver period is certain to be diminished. In the meantime, poverty remains—hidden somewhat by a war-time economy but just as bitter and grinding as ever.

The OEO idea did not succeed. It was, at best, only an interim effort. So the search for other, better ways to end poverty is underway. Model Cities is the newest approach to community organization —proceeding cautiously and safely, under full control of the mayors. And the President, early in 1968, finally appointed a promised Commission on Income Maintenance to look into the possibilities of a guaranteed-income plan, a negative income tax, or some variation of such an approach.

Compared to the OEO efforts, plans for income maintenance have two advantages—the results are immediate and mayors have little to fear from them. But the estimated cost—perhaps $25 or $30 billion a year—is beyond anything any President has ever been willing to commit for domestic welfare. Certainly not while equivalent amounts are being spent to fight communism in Asian jungles.

Notes

1. Sargent Shriver, at a press briefing in his office following House passage of the 1967 Economic Opportunity Amendments.
2. John C. Donovan, *The Politics of Poverty* (New York: Western Publishing Co., 1967) , p. 38.

3. *Public Papers of the Presidents of the United States, 1963–1964*, Vol. I, p. 114.

4. Interview with Rep. Albert Quie, November 1967.

5. President Johnson, *Public Papers, 1963–1964*, Vol. I, p. 379.

6. U.S. House of Representatives, *Hearings Before the Subcommittee on the War on Poverty Program of the Committee on Education and Labor: The Economic Opportunity Act of 1964*, 88th Congress, 2nd Session, 1964, p. 18.

7. U.S. Senate. *Hearings Before the Select Committee on Poverty of the Senate Labor and Public Welfare Committee: The Economic Opportunity Act of 1964*, 88th Congress, 2nd Session, 1964, pp. 176–177.

8. House Hearings, *op. cit.*, p. 64.

9. Senate Hearings, *op. cit.*, p. 185.

10. Interview with Rep. Sam Gibbons, November 1967.

11. Senate Hearings, *op. cit.*, p. 54.

12. *Ibid.*, pp. 183, 202.

13. *Ibid.*, p. 183.

14. U.S. House of Representatives. *Hearings Before the House Rules Committee* (June 16–18, 1964), 88th Congress, 2nd Session, 1964.

15. Senate Hearings, *op. cit.*, p. 176.

16. Senate Hearings, *loc. cit.*

17. Johnson, *Public Papers, 1963–1964*, Vol. II, p. 989.

18. U.S. House of Representatives. *Hearings Before the Subcommittee on the War on Poverty Program of the Committee on Education and Labor: Examination of the War on Poverty Program*, 89th Congress, 1st Session, 1965, p. 2.

19. *Ibid*, pp. 19–20.

20. U.S. House of Representatives. Committee on Education and Labor, *Economic Opportunity Amendments of 1965:* Report, 89th Congress, 1st Session, 1965.

21. U.S. Senate. *Debate on the Economic Opportunity Amendments of 1965, Congressional Record* (August 19, 1965).

22. Statement by Rep. Peter B. Frelinghuysen, June 17, 1965.

23. Mayors Samuel W. Yorty and John F. Shelley, Draft resolution for presentation at the Annual Meeting of the U.S. Conference of Mayors, May 29 to June 2, 1965.

24. U.S. House of Representatives. *Debate on the Economic Opportunity Amendments of 1966, Congressional Record* (September 26, 1966).

25. Interview with Rep. Sam Gibbons, November 1967.

26. U.S. House of Representatives. *Debate on the Economic Opportunity Amendments of 1966, Congressional Record* (September 26, 1966).

27. "Republican Poverty Memo," Republican Members Poverty Subcommittee, March 15, 1966, No. 1.

28. "Republican Poverty Memo," Republican Members Poverty Subcommittee, March 25, 1966, No. 9.

29. *Ibid.*

30. "Republican Poverty Memo," Republican Members Poverty Subcommittee, April 29, 1966, No. 21.

31. U.S. Senate. *Report of the Committee on Labor and Public Welfare: Economic Opportunity Amendments of 1967*, 90th Congress, 1st Session, Senate Report No. 563 (September 12, 1967), p. 2.

32. *Ibid.*

33. U.S. House of Representatives. *Hearings Before the Committee on Education and Labor: Economic Opportunity Amendments of 1967*, 90th Congress, 1st Session (June 12 and 16, 1967), Part 1, p. 76.

34. *Congressional Record*, November 7, 1967, p. H14738.

35. *Ibid.*, p. H14739.

36. Eve Edstrom, *Washington Post*, November 10, 1965.

37. Quoted in *The New York Times*, November 6, 1965.

38. House Hearings, 1965, *op. cit.*, p. 637.

Chapter 9

⊂⊇ *Evaluating the War on Poverty*

ROBERT A. LEVINE

Policy evaluation is the art—not the science, not for social programs anyhow—of measuring the results of a program and weighing them against a set of criteria. At least, defining evaluation in this way is both convenient and close to the common understanding of the word. This sort of evaluation should play a crucial role in the making of policy decisions. In fact, at least until the recent institution of the Programming, Planning and Budgeting System (PPBS) throughout the government, it has played such a role only on a casual basis, but there is hope that PPBS may change this. At least we think that such evaluation is being done in the War on Poverty and is affecting policy decision.

Because the War on Poverty is new, it can provide a relatively clear example of the role of evaluation in policy. In the beginning, there was the plan, a set of proposals based on conceptual and quantitative analysis of what poverty is and what programs are needed to eliminate it. Second came the program, the translation of the plan into dollars and cents, into administrative arrangements, and into chronological phases. Then was the budget, the allocation forced on the program by limits to the funds available. For the first two years of the War on Poverty, the cycle went through plan, program, and budget. But now, three years after the official beginning of this war, programs have been in effect long enough to produce results, and

NOTE: The numbers in this chapter are accurate as of mid-1967. No attempts have been made to update them.

perhaps for the first time it is reasonable for the authorities at every executive and legislative level to demand the evaluation of these results and their building back into the next year's plan. This is where we are now. Evaluation must complete the cycle between budget and next plan.

Criteria for evaluation and methods of measurement are needed at three levels. First, we must define success for the War on Poverty as such and, having defined it, be prepared to measure the effects of the entire $27.7 billion a year worth of anti-poverty programs [1] against these criteria. Second, we must have criteria and measurements for the evaluation of individual programs that comprise the War on Poverty—particularly but not exclusively the newest ones run by the Office of Economic Opportunity (OEO); hard evaluation of OEO programs is a prime political necessity, even more than for programs run by other agencies. Third, we need criteria for comparing the effects of the individual programs against one another in order to aid in decisions concerning the allocation of funds and efforts.

These three—War on Poverty evaluation, individual program evaluation, and relative program evaluation—provide a reasonable sequence for evaluating the evaluations themselves.

THE WAR ON POVERTY AS A WHOLE

Let it be said at the outset that we define poverty in terms of command over economic resources and that this definition is not universally acceptable. There are those who would define it in terms of some bundle of individual, social, and cultural attributes including, but not limited to, command over resources. Matters of definition come close to being matters of taste; we think that command over economic resources describes what is meant by poverty both conventionally and legislatively, but we cannot swear that this definition is abstractly correct. Let it be said in partial pacification of those who would define poverty in less economic terms that the economic definition goes back through the intricacies of poverty to end up with no less emphasis on noneconomic programs than would a noneconomic definition itself.

Command over resources is determined by both the current flow of income and the stock of assets held by an individual or family. Since we do not yet have usable data on the assets of the poor (although such data should soon be available from the Survey of Economic Opportunity sponsored by OEO and taken by Census in 1966) , the working definition can concern only income.

The "poverty line" used by the Federal Government is one designed by Mollie Orshansky of the Social Security Administration that, on the basis of estimates of food budgets and their relationships to total family budgets, defines a family of 4 as poor if it has less than roughly $3,200 income at current prices, with an adjustment of about $500 up or down per person for larger or smaller families. Although this definition has a rationale, it is essentially arbitrary, as would be any single poverty line for a particular group of families. Obviously, something is lacking when we define a family with $3,199 as poor and a family with $3,201 as not poor. This arbitrariness bears on the different uses that can be made of this poverty line as a criterion for evaluating the success of the War on Poverty. The simplest use that can be made of the line and the way it is being used now is to count the number of Americans below the line. Year to year decreases in this number, to the extent that they can be traced back to the War on Poverty, are indicators of program success. This method has validity, so long as decreasing the number of poor is taken not as *the* objective of the anti-poverty program but as a reasonable and simple indicator of the more complicated real objectives.

One immediate way to add complexity and realism is to measure not the number of poor but the "income gap"—that is, the number of dollars of additional income that would be necessary to bring all poor families up to the poverty line. This has the advantage over the first method of giving weight not only to the number of people below the poverty line but the distance they have to go to reach that line.

This second measure, however, still has a disadvantage that only movements *below* the poverty line are counted. Surely we should take some credit for the movement, say, of a $3,201 family to $4,000 even though neither level is poor for a four-person family. A method that accounts for this, and probably brings the command-over-resources criterion to its ultimate sophistication, has been suggested by Harold Watts.[2] Professor Watts, director of the Institute for Research on Poverty at the University of Wisconsin, suggests a method by which income movements are counted whether they are above or below the poverty line, but they are weighted more heavily the further below the line they start and less heavily the further above the line they go.

Given the data currently available, we have so far made use only of the first method, counting the number of the poor. This count shows that in 1964, the year the War on Poverty was officially declared, there were 34.1 million poor people in the United States, according to data gathered by the Current Population Survey. In 1966, which is the last year for which data are available (since these data are based on a full-year income), there were 29.7 million poor; a drop of almost 4½ million in the first two years of the War on Poverty.

Depending on how broadly we define the War on Poverty, all or part of the 4½ million drop in the number of poor can be taken as an evaluative measurement of success. For us to count the entire drop, however, we would have to count economic growth and decreasing unemployment in their entirety as parts of the war and this may be stretching it a bit.

In attempting to isolate the effects of the newer programs more commonly thought of as comprising the War on Poverty (primarily the programs of OEO, the Department of Labor, and Health, Education and Welfare [HEW]), we tried to project the number of poor from data enumerated during the pre-1965 years when most of the new programs were not in effect and to compare these projections to the actual changes in the number of poor since the new programs came into being. For two reasons, these comparisons are inconclusive. The first reason is that such projection models are necessarily inexact and variations of a million or so poor people in one direction or another are well within the noise level. The second reason is that a necessary independent variable in any such model projecting poverty from a pre-1965 data base is the unemployment rate, but the unemployment rate itself is a variable highly dependent on poverty programs. That is, since a very large portion of War on Poverty funds are devoted to job training and even larger portions to other programs, such as education, that are supportive of job programs, we would hope that the success of these would directly affect the rate of unemployment. In fact, in a statistical sense, we know that there has been some such effect because participants in programs such as the Neighborhood Youth Corps (NYC) are counted as employed.

In any case, for projections from pre-1965 data to provide a valid basis for comparisons with actual post-1965 data it would have to be assumed that the unemployment rate, which was unaffected by poverty programs before 1965, is still unaffected by poverty programs.

This assumption is demonstrably untrue, but until we can build the equations that measure changes in unemployment rates due to War on Poverty programs, this method of deriving effectiveness by such comparison breaks down because of its own circularity.

Thus we know that the number of poor has been reduced by 4½ million since the War on Poverty was begun, we know that the major portion of that drop has been due to economic growth, we know some of the improvement has been due to the War on Poverty, but we do not know how much improvement is in each category.

Or at least we know only one other fact. All of the drop in poverty cannot be attributed to our efforts, but as Sargent Shriver has said, had there been an increase in poverty, it would have all been blamed on us.

EVALUATION OF INDIVIDUAL WAR ON POVERTY PROGRAMS

To complicate matters even further, when we move to the next level, the evaluation of individual components of the War on Poverty, each of these programs must be evaluated by two different sets of criteria. They must be evaluated for their proximate effects, for example, the effectiveness of a health program in improving the health of the poor—and they must be evaluated for their anti-poverty effectiveness. The latter measure must ultimately be carried out in terms of criteria like those discussed above for the overall effectiveness of the War on Poverty, but the current essential is merely to connect proximate effectiveness with poverty. What has health improvement got to do with getting the poor out of poverty, for example?

For purposes of analysis, we divide the programs of the War on Poverty into four categories: manpower programs, the purpose of which is to provide jobs or job training for the poor; individual-improvement programs, including education and health, designed to change at an early and more fundamental level the factors that prevent people from taking advantage of job and other opportunities; community-betterment programs to change the stultifying environment that holds the poor down; and income-maintenance programs that recognize that, for many of the poor, opportunity is meaningless and the need is simply more money (and also recognize that for many, money itself increases the range of opportunity) . Rather than being alternatives, these programs support one another. Better education, for example, will increase the capability of the poor to profit from training and to hold jobs, but a decent job program is necessary to make education meaningful and to motivate people to learn.

In each of these four categories, the relationship of evaluation for proximate effects to evaluation for ultimate War on Poverty effectiveness varies. For manpower programs, proximate and ultimate evaluations are quite similar. The number-of-people-in-poverty criterion for evaluating War on Poverty effectiveness is not easy to use for manpower programs, but as it turns out, the more sophisticated War on Poverty criteria—the dollar-poverty gap and the Watts weighted-income-gain criterion—are conceptually quite close to the criteria ordinarily used in evaluation of training and employment programs. The benefits of manpower programs are ordinarily measured by the earnings gain attributable to the programs, and measures of such gains can obviously be tied directly into dollar measures of effectiveness of these programs as anti-poverty tools.

For individual improvement, however, the proximate and ultimate criteria begin to diverge. In the case of education, it is possible to tie gains directly to income and thus derive an evaluation measure closely aligned with the ultimate War on Poverty measure, as in the case of manpower programs. (In fact, as will be discussed below, the evaluation of Job Corps as a manpower program was based on educational gains within the program.) But for early-year and in-school education programs, the ties to later earning capabilities are difficult to derive, and the art of evaluating the proximate effects of such early-year programs (for example, the effect of an in-school program on raising subject-matter achievement levels) is still at such a primitive level that much work is needed to develop these proximate measures before we attempt to tie them directly to the War on Poverty.

The conceptual status of evaluation for community-betterment programs is even worse. For many of the specific programs that fall into this category, such as housing, evaluating the proximate effects may be relatively straightforward. Does a housing program build decent housing? But for most of these component programs falling under community betterment, the ties to anti-poverty effectiveness are unclear. That better housing will help people get out of poverty has never really been established.

And to complicate matters, the community-betterment category is not merely the sum of its component programs but is explicitly designed to bring about a poorly defined something called "social change," which we do not know how to measure at all.

Finally, for income-maintenance programs, the tie between proximate and ultimate measures is simple because they are virtually the same. Income-maintenance programs are primarily designed to increase income and thus to decrease the income gap that was suggested as a second measure of War on Poverty effectiveness; they can easily be weighted according to who receives the gains in order to derive a Watts criterion.[3] But some of the subordinate measures for evaluating income maintenance are more complicated. For example, it does not suffice to evaluate these programs for their direct income-gap-reducing effects; it is also necessary to observe their effects, favorable or unfavorable, on such matters as work incentives of the program recipients and family stability in recipient families.

In each of these categories, the effort is made to measure program results quantitatively, if possible, and to evaluate the programs by comparing these results to quantitative criteria. One such quantitative criterion is the cost of the program, and such a comparison can be expressed as a benefit-cost ratio. The ordinary formulation of such a ratio means two things. First, a ratio of benefits to cost, which is greater than unity (that is, greater than 1 to 1), means that the dollar benefits exceed the dollar costs; conversely, a ratio less than 1 means the dollar costs are greater. Second, as such ratios are computed for anti-poverty programs, a ratio greater than one means that a greater long-run anti-poverty effectiveness per dollar can be obtained from the program being measured than from the alternative of a simple stream of federal income-transfer payments paid to the poor recipient; and conversely.

Several points should be made quite clear about benefit-cost ratios as they are used for anti-poverty program evaluation:

1. A ratio less than one does not mean that a program is unsuccessful. There are usually many intangibles that cannot be computed into benefits; costs are all too tangible. Further, even though a ratio less than one might indicate that income-transfer payments are cheaper, a program that leads to increased earnings is ordinarily considered socially preferable to one of transfer payments,[4] and allowance must be made for this.

2. The state of the art and the state of the data for benefit-cost comparison are both primitive enough that it is almost always unwise

to compare even similar programs on the basis of computed ratios unless the ratios were specifically computed in a single study for purposes of such a comparison.

3. A program is not counted as preferable simply because a benefit-cost ratio (or other quantitative evaluation) is computable, whereas it is not for another program. For most anti-poverty programs, quantitative analysis is not yet possible; for some it never will be—and these include some of the most important programs. Effectiveness and quantifiability should never be confused, and it is an error to substitute the concrete for the important. Benefit-cost analysis, when possible, plays a role in the evaluation of programs, but it is only a part of evaluation. Conversely, however, when benefit-cost analysis is possible, it can play an important role in the defense of programs because if a program can be justified by counting *part*—the measurable part—of its benefits and *all* of its costs, an a fortiori case can be built by reference to the benefits not counted.

Given all these caveats, the current results of individual program evaluation in OEO can be summarized by saying that most of the evaluations are ambiguous, due primarily to the lack of unambiguous quantitative or qualitative data; that the few programs for which good data were available come out looking very good; and that two programs can be evaluated unfavorably, indicating the need for substantial program changes and perhaps phase-out.

MANPOWER

Manpower programs are relatively easy to evaluate because the proximate and ultimate criteria are similar. To evaluate a training program, our primary data needs are for characteristics of the trainee before entering the program and after passing through it. Such characteristics include both items of the demographic type such as age, race, and education as control variables; and also job-holding experience and earnings as variables of direct interest.

It is not proper, of course, to evaluate the effectiveness of a training program by comparing earnings after to earnings before because change may be an effect of lapsed time or of other factors outside the program, as well as a direct effect of the program. Just as obviously, even though such before-after comparison is not really legitimate, we do it because we frequently have nothing else to fall back on. But the really important and legitimate form of evaluation compares the before-and-after experience of trainees to the similarly time-phased experience of nontrainees in a carefully selected control group. This makes things a lot less simple, particularly when we talk about youth training. Youth control groups are particularly difficult to come by, both because so many young people between the ages of sixteen and twenty-one have passed through OEO programs and because the self-selection process for youth training programs means that the possible members of a control group may differ from the trainees in certain specific (but undefined) characteristics that led them to avoid the training program. Because of these difficulties, we are proceeding rather carefully in setting up the youth control group that is vital to our program evaluation. We are, however, already collecting substantial data on the pretraining characteristics and some data on post-training characteristics of our program participants and are in the process of setting up a youth control sample.

A pilot study is now underway to determine the feasibility of setting up a large national sample of poor youth, sixteen to twenty-one, that could be tested and then re-interviewed and retested two or three years later. The objective is to create a sample that is large enough to allow the establishment of groups of youth that are statistically similar in terms of relevant socioeconomic variables, some of whom have participated in training programs, Job Corps, NYC, and Manpower Development and Training Act (MDTA), and some of whom have not. Hopefully, such a sample would allow both cross-sectional and longitudinal comparisons that would provide some of the sort of evaluative information, admittedly crude, that is necessary for realistic judgments about reasonable program mix. Elements of this sample would serve as a control group, so that program effects could be separated to some degree from effects due simply to growth of the youths and to changes in general economic and social conditions. In addition, it may be possible to determine which types of programs are best suited for which types of poor youth and, within programs, which program characteristics seem to be related with favorable results. We are fully aware of the limitations of such an approach to the problems of evaluation—and this is one of the reasons for proceeding first on a pilot basis—but it seems to us that the logic of the program-evaluation efforts leads inevitably to this type of an approach. If the limitations of this type of evaluative method prove too severe, I suppose we must re-examine the logic of program evaluation as it now stands.

Given all this, we have been able to carry on some real evaluation in the manpower area. Professor Glen Cain of the University of Wisconsin has designed and carried out a benefit-cost evaluation of the Job Corps, the residential Youth Training Program, that not only throws a good deal of light on the effectiveness of this program but also makes a substantial advance in the state of the art of manpower evaluation.[5] Cain's study shows that the benefit stream attributable to the Job Corps, discounted back to a current capital value, can be estimated to be in the interval between 1.02 and 1.70 times the current cost. This estimate is quite conservative. It bases the benefit calculation entirely on measured educational gains for Job Corps enrollees, as based on periodic testing within Job Corps camps. In this particular case, it was possible to get around the control-group problem by using the reasonable assumption that for out-of-school youth at this age, educational gains in fields such as reading and math would be nonexistent (or negligible, lacking a formal program). The earnings gains stemming from the Job Corps educational gains are then estimated by using the known benefits of education to others in similar age and demographic cohorts.

The reason the study is conservative, then, is that it can be assumed that there are many other benefits for which credit has not been taken obtained by youngsters from Job Corps. Some of these gains are measurable but have not yet been measured—gains from vocational training and possible reductions in crime and welfare rates, for example. Others may never be measurable, but are still tangible and important, such as the benefits to earnings capabilities gained from what Job Corps calls the "socialization process"—the ability to get along with other people in a work situation. Still other gains not credited in the Cain study are less tangible but perhaps the most important of all. An example here would be effectiveness of Women's Job Corps in maintaining the stability of the future families of girls currently passing through the program, which, since a broken family is much more likely to be poor than an intact one, has a direct anti-poverty effect. A guess is that adding those benefits that have not been measured to the conservative estimates of the benefit-cost ratio, which ranged from 1.02 to 1.70, would lead to a benefit-cost ratio of at least 2.0—a current value for the stream of benefits worth twice the current cost of the program.

We have no other evaluations in the manpower field comparable to that done for Job Corps. Job Corps is a separately definable program whose effects can be readily measured; in fact that it is a relatively long-term high-cost program means that there is more leeway for testing and more money for data-gathering than for some other programs. Another seemingly similar program, the Out-of-School NYC, a nonresidential training program for school dropouts, has not been able to provide data for a similar sort of evaluation. In any case, NYC is a different enough program so that evaluation would have to be done on other bases than Job Corps, and the results would not be readily comparable between the two programs. Job Corps was evaluated initially on the basis of educational gains, but Out-of-School NYC has no educational component. It is at a minimum an aging vat for kids at a difficult age who have dropped out of school; it is at most a source of valuable counseling and work experience. And adding to the distinction between NYC and Job Corps is that both are voluntary programs, and the self-selection process may lead quite different sorts of youngsters into each of the two programs. This last is likely to be true even though the gross demographic characteristics of the Job Corps and NYC populations are quite similar.

The difficulties of comparing NYC to Job Corps provide an illustration of a general caveat about evaluation, mentioned above. It is so difficult to do evaluations of similar programs on precisely the same bases that very few evaluations have been accomplished yet that can be used for comparing programs to one another. The benefit-cost ratios cited above for Job Corps are favorable ones, for example, but they are lower than benefit-cost ratios produced by the Planning Research Corporation for the Labor Department in a study of MDTA institutional and on-the-job training programs.[6] In fact, the MDTA study was done in a different way, and the benefit-cost ratios produced bear no relationship to Job Corps benefit-cost ratios. The use of ratios like these to compare different programs on the basis of different studies just because two different statistics are both called "benefit-cost ratios" is a dubious process.

Until recently, virtually all the OEO manpower programs were aimed at youth below the age of twenty-one. The one exception was the Work Experience Program (Title V of the Economic Opportunity

Act), for training of adults on relief plus certain others, primarily adult males, in categories that might become eligible for relief. Although no benefit-cost studies have been done on this program, data have been gathered indicating a relatively low "success" rate and showing other flaws in the program. We have analyzed these evaluative results and have come to the conclusion that it seems likely that training programs, whether for adults or youths, can be more effectively run by manpower experts than by public-assistance authorities; and that welfare recipients can be more effectively trained if they are not separated out as welfare recipients.

Much more OEO money is now going into adult-training programs, primarily through monies delegated to the Department of Labor for the Concentrated Employment Program designed for the worst poverty areas of large cities and some rural communities and for the Job Opportunities in Business Program for private training of the hard-core poor. As we plan to evaluate these programs, it is becoming clear that evaluation of adult-training programs is going to be even more difficult than that of youth programs. For poor adults in general, educational gains seem unlikely, and since we are dealing with a group that for the most part has substantial, if spotty, previous work experience, a comparison between what they do after the programs and what they were doing immediately before will be imperfect. Adding to this the fact that the success rate of adults in programs is likely to be due to a very wide variety of factors—individual, family, and social—and we have an evaluation situation that can be quite complex. At this stage of the game, what we can say is that we are setting up data systems to bring in the relevant numbers of the program, and with the assistance of the RAND Corporation, we are attempting to create systems of evaluation for these programs.

INDIVIDUAL IMPROVEMENT

The programs we count in the individual-improvement category are primarily athough not exclusively educational ones. The evaluation of education programs is less straightforward than manpower. Remarkably little has been done along the lines of systematic comparative evaluation of different educational techniques for reaching the underprivileged. The Office of Education, which disposes of a billion dollars or more a year for the education of the poor under Title I of the Elementary and Secondary Act of 1965, is beginning a comprehensive evaluation program, although this will not be simple because the Office of Education statutorily provides monies without being able to control them, and local school authorities don't like to be evaluated. Up until this effort, virtually nothing has been done on a systematic basis.

Table 9–1 brings together an inventory of federal programs that are intended to contribute to the compensatory-education effort or that are or can be used to contribute to the compensatory-education effort. In addition to identifying federal programs and administering agencies, Table 9–1 estimates the number of beneficiaries and the amount of funding through 1967.

The two right hand columns briefly summarize the kind of evaluation information available about each program. It is important to note that while there are several inventories of federal educational programs for the poor, this table represents the first attempt to summarize what is known about the impact of such programs on the amount of rate of learning, whether this be measured in cognitive, behavioral, or attitudinal terms.

Obviously, the findings reflected by this table do not pretend to be definitive. It is important, however, that it represents the first time evaluative findings to date have been set down cheek by jowl with measures of the numbers to be served and dollars to be spent in the federal effort. This table drives home the need for a major effort to evaluate the essentially experimental programs being funded. Immediate steps should be taken to provide that every program and every experiment include an evaluation design from the start. Only then can we increase our capacity to know what works, or what works best, in compensatory education. As we now stand, the state of evaluation of educational programs is such that we cannot even be sure that when favorable program results are obtained, they are the result of good program design or merely a Hawthorne effect.

The evaluation of various programs for federal aid to education is primarily the responsibility of the Office of Education in HEW. They are moving forward on this through the very difficult barriers of state and local rights and school board defensiveness that thus far have been insuperable obstacles in the way of effective federal *programming* in education, never mind evaluation.

OEO educational evaluation is at least institutionally easier because OEO educational programs are run on a national basis. The

TABLE 9-1. *Summary of Federally Funded Compensatory Educational Services and Financial Assistance to the Poor*

KIND OF PROGRAM	FEDERAL AGENCY AND AUTHORITY	BENEFICIARIES (THOUSANDS)			FUNDING (MILLIONS)			IMPACT ON LEARNING OF DISADVANTAGED	
		65	66	67	65	66	67	EXPERIMENTAL (CONTROLS)	OPERATIONAL (NORMS OR JUDGMENTS)
Preschool (3-5) Headstart	OEO-CAP	561,000	500,000	500,000	$85	$180	$310	Deutsch—modest gains of pre-school year were retained and expanded in K and 1st grade.	1% survey showed gains, 5 points on nonverbal tests of intelligence. No retention data available yet.
		20,000	100,000	210,000					
Other preschool programs	OE, Title I, ESEA Preschool only Preschool and kindergarten		60.0	See below	—	See below	See below		
In-school children (5-15) Compensatory, remedial tutorial programs in schools and complementary to schools	OEO, CAP Education Components (including Upward Bound)		348.0	339.0		—	77.0	Control groups suffered cumulative slippage in K and 1st grade.	Scattered evaluations, largely subjective. Tutorials and Upward Bound projects show most observers think these experiences beneficial.
OE ESEA	OE-ESEA Title I	—	6,600.0	7,000.0		775.0	1,070.0	Systematic evaluation in planning stage. No information as yet.	Preliminary analyses of 500 project samples showing types of projects only. No big cities included.
In-school youth (16-21) Counseling and guidance	OE-NDEA, counseling and guidance	(2,800.0)	(3,400.0)	(3,600.0)	(156.2)	(209.4)	(209.7)	N/A	Descriptive and judgmental evaluations and periodic administrative assessments.
Vocational education NYC in-school work programs	OE-Voc. Ed. Act of '63 OEO-Labor EOA	102.2	115.0	125.0	28.4	75.0	81.2	N/A	Increased attendance and retention in school, but slight negative impact on academic achievement.

TABLE 9-1 (continued).

KIND OF PROGRAM	FEDERAL AGENCY AND AUTHORITY	BENEFICIARIES (THOUSANDS) 65	66	67	FUNDING (MILLIONS) 65	66	67	IMPACT ON LEARNING OF DISADVANTAGED — EXPERIMENTAL (CONTROLS)	OPERATIONAL (NORMS OR JUDGMENTS)
Work Study—vocational education	OE-HEA	114.4	115.0	125.0				N/A	—
		15.0	85.0	—					
Opportunity grants (HE)	OE-HEA		115.0	220.0		60.8	122.0	N/A	No information.
Higher education loans	OE-NDEA		(400.0)	(375.0)		(179.3)	(190.0)	N/A	No systematic evaluation by income level of recipients.
Guaranteed student loans	OE-HEA		(193.0)	(775.0)		(9.5)	(45.0)	N/A	No systematic evaluation showing impact on entry, retention, or achievement of low-income students.
Work study, higher education	OE-HEA		110.0	150.0		99.0	134.1		
			60.0	90.0					
			150.0	210.0					
Out-of-school youth (16–21)									
Job corps Men	OEO-EOA	15.6	325.8	39.0	183.0	310.0	228.0	N/A	Information on basic educational attainment of enrollees not available yet.
Women		1.3	4.2	6.0					
NYC out-of-school program	OEO Labor (little basic education)	(61.7)	(60.0)	(64.0)	(44.8)	(97.0)	(138.6)		
*MDTA institutional	OE-Labor	10.4	10.4	—					See below MDTA.
OJT	MDTA-Labor	(125)	(125)	( )					
Adult education—(basic education only)		(—)	( )	( )					
CAP Adult and Adult Basic Projects	CAP-Sections 206, 207 largely basic literacy or remedial subjects, taught alone as prerequisite to vocational education	23.9	87.5	117.0		15.3	47.0		No information.

KIND OF PROGRAM	FEDERAL AGENCY AND AUTHORITY	(THOUSANDS)			FUNDING (MILLIONS)			EXPERIMENTAL (CONTROLS)	OPERATIONAL (NORMS OR JUDGMENTS)
		65	66	67	65	66	67		
Adult basic (literacy) education	OE-OEO Title II B	—	75.0	100.0	—	21.0	30.0		Preliminary findings by Greenleigh not yet available. No information on basic educational attainment of enrollees.
Adult Education—(basic education combined with vocational or other adult education) Work experience	OEO Welfare Administration, Title V (provides adult basic in absence of II B program).	(88.0)	(109.3)	(105.0)	(110.0)	(150.0)	(158.7) (No information on % receiving basic compensatory education)		
† MDTA institutional training	OE-Labor	14.5 (125)	14.5 (125)	—	(No information on funding of programs basic education components)			None	Four experiments showed average gain of 1.5 grade levels in basic subjects in 15–20 weeks. No systematic information on basic educational attainment of enrollees.
OJT Vocational education	Labor OE Voc. Ed. Act of 1963 et al.	(2,281.0) ‡	—	—	(18% of total funding for adult classes)			None	None

NOTE: Numbers in parentheses are total of beneficiaries or total funding, when it is not known how many enrollees actually receive literacy or other compensatory education, or are poor.

* MDTA institutional programs. About 42 per cent of enrollment is under 21 years of age. Twenty per cent of these receive compensatory basic education. All of these latter number were counted as poor.

† Adults over 22 years of age accounted for 58 per cent of enrollment in MDTA institutional training programs. Again about 20 per cent of these are receiving significant amounts of basic education. All these have been counted as poor in enrollment figures without parentheses.

‡ Does not include basic compensatory. Enrollments often for single evening course.

most rigorous evaluation done for an OEO educational program is that of Upward Bound, a program designed to take poor youth in the upper grades of high school who have been getting poor marks but show a spark of basic capability and convert them into college material by intensive summer and other training. Benefit-cost ratios have been computed using techniques similar to those of Job Corps, estimating stream of increases in future earnings stemming from increases in education due to the program. Our estimates show that the Upward Bound effect in preventing high-school dropouts among those who might otherwise have dropped out gives benefit-cost ratios of 2.5 to 1. Considering both the additional benefits and the additional public and private costs to that portion of the group who enter college and stay for at least a year, the overall ratio for these is at about 1.6 to 1 to cost. For college graduates, the overall benefit-cost ratio will be 2.8 to 1, although the program is so new that none of its enrollees have yet finished college, and completion rates must be estimated.

Beginnings are being made on good evaluation of In-School NYC, a program designed to keep youngsters in high school by providing them with the experience and pocket money that go with part-time jobs. No data sufficient for rigorous analysis are yet available, but preliminary analysis done locally in a few cities, notably Washington, D.C., indicates that enrollees in the program do have a significantly lower dropout rate than similar youth not in the program. Since the value of high-school completion to a poor youngster is high, this effect is a favorable one, though we do not yet know how favorable relative to the cost of achieving it.

The largest and best known OEO education program, of course, is Headstart. Headstart is a surprisingly difficult program to evaluate for three major reasons. The first is that test instruments fully adequate to measure the capabilities and achievements of underprivileged preschool children have not yet been designed. Since what we are trying to measure is change due to the program, this defect becomes even more important. Second, summer Headstart became so big so fast that we have not yet been able to obtain a control group for the program. It is difficult to find poor preschool youngsters in the United States who have not been in Headstart without wondering whether there are not other than random factors that distinguish them from the Headstart kids. Third, although Headstart is sometimes thought of as being a preschool education program, it is much more than that. Even if the educational gains stemming from Headstart were negligible, health gains alone, for example—the very fact of having all these kids examined by physicians, many for the first time—might justify the program or at least they would substantially expand the basis for evaluation in a way that is difficult to combine with the other bases.

Given all these obstacles, evaluation has made some discoveries about Headstart, both favorable and unfavorable. There is no doubt that summer Headstart programs, taken as a whole, do increase the cognitive abilities of their enrollees and do so significantly more than these abilities would have been increased for the same kids without the program. On the other hand, there is only marginally more doubt that over a period of the first school year following Headstart, poor kids who have not been in the program tend to catch up with those who have been. The data on both these effects are insufficient to quantify them very well, particularly because of the control-group problem, but the effects do seem to exist.

These evaluations have had two effects on Headstart programming. They have led to the thrust toward a full-year Headstart program, which it is hoped will have more lasting effects than the rather meager summer program, although the evaluative data on full-year Headstart are not yet in to prove this belief, and although the summer program still has value at least as a net for catching a much larger number of poor kids at the same cost and providing some benefits such as health and family involvement. The second effect of the Headstart evaluation has led to the Follow-Through program designed to work with Headstart "graduates" in their first school year to try to preserve the benefits of Headstart. Since this program has not been really begun, it has not been evaluated, although plans are underway for continuing evaluation as the program begins.

In addition to the difficulties of obtaining proximate evaluations for Headstart, substantial conceptual problems exist in trying to connect these proximate results to the evaluations of ultimate effects and in producing analyses of anti-poverty effectiveness. Ribich [7] notes that, on the basis of a small bit of data available to him early in the program, Headstart, taken alone, does not seem to have a very high benefit-cost ratio. Even with more and better data showing positive proximate-program results this might very likely be the case, for two reasons. First, any earnings increase attributable to Headstart is not likely to begin until ten to fifteen years after the program for a five-year-old child. Because benefit-cost ratios are computed by discounting increases in earnings more heavily the further into the future they are, Headstart begins with ten to fifteen years against it. Second, Headstart, to be truly successful, will have to be just the beginning of a changed educational system for poor kids. The evaluations above showing catch-up of non-Headstart kids to Headstart kids in first grade might be slightly surprising, but there could be no doubt that given the low quality of slum schools, urban and rural, the favorable effects of a one-year preschool program would be bound to fade out in twelve years of unchanged poverty schooling.

Both of these statements lead to the same point. If Headstart is not the beginning of a changing and changed education for poor kids, then it will not be a successful educational program, although some of the other effects might still be valuable. The Follow-Through program is one attempt to adapt policy to the results of this kind of evaluation. The Title I program is another sort of attempt. Neither one of them is any more than a mere beginning, either in concept or scope. A true improvement in the educational system for the poor is likely to be very expensive, both financially and in terms of political bruises. Yet, just as preschool education may be a *necessary* condition for decent anti-poverty education, but is demonstrably not a *sufficient* condition, it is pretty clear that a decent educational system is a necessary condition for ending poverty in the United States, even though it is not sufficient.

The other major set of programs in the individual-improvement category is health programs, in the case of OEO primarily the comprehensive neighborhood medical centers. This program originated from an evaluation of existing health programs for the poor, which led to the conclusion that what was needed was not more money so much as a better organized and less fractionated delivery of services in poor neighborhoods, essentially as a slum substitute for the family physician. No real evaluation has been done yet of the neighborhood medical centers, which are relatively new. We expect to be able to do so on the basis of before-and-after neighborhood health statistics, among other techniques, that should tell us something about the proximate effects of these programs. Analysis of ultimate effectiveness as anti-poverty programs is pretty much still down the pike.

The one completed evaluation effort on the health programs at least shows that these services are delivered to the poor at a cost less than that for which they could be purchased on the open market;

thus, the program at least can be evaluated favorably for the efficient delivery of its product.

COMMUNITY BETTERMENT

Probably the most complex category of programs is that of community betterment—programs for environmental change. Among OEO programs, these fall primarily into the community-action category, although the VISTA program falls here, too, as do major non-OEO programs such as housing.

Community-betterment programs are hard to understand and evaluate because they have a double purpose: the delivery of certain services that it is hoped will change the environment of the target areas; and the inducement of social change in these areas and in larger areas of which they are part.

Some of the specific programs under community betterment are relatively easy to evaluate for their proximate effectiveness. For family-planning programs, for example, it was possible to compute benefit-cost ratios ranging from 3.3 up to 18.8 depending on assumptions as to how many of the women reached make use of the program. The benefit computation is based simply on the idea that for every additional family member the poverty line increases by $500 a year, and thus the benefits of not having an unwanted child can be computed roughly at $500 a year.

Another evaluation within this community-betterment category, by Kirschner Associates [8] of Albuquerque, New Mexico, came to the conclusion that the Small Business Development Center program of OEO was unable to reach the poor. In its initial purposes, first making business loans to poor people with entrepreneurial capability, and second, getting the poor into employment in small businesses, the program had not worked well. The first objective had not worked out because people below the poverty line simply did not have entrepreneurial capabilities in sufficient quantity to work with the program; the second because imposing on an already burdened small businessman an additional problem of having to employ poor people rather than choosing his employees did not add to the likelihood of business success. As a result of these difficulties, the employment-of-the-poor criterion was dropped, and the eligibility for loan assistance was raised to income levels well above the poverty line in order that

small business loans could be made at all under the program. Kirschner reported all these difficulties and changes and recommended that
the program be continued with loan recipients above the poverty
line, primarily in order to aid minority businessmen in ghetto areas.
OEO accepted Kirschner's evaluation results but rejected the policy
conclusion, believing, rather, that aiding minority businessmen was a
good thing but not part of a poverty program. OEO tried to drop the
program, but the Congress has indicated a preference for the policy
of aiding minority businessmen. All of which goes to show that the
use of evaluation results is seldom straightforward.

Other evaluations of community-betterment programs have been
taking place or are underway. The neighborhood-centers program
was also evaluated by Kirschner [9] who highlighted a possible problem in reconciling the service delivery and organizational functions
of the neighborhood center. The legal services program of OEO was
examined, with the same result mentioned above for health centers:
It is still too early and too difficult to evaluate the real effectiveness of
the program, but at least we can say that this new form of organization provides the poor with services at a lower cost than that for
which they can be obtained on the open market.

Even in the case of these component evaluations, the logical
connection to ultimate anti-poverty effectiveness is difficult to map
out, although in the family-planning case it was possible. Matters are
much more difficult in evaluating the overall social change that
community-betterment programs are supposed to be bringing about.

We have some inkling of how to define social change. That is, we
know what kinds of things we would want to change—school systems
and employment services, for example—but we do not know well
how to measure these changes, nor do we really know what these
changes have to do with getting people out of poverty. Given all this,
we are starting out on several tacks to try to achieve evaluations, both
generalized and systematic. Almost two years ago, OEO funded universities or other organizations in six cities and in two rural areas to
evaluate the community-action programs in their areas. Rigid specifications for the evaluation were not set forth nor was an attempt
made to have these evaluations made on a common basis. The objective was to find out *how* to evaluate from these efforts, not to compare programs on any common basis.

At the same time, an internal OEO effort was begun to bring
scattered knowledge of program results in a number of cities into a

common pattern to see what could be found out about the effectiveness of the program in these cities and the reason for this effectiveness. The sources here ranged from reports on OEO prerefunding visits, which typically take a several-man team a few days to accomplish, to newspaper reports, to special visits. Enough data, quantitative and nonquantitative, were gathered to make it possible to at least come to some general verbal conclusions about community-action programs. These were stated as follows in a report to the director of OEO:

Any evaluation of CAP must begin with the admission of the vagueness and intangibleness of the criteria for determining success. Added to this fundamental problem is the paucity of usable data from the agencies. Despite this caveat, however, we do have evidence that the better urban programs are having substantial and demonstrable impact on the slum communities of poverty. They are providing services to the poor that were simply not available before, and we can quantify this claim. We have hard data to show that they are giving people non-poverty jobs. They are changing the community structure which has kept the poor down, and we can demonstrate that, although it is not quantifiable. Even the best urban programs, however, are reaching only a fraction of the problem at current funding levels. If I were to sum up in a single sentence the major evaluative results of Community Action, it is that we have demonstrated what can be done for people where programs are run well, but we have also demonstrated that current funding levels are not going to change the world fundamentally for a long, long time. One additional problem of many programs is that they have not yet reached the really hard-core in any important way—in some sense, they are "creaming."

The above statements concern the best urban Community Action programs. We can also demonstrate that we have some pretty bad ones. Rural Community Action has very seldom gotten off the ground.

In addition to this general statement, we have tried to analyze our sample of cities for variations among community-action programs and the reasons for these variations. In general, among urban community-action programs we can describe two polar types of community action, with a continuum between. On one end are those community-action programs that are tied tightly to the official structure of the cities in which they are located, that are controlled by the official structure, and in which the poor and minority groups have only a nominal effect on program decision. At the other end are those cities in which the community-action program is in the state of open warfare with other city institutions, particularly the official ones. A variation on this last polar situation comes when the official community-action program is not far distant from the official city government but the local program employees and participants are in revolt against both the community-action officials and the city officials. The hostility model seems particularly endemic in California, although not confined exclusively there.

In general, the optimum in terms of program effectiveness lies between the poles (of course). Those programs that seem to be working best are in cities in which the public establishment participates heavily but allows program flexibility and influence by program recipients. The idea here is that the abdication of some real power by local officialdom can in the long run or even in the short run add to program effectiveness for the purposes desired by both officialdom and the poor themselves. It is quite possible, in fact, that such partial abdication can lead to more, rather than less, political strength for ongoing public officials.[10]

All this is highly speculative, however. It may be that in the long run an extreme hostility model will be most effective, allowing the poor to build institutions and political power. It is notable that in California, where hostility is sharpest, there were no major riots during the summer of 1967—in part, because those who might have rioted were too heavily engaged in small-and-large-group political hostility against the "establishment" and against each other. In Detroit, which should still be considered an example of the optimum, many minority members, poor and otherwise, were brought into active participation in community action and other programs, but enough people were felt left out of programs and society to carry out a major riot. One possible conclusion (on riots, not on poverty) might be that the first essential for a city to avoid a civil disturbance is to have had one already.

In any case, we are now in the process of trying to systematize our highly impressionistic evaluations of community action and social change illustrated above. The first step in this process seems to be taxonomy—analysis into highly detailed classifications of what we know about differences among programs and differences in events in the areas in which these programs are taking place. Once this is done, it may be possible to cluster characteristics thus categorized into related groups and to chart paths of flow and causation among them.

For example, it may be that a community-action program characterized by a close tie to public authority, a large number of neighborhood centers, and a heavy investment in manpower has brought about more observed social change (for example, city investment increases in the poverty area) than has a program with a looser tie to the city, a relatively big Headstart effort, and fewer but larger neighborhood centers. All this may begin to give us a leg up on a theory of what works and how well it works, which is the essence of evaluation in this area. The Cambridge firm of Barss and Reitzel is beginning in these directions under contract to OEO.

One final negative note is necessary on evaluation of community betterment and community action. The obvious way to evaluate programs like these is to look at external indicators like crime rates, people on welfare, and so on. It is obvious, and we have tried it, and it doesn't show anything except that data and program changes in fields like welfare dominate any effect on these indicators that the new poverty program might have. Considering the fact that the typical community-action investment in a city is unlikely to be as high as 5 per cent of the city's total budget, this does not seem surprising.

In other words, given current funding of community action we can use early indicators for evaluation, but it is unreasonable to expect fundamental change at this point in time.

INCOME MAINTENANCE

OEO funds no income-maintenance programs, yet these programs, particularly public assistance and that portion of Social Security going to the poor, make up a larger portion of the total War on Poverty than any other group of programs—more than half of the $25 billion. Thus, it is as necessary here for us to think about evaluation as it is anywhere else.

In one sense, the evaluation of income-maintenance programs is extremely easy. That is, the objective of such programs is to increase incomes, and they can be evaluated on the basis of the number of dollars that go to increasing these incomes—in other words total expenditures minus administrative costs. Slightly more sophisticated is the evaluation by that portion of the dollars that goes to increase the income of those who are the primary target of the program. For example, if the objective is to increase the income of the poor, then an income-maintenance program of the family-allowance type, which puts several dollars into the incomes of non-poor recipients for every dollar to poor recipients would be inefficient relative to one that is targeted better on the poor.

Such evaluations are straightforward and, indeed, do not even require program experience to carry them out; national statistics are adequate to estimate the effects of these programs in advance. But things are never so simple and there are, of course, a good many unknowns in programs of income maintenance that can only be evaluated on the basis of experience. For example, the chief income-maintenance program currently directed at the poor as such is public assistance. It is known beyond any doubt, on the basis of experience and evaluation, that public assistance as it is now administered is arbitrary, degrading to the recipients, and spotty geographically, and that it reduces people's incentives to get off welfare by going to work. This is true in spite of the fact that it is not terribly deficient in terms of dollars delivered to the poor relative to total dollars spent. But the other drawbacks of public assistance are substantial, and if other programs are available to deliver dollars as effectively or nearly as effectively, then evaluation may lead to choice of an alternative.

The two major programs that have been discussed as general alternatives to public assistance are the family-allowance program and the negative income tax. As suggested above, some of the evaluation of the family-allowance program can be carried out without experience, based purely on quantitative logic. A major part of the evaluation of each of these two, however, must stem from experience. In addition to their effectiveness ratios in providing dollars to the poor, it must be discovered whether they can in fact avoid the difficulties of current public-assistance systems. It must be discovered what effect they have on maintaining or increasing the stability of families receiving payments; it must be discovered what effect they have on the work incentives of recipients. On the latter two questions, current public assistance has already been found badly wanting. It decreases family stability by giving preference to recipients in broken homes; it decreases work incentives by subtracting a dollar of assistance payments for every dollar earned.

Whether family allowances or negative income taxes are preferable to public assistance still remains to be discovered, but there is some presumption that they will be. Both of them remove the absolute incentive to break up the family, and both of them return at least some fiscal incentive to work. But how much and how effectively is not known. What presumably will be needed politically for any large-scale adoption will be to discover the importance of such "side effects." OEO is currently beginning in the state of New Jersey one such experiment, planned by the University of Wisconsin Institute for Research on Poverty. The experiment is intended to discover the effects on work incentives and stability of families headed by able-bodied males of a graduated work-incentive plan similar to the negative income tax model. We expect that other agencies, public and private, will be doing additional experimentation.

EVALUATION OF RELATIVE PROGRAM EFFECTIVENESS

The relationships and relative importance among the various programs that comprise the War on Poverty can be evaluated on three levels: relations among programs within the four categories; the relationships of the categories to one another; and the relationships of major thrusts, such as service delivery versus social change.

As mentioned above in the discussion of manpower programs, we are already beginning to work on relative effectiveness of programs within categories. Although the difficulties of preparing evaluations of programs even as similar as Job Corps and Out-of-School NYC are substantial, such comparisons are being made. Indeed they must be made. The allocation of monies among similar programs is dependent in part on estimates—still not quantitative—about relative effectiveness. As more knowledge is gained, much more qualitative evaluation of similar programs will be possible; conceptually, it presents few difficulties.

At least the within-category comparison compares like to like. Comparison among categories to estimate the relative effectiveness of each and therefore the relative allocation of investment among them is conceptually far more difficult. We know some things to begin with. We know, for example, that these four categories are complementary rather than alternative. It is nonsense, for example, to talk about a "community action" strategy or an "income maintenance" strategy as if they were either-or alternatives. They are useful in part for different people; in part, they support one another rather than being exclusive. The real issue is, given highly limited budgets, how much should be invested in each.

Thus far, except on the softest possible theory, we have not gotten very far along these lines. Some progress is beginning, however. Professor Lester Thurow of the Massachusetts Institute of Technology Department of Economics has derived, for a forthcoming Brookings publication,[11] a number of models that purport to show the *relative* contribution to getting people out of poverty that can be made by manpower programs, education programs, and by several others. Thurow's models are by no means perfect. The way in which they are derived may not satisfy the requirements of rigorous statisticians because the data from which they are derived do not satisfy these requirements. Further, important categories, particularly in the social change field, are simply not amenable to these techniques. Nonetheless, Thurow provides a start, and an important one, on the long-run process of obtaining a unified theory that will enable us to evaluate the relative importance of different programs in eliminating poverty.

CONCLUSION

To conclude this evaluation of evaluation, we can say that surely in terms of comprehensive evaluation of the Poverty Program at any level, we are not nearly where we would like to be. I think it is also fair to say that we are far ahead of any similar program past or present. At least, I think we know what evaluation means, and we are trying, given their complexity, to evaluate our programs as honestly as we can.

We are able to do this because a relatively simple unified objective like getting rid of poverty means that we at least are able to define what it is that we are evaluating for. Other programs that are cut functionally (for example, manpower, housing) have more conceptual difficulty because the size of effects and distribution of effects among different groups ot people are very difficult to compare with one another. In poverty, we assume away such distribution problems by defining a group of people—the poor—who are the only ones for whom program gains will count.

We have done more evaluation than other programs for the fortuitous reason that the beginning of the poverty program pretty much coincided with the beginning of the Federal Programming, Planning and Budgeting System, so that we were able to start anew, without encountering so many of the encrusted "we know that our program is good, don't bother us" interests that encumber other programs and agencies.

Finally, we are able to evaluate our program because we know we must. The War on Poverty and OEO are in political trouble that is beginning to seem perpetual. And a program that is in trouble is politically the easiest to evaluate because we know that there are many good things about it that, if they could be demonstrated by rigorous methods, aid in the perpetuation and political salvage of parts of the program. A politically popular program resists evaluation because everyone knows it's good, and it would be a shame if an evaluation showed that the emperor had no clothes after all. But because of the political difficulties of the Poverty Program, our ability to carry out evaluations of the whole program is enhanced.

All this is well and good. The proposition that OEO is doing a lot of evaluation and pointing it in many of the right directions is not a difficult one to defend. The final question, however, is what use is made of this evaluation in helping to make policy decisions?

Part of the answer is implicit throughout this chapter. Decisions like the disposition of the small-business program, the phasing-down of the work-experience program, and the new directions for Headstart all have been demonstrably affected by evaluative results. Beyond this, it can be stated, although not proved, that evaluative results as they come in have a substantial effect on day-to-day planning and operational decisions. It would be difficult to show that the entire War on Poverty program is directed by scientific use of evaluative methods or, for that matter, by the program-planning processes as a whole; it would be naïve to think that it might be so directed. Policy decision in the United States is achieved through political processes, not scientific ones—fortunately. The role of evaluation and planning is to contribute to these processes, not to overwhelm them. In the War on Poverty, this contribution is being made.

Notes

1. The $27.7 billion of federal aid to the poor in the President's budget request for fiscal year 1969 is divided functionally into: $15.9 billion in cash-benefit payments, primarily public assistance and that portion of Social Security going to the poor; $4.7 billion for health; $2.5 billion for education; $1.6 billion for work and training; and $2.9 billion miscellaneous. The OEO budget is $2.2 billion, with almost half in the work and training category, but OEO PPBS covers the entire $28 billion.

2. Harold Watts, "An Economic Definition of Poverty," in Vol. I, this series: Daniel P. Moynihan, ed., *On Understanding Poverty: Perspectives from the Social Sciences* (New York: Basic Books, 1969) .

3. *Ibid.*, p. 325.

4. Although, since transfer payments may have favorable social effects in themselves (e.g., family stability) , the ordinary formulation may be based on an oversimplification.

5. Glen Cain, "Benefit/Cost Estimates for Job Corps," University of Wisconsin, Institute for Research on Poverty, discussion paper, pp. 9–67.

6. Planning Research Corporation, "Cost-Benefit Analysis of Institutional and On-the-Job Training Programs," November 1967.

7. Thomas Ribich, *Education and Poverty* (Washington, D.C.: Brookings Institution, 1968) .

8. Kirschner Associates, "A Description of the Economic Opportunity Loan Program," February 1966.

9. Kirschner Associates, "A Description and Evaluation of Neighborhood Centers"—A Report for the Office of Economic Opportunity Contract No. OEO-1257, December 1966.

10. It should be noted that such *voluntary* abdication of some decision-making power is entirely consistent with the 1967 Green Amendment to EOA, which clearly gave local officials the right to decide who should make decisions.

11. Lester C. Thurow, "The Economics of Poverty and Discrimination," prepared for the Brookings Institution, Washington, D.C., September 1967. (Draft I, mimeographed.)

Chapter 10

⊂⊋ *Practice, Method, and Theory in Evaluating Social-Action Programs*

PETER H. ROSSI

INTRODUCTION

In the thirties, when the New Deal programs got underway, the behavioral sciences were mainly the recipients of program assistance: Works Progress Administration (WPA) and National Youth Administration (NYA) clerical help made it possible to conduct social research on a larger scale than heretofore possible.[1] But, little research was conducted on the programs themselves.[2] As a consequence, the effectiveness of New Deal programs is unknown.

In contrast, the behavioral sciences were explicitly invited into the current War on Poverty by the initial enabling legislation, funds being explicitly set aside under the act for evaluation research. Behavioral scientists this time were not to be merely recipients of help in the form of free labor; they were to participate in the policy-making process through the exercise of special skills. As a consequence, one could imagine a considerable flowering of evaluation research and advances in evaluation-research methodology. In some sense, indeed, there has been a flowering: Behavioral scientists throughout the country have been engaged in undertaking evaluations, and new research firms have sprung up to provide the needed

An earlier version of this paper was given at the 1966 Meetings of the American Statistical Association. This paper was revised with the help of a grant from the Russell Sage Foundation, whose help is hereby gratefully acknowledged.

services. In another sense, however, the flowering has meant more the encouragement of weeds than of more desirable species. Few of the researches conducted under the Poverty Program have been the best that behavioral scientists could offer (or the best they attempted to offer). Rather, much evaluation can be called research only by the most charitable extension of the meaning of that term. Only a few delight the connoisseurs: Few have that elegance of design and clarity of execution that would achieve widespread admiration among social researchers.

Nor is this condition a peculiarity of Poverty Program evaluation researches. Research on the effects of educational programs, on the effectiveness of police methods, even on the effectiveness of publicity campaigns, all have the same characteristic of falling far short of the potentialities of currently acceptable research methodology. Evaluating the effectiveness of social-action programs is a depressed area within the realm of behavioral science.

The purpose of this chapter is to explore some of the main reasons why evaluation research has fallen so short of its potential and to suggest some ways in which these difficulties can be overcome. Providing much of the materials on which this chapter has been based have been experiences as director of a university-connected research center [3] and a survey of researches conducted by the Office of Economic Opportunity (OEO). Although these sources of information cover the OEO research program quite well, with the exception of those researches for which no reports have been submitted to OEO, they do not cover the total spread of evaluation researches over the full range of current social-action programs.

The methodological standpoint on which this view of evaluation research rests is that, in principle, the evaluation of social-action programs is best undertaken through the use of experimental designs. All the elements that would strongly recommend such designs are usually present: The program to be tested is some treatment that is either added on to or is designed to supersede some existing treatment. Programs of this sort are under the control of someone or some agency and hence can be fitted into an experimental design if proper steps are taken to set up reasonable experimental and controlled situations. In addition, such programs are usually not designed to cover the entire population to which they are directed, but only some portion, so that withholding treatment from control groups is not radically different from what would ordinarily happen in the administration of such programs. In practice, however, there are many obstacles to the employment of experimental designs, as a later section of this chapter will show.

THE MAIN DESIGN PROBLEM—WEAK EFFECTS

Although a social historian might deplore the lack of good research on the New Deal programs, it may well be the case that research in that instance would have been superfluous. The impact of the Great Depression was so great that any program would help, provided it included some income-maintenance provisions. The problem in the thirties was not conceived so much in terms of rehabilitation as in terms of providing for needs that a weakened economic system had neglected.

In contrast, the present historical period is perhaps the wrong one in which to develop a heavy conscience concerning the poor. The treatments we can devise cannot be expected ordinarily to produce massive results. It appears that we are in much the same situation with respect to social ills as we are with respect to physical ills. The introduction of modern medicine and especially modern sanitation practices into a country that has neither can be expected to produce dramatic results in the forms of reduced morbidity and mortality. But, in the United States of today, each new gain in the reduction of morbidity and mortality can be expected to be smaller and more difficult to achieve. Providing potable water in a community that has used polluted water supplies will achieve dramatic reductions in mortality. Expensive research on lung cancer or attempts to reduce the amount of smoking will not, even if very successful, reduce mortality by very much.

Similarly with respect to our social ills: Dramatic effects on illiteracy can be achieved by providing schools and teachers to all children. Achieving universally a high enough level of literacy to assure that everyone capable of learning is qualified to obtain and hold down a good spot in our modern labor force will be very much more difficult. Hence, the smaller our rates of unemployment, the more difficult it will be to affect the employment status of those who are unemployed. The more social services we have already supplied, the more difficult it is to add to the benefits derived by additional services.

Part of the reasoning behind this pessimism lies in the assumption that affecting the course of a marginal social problem is more difficult than affecting the course of a central one. Thus, affecting the unemployed in a labor force with a high unemployment rate is quite different from affecting the same group under conditions of high employment.

In part, the reasoning flows from the types of effects that are desired. The goals of social programs that are directed toward affecting institutions and hardware are easier to achieve than those of programs directed toward changing the behavior and attitudes of large numbers of individuals. Thus, the armed forces have made stronger progress toward removing discriminatory practices than have government attempts to influence thousands of private employers. Or, the provision of a modern sanitary sewer is easier to achieve than convincing millions of smokers to stop smoking.

Thus, the problem of evaluation in this historical period is that new treatments can be expected to yield only marginal improvements over existing treatments and, hence, that cost-to-benefit ratios can be expected to rise dramatically as target problems and populations constitute smaller and smaller fractions of their universes. When only marginal effects are to be expected, evaluation becomes more difficult to achieve and at the same time program administrators can be expected to be more and more apprehensive concerning the outcome of evaluation research.

To illustrate, consider the case of Project Headstart: We have apparently wrung most of the benefits we can out of the traditional school system. We have learned how to deliver education to every educable child and for the large majority of children succeed quite well in providing sufficient skills to obtain places in the labor force. Everyone would agree that universal schooling for children up to approximately age sixteen has been a huge success, compared with no schooling at all or schooling mainly for those who can pay. Yet, there remains room for improvement, especially in the education of the poor and otherwise disadvantaged. A supplementary preschool program attempting to bring such children into parity with those better off because of family background would appear to be an excellent program. But any such program is not likely to produce as much benefit as did the introduction of elementary schooling. Nor is such a program likely to move underprivileged children into a position of true parity with others because no part-time supplementary program is likely to compensate for what a full-time total institution, the family, was supposed to do.

Effective new treatments that produce more than equivocal results can be expected to be expensive. For example, each trainee at a Job Corps camp costs somewhere between five and ten thousand dollars a year as compared to considerably less than one thousand dollars per year in the usual public high school. Yet, a year in a Job Corps Training Center is not going to be five to ten times more effective than a year in a public high school.[4]

To compound difficulties, the costs of evaluation for programs that are marginally effective are higher (for the same quality) than for programs that are very effective. If effects can be expected to be small, then greater precision is needed in research to demonstrate their existence unequivocally. Thus, we are presented with the paradox that precisely in the cases in which the most powerful research instruments are needed, they are unlikely to be used. It is almost as if we do not want to know whether the social-action programs are really effective.

Although as social scientists we can expect the new social programs to show only marginal effects, the practitioner does not ordinarily share our cautious outlook, at least not when he faces the congressional appropriations-committee hearings. The public claims made for the programs are ordinarily pitched much higher than one could reasonably expect to be able to show. However, although with the best of research we could show only very slight results, with the worst of research we could show anything. Thus it turns out that some of the major obstacles to good research lie in the interests of administrators in program maintenance. The worst of evaluation research is not research at all, but some other type of activity that goes under the name of research.

THE PRACTICE AND THEORY OF EVALUATION RESEARCH

In order to properly display the range of activities going under the name of evaluation research under OEO, we surveyed a sample of evaluation reports contained in the library of that agency.[5] Some 294 reports were contained in the library as of December 1967, a subsample of a larger group of 1,123 research projects contracted for by OEO as of June 1967.[6] The first 200 reports catalogued form the basis of the discussion that follows.

One hundred and seventy of the reports (or 85 per cent) were primarily descriptive accounts of how many people were being reached by the program in question or descriptions of the activities that took place within the program. They tended to be written in a loosely narrative form, with virtually no systematic observations on the effectiveness of the programs included. Five reports were missing. A remaining twenty-five reports were judged to be based on procedures sufficiently systematic to be at least considered research. These were read carefully and abstracted for later analysis.

Most of the reports contained what might be called systematic social bookkeeping data. For example, a purported evaluation of the Community Action Program (CAP) [7] involved interviews with residents of areas affected, obtained by sampling in ever-widening circles around the CAP headquarters. The nonresponse rate was more than 50 per cent. Data were presented to show how many persons had heard of the programs and participated in them and how many rated each program as effective or ineffective. Or, another report [8] was based on interviews with the personnel of nineteen small-business development centers in operation at the time of the study. Staff members were asked about their backgrounds and the social characteristics of the clientele of the program. Conclusions were drawn concerning whether or not the small-loan program was reaching its presumed target population.

The last example cited above illustrates that such social-bookkeeping studies can be useful. It is on the basis of this study that OEO concluded that its small-business loan program was not effective.[9] At this point, it is useful to distinguish between two meanings of effectiveness: "coverage" and "impact." By coverage is meant the ability of a program to reach the units that it is expected to affect. Thus a small-business loan program that was not giving loans to poor people is obviously having poor coverage and is in that sense ineffective. But, a program may have a proper coverage and not affect the people whom it is reaching. Thus, the same small-loan program even when making loans to the poor may not be helping small business to survive (if that is its goal) beyond what would ordinarily be the case without such a program. This last type of effect may be called a program's impact.

In this sense, most of the studies found in our survey were descriptions of coverage but not impact. Obviously, a program must have some coverage as a necessary but insufficient condition for being judged effective. But even with coverage, impact may be high or low.

Impact studies may be illustrated in the group of reports containing evaluations of Headstart programs. Typically, children are tested before and after participation in the program, and gains in test scores are judged to be the result of the program.[10] About half of the twenty-five evaluation reports studied in detail contained information designed to measure the impact of programs.

Not a single report contained by the most charitable definition the results of a controlled experiment.[11] At best, individuals exposed to a program (for example, Headstart, Job Corps) were compared with persons who were not exposed to the program, the comparison group presumed to represent an approximation to a control group. The range of quality represented by these researches runs almost the full gamut, from "moseying around" to quasi-experimental designs. But the distribution is weighted toward the poorer quality end of the range; the vast majority of the reports can best be characterized as "moseying around," with the best studies representing estimates of program coverages rather than impact.

This is not the place to lay out in detail the importance of experimental designs in the study of the impact of social-action programs.[12] It is sufficient to state at this point that without such designs it is difficult to unravel the effects of self-selection and other biases from the effects of administered programs. Surveys and quasi-experimental designs have some value, however, as I will attempt to show later on in this chapter.

THE POLITICS OF EVALUATION

The will to believe that their programs are effective is understandably strong among those who conceive and administer them. After all, they have committed their energies, careers, and ideologies to the programs, and it is difficult under such circumstances to take a tentative stance concerning outcomes. Hence, most administrators who have some sort of commitment to their programs have a strong incentive to believe that evaluations will prove their worth. They hope and expect that evaluations will come out with positive, or at least not negative, results.

As long as results come out positive, relationships between the practitioners and the researchers are cordial and perhaps even effusively friendly. But it often enough happens that results are not positive. A dramatic illustration of what occurs under these circumstances helps to underscore the resulting deterioration of relations. A few years ago, the National Opinion Research Center (NORC) undertook research, with the best of sponsorships,[13] on the effects of fellowships and scholarships on graduate study in the arts and sciences. It was the sincere conviction of the learned societies that sponsored the research that the availability of fellowships and scholarships was an important determinant of how many students went on to graduate work and, furthermore, that such stipends affected the distribution of talent among fields within the arts and sciences. The results of the research were nonpositive: It did not appear that financial support had much to do with going on to graduate study nor did the availability of stipends in one field attract students from another. Those who were committed found some way to get their advanced degrees, often relying on their spouses to make investments in their training. It certainly did not appear that stipends were holding back graduate training, but it also did not appear that stipends were doing much more than providing relief to overworked spouses. These results were quite disappointing to the sponsors, whose first reactions were to question the adequacy of the research. Humanists and biophysicists suddenly became experts in sampling and questionnaire construction as they looked for some fault in the study design that would undermine the plausibility of the results. One of the social scientists on the advisory committee obviously spent hours adding up frequencies in statistical tables and cross-checking tables for internal consistency. Some question was raised as to whether or not the results of the study should be published.

Needless to say, the relations between the researchers and the sponsoring learned societies have been relatively cool ever since. The learned societies believe that their problems have been badly researched, and the researchers believe that their research has been badly treated. The findings have affected policy not one whit: The sponsoring groups are still adamantly claiming more and more in the way of financial support for graduate students.

It is difficult to recall any social-action program that was put out of business by a negative evaluation.[14] Why is this the case? Why do negative (or nonpositive) results have so little impact? The main reason is that the practitioners, first of all, rarely seriously entertain in advance the possibility that results may come out negative or insignificant. The rules of the game of evaluation of social-action programs have not yet become institutionalized in the same way that the rules of evaluation for drugs have become institutionalized.

Proper rules for the game of evaluation would require that action alternatives for the contingencies of positive and negative findings be thought through and that administrators and practitioners alike become committed to following through such alternatives. Without commitment to such alternatives, the gamblers usually welch.

The ways in which welching is accomplished are wonderfully varied. It is easy to attack the methodology of a study: Methodological unsophisticates suddenly become experts in sampling, questionnaire construction, experimental design, and statistical analysis, or borrow experts for the occasion. Apparently, you can always find some expert who will be able to find something wrong with the research.[15]

Further replication may be called for to more firmly establish the findings. The best example here is the long history of research on the effects of class size on learning in which each new generation of educational psychologists attempt anew to find a negative relationship between class size and learning—so far without success. The net effect of the more than two hundred researches finding little or no relationship has been nil on social policy. Every proposal for the betterment of education calls for reductions in the size of classes.

Most often of all, it is "discovered" that the "real" goals of the social-action program were not the goals that were evaluated in the research after all. Thus the important goals of a job-retraining program were not to get jobs for the trainees but to train them in the etiquette of work. Or, the goals of a community organization in an urban renewal area were not really to affect the planning process but to produce a commitment to the neighborhood on the part of residents while planning took place. Or, the goals of a community-action program may not be to produce any specific benefits but to increase the satisfaction of the poor with their lot.

Perhaps the best example of how "real" goals are discovered

after goals that were evaluated were found to be poorly attained can be found in the work of a very prominent school-administration group.[16] Fully committed to the educational modernities of the forties and fifties, this group found to its apparent surprise that whether or not a school system adopted innovations it was sponsoring had little to do with the learning levels achieved by the students. Hence, they dropped achievement tests as a criterion of the quality of a school system and substituted instead a measure of the flexibility of the school administration in adopting new ideas, thereby producing an evaluation instrument, which, in effect, stated that a school system was good to the extent that it adopted policies that were currently being advocated by the group in question.

The main point to be made here is that the proper employment of evaluation research requires a commitment *in advance* on the part of the administrators and other practitioners to action based on whichever of the alternative potential outcomes in fact occurs. Without such commitment, it becomes all too easy to brush aside disappointing results, making the research effort a fatuous enterprise.

As mentioned earlier, few evaluation researches employ controlled experiments as their basic research design. It is important to understand that a key reason for this condition lies not so much in the difficulty of designing such experiments as in the impediments to their use in practice. The key feature of a controlled experiment lies in the control exercised by the experimenter over the processes by which subjects are allocated to experimental and control groups. In a well designed experiment, such allocations are made in an unbiased fashion, that is, potential subjects have a known probability of falling into one or the other group. But there are many ways in which a well thought out plan for unbiased allocation can go awry.

Perhaps the major obstacle to the use of controlled experiments in evaluation research is a political one. The political problem is simply that practitioners are extremely reluctant to allow experimenters to exercise proper control over the allocation of potential subjects to experimental and control groups. For example, the proper evaluation of the Job Corps would require that potential trainees be separated into experimental and control groups, the former receiving Job Corps training and the latter receiving either no treatment at all or some sort of training differing in essential respects from Job Corps treatment. The contrasts between the later performance of both groups provide a measure of the effectiveness of Job Corps experiences. The political sore point is that a controlled experiment means that some potential trainees who are otherwise qualified are barred "arbitrarily" from training, an act that public agencies are extremely reluctant to authorize.

In part, the political problem arises because researchers have not thought through sufficiently the problem of what constitutes a control or nonexperimental experience. The logic of experimental designs does *not* require that the control group be completely neglected —not given any treatment. The logic *does* require that the control group not be given the same treatment as the experimental group. One could administer to the control group another type of treatment designed to improve their job skills that was nonresidential and that lacked certain other critical features of Job Corps training. In short, we have not been ingenious enough in inventing *social placebo* treatments that are realistic enough to give public officials who have to authorize such experiments the security that they are not merely slighting individuals at random.

Such social placebos are not difficult to invent. For example, a social-placebo treatment for a job-retraining program could be designed to help men get jobs that do not involve retraining and over which the job-retraining program ought to show some advantage. Perhaps testing and intensive counseling might be an acceptable placebo treatment for a job-retraining program. Or, a placebo treatment for a Headstart program might be traditional nursery-school experience.

Note that the placebo aspect of the control-group experiences suggested above is directed not at the potential subject—as is the case in the usual meaning of placebo—but is designed to placate the administrators and public officials. In other words, control groups have to be given politically acceptable alternatives to the programs being tested.[17]

However, even in the best of circumstances and with the best of sponsors, the carrying out of controlled experiments can run into a number of boobytraps. For example, early in the history of the Job Corps, NORC attempted to set up an experimental evaluation of the Job Corps, but the program did not generate enough qualified volunteers to fill up both experimental and control groups. Under these circumstances, the administrators chose to fill up the experimental groups, abandoning all attempts to segregate qualified volunteers into experimental and control sections.

There is also the example of a well-designed experiment in the effectiveness of certain means of reaching low-income families with birth control information whose design was contaminated when the City Health Department elected to set up birth control clinics in those areas that had been designated as controls.

There is also a special risk that is run by long-range experiments. The world may change the experiences of control groups so that differences between their experiences and that of experimental groups are minimized. For example, an evaluation of the effects of public housing unfortunately took place in a period when the quality of the general housing stock of Baltimore was improving at such a fast rate that differences in the housing conditions between experimental and control groups had greatly diminished by the end of the experimental period. Similarly, a job-retraining program in a period when unemployment rates are declining cannot be expected to show as much of an effect as a treatment for a control group as would be the case in a period in which unemployment rates were either steady or increasing.

STRATEGIES FOR EVALUATION RESEARCH

There are a number of lessons to be drawn from the experiences discussed in this chapter that hopefully could help in devising a strategy for the conduct of evaluation research. Although it is true that in the best of all possible worlds the best of all possible research designs could be employed, in a compromised, present-day real world, full of evil as it is, it is necessary to make do with what is possible within limits of scarce time and resources available to us. The problem facing social scientists and policy makers alike is how to set up conditions for doing the best job we can in producing research that contains powerful enough information to permit making sensible judgments about the worth of social-action programs, without at the same time making political errors and within a time period that makes it possible to modify programs.

Although the idea of evaluation research has gained wide acceptance, we are a long way from full commitment to the outcomes of evaluation research. It is part of the researcher's responsibility to bring to the practitioners awareness of the possibility that in most cases the effects of social-action programs are not going to be spectacular and that there is more than an off-chance possibility of negative or at least nonpositive evaluations. As already indicated, the policy implications of such findings must be worked out in advance, with the practitioner firmly committed to acting on them if evaluation research is not to be turned into either fatuous or just plain irrelevant exercises.

A second lesson to be drawn is that we have a long way to go in divising acceptable ways of applying controlled experiments to evaluation. Political obstacles [18] to the use of controls often make it difficult to get acceptance of such designs. The difficulty of maintaining controls in a nonsterile world makes full-fledged use of experimental designs over long periods of time relatively rare. Earlier in this chapter, I suggested that we take a lesson from medical research and search for the social analogues of placebos to be administered to our control groups.[19] There are other directions in which experimental designs should go: For example, considering that there is a high likelihood that treatments for social ills will have small effects, we need very powerful designs to demonstrate positive results. But, because power costs money, it is worthwhile to consider research designs that evaluate several types of treatment simultaneously, thus increasing the amount of information obtained at a relatively slight increment in cost. To illustrate: It would be considerably more useful in terms of the amount of information gained if OEO were to provide experimental evaluations of several types of Job Corps programs rather than merely a single experiment that regarded all Job Corps centers as a single experimental treatment. Looking at the differential effectiveness of different Job Corps programs would provide information that would make it possible to construct better programs as well as information that would provide estimates of how much difference attendance at any Job Corps camp makes.

This chapter has stressed desirability of the model of the controlled experiment for evaluation research. But it is abundantly clear that controlled experiments are not being used and that they are difficult to employ. Most frequently found are one or another variant on quasi-experimental designs in which control groups are constructed by methods that allow some biases to operate,[20] for example, correlational designs in which persons subjected to some sort of treatment are contrasted with persons who have not been subjected to this treatment, controlling statistically for presumably relevant characteristics.

The important question that faces evaluation researchers is how bad are such "soft" designs? How much credence can be placed in their results, and what are the circumstances under which they can be employed with relatively strong confidence in their outcomes?

When massive effects are both desired and expected, "soft" techniques are almost as good as subtle and precise ones. To illustrate: If what is desired as the outcome of a treatment is the remission of symptoms in each and every individual subject to the treatment in question, then it is hardly necessary to have a control group. Thus, if a birth control technique is to be judged effective *if and only if* it completely eliminates any chance of conception, then the research design is vastly simplified. The question is not whether those who use the method have fewer children than a control group, but whether they have any children at all, a question that can easily be decided by administering the technique to a group and counting whether any conceptions appear at all.

Of course, with respect to social-action programs one is rarely confronted with the evaluation of a technique that is expected to accomplish complete remission of symptoms in every person subject to the treatment. But there are approximations to this condition. For example, an income-maintenance program may be designed to cover each and every person or household whose income falls below a certain minimum. An evaluation of the program might involve finding out how many eligible persons are being missed for some reason or other. Or, a training program designed to produce computer programmers must at least graduate students who have the ability to pass minimum standards in computer programming.

The obverse of the above also holds. If a soft method of evaluation does not show that a program or treatment has had any effect, then it is not likely that a very precise method would show that it has had more than very slight effects. For example, if a Headstart program produced no improvement in the verbal ability of its subjects in a before-and-after type of research design, it is not likely that a controlled experiment would show anything different. The existence of complex and large interaction effects that suppress large differences between a group subject to a treatment and a statistically constructed control group seems highly unlikely.[21]

Of course, if a correlational or before-and-after design does show some program effects, then it is never clear whether selection biases or the program itself produced the effects shown. Thus, testing children who have gone to Headstart programs and comparing them to those who have not may indicate only that those whose parents sent them are providing a cognitively richer home environment.

These considerations lead to the following strategy: It is worthwhile to use soft methods as the first stage in a program of evaluation, discarding treatments that show no effects and retaining those with more favorable showings to be tested with more powerful designs of the controlled-experiment variety. Thus, if a training program shows no increment in learning on the part of its participants, then it is not worthwhile to go into a controlled experiment. Or, if an optional food-stamp plan does not appreciably increase the quality of household diets, compared with those of eligible persons who do not elect to participate, then it is not worthwhile to conduct further, more precise evaluational research.

Although ex post facto designs of a correlational variety have obvious holes in them through which may creep (or even gallop) the most insidious of biases, such designs may be extremely useful in the investigation of effects that are postulated to be the results of lengthy treatments. For example, if one is concerned with the effects on the occupational adjustment of Negroes of attendance at integrated schools, the comparisons between adult Negroes who have attended such schools with those who have attended segregated schools will indicate at least whether it is likely that such effects exist without having to wait for a cohort of Negroes to go through their schooling experience and reach the labor force. If, as one study has shown,[22] such correlations do in fact exist, it is still not clear whether Negroes who did go to integrated public schools as childen were more highly motivated intellectually or whether it was the fact of attending integrated public schools that produced the effect.

A more dramatic example can be taken from the correlational studies of the association between smoking and lung cancer. Despite the fact that the association may be caused by factors common to both smoking and lung cancer, the evidence from ex post facto studies can hardly be ignored and certainly justifies the expenditure of considerable sums of money in before-and-after studies.[23]

Similarly, our study [24] of the effects of Catholic education on subsequent religious behavior and occupational attainment of adults can still be easily objected to on the grounds that self-selection biases could have produced the effects we have shown, even though we made every attempt to hold obviously relevant factors constant.

Nevertheless, we have gained a great deal of knowledge concerning the order of effects that could be expected, were controlled experiments to be conducted. The net differences between Catholics who attended church schools and those who did not are so slight that we now know that controlled experiments assigning Catholics randomly to Catholic and public schools would not produce results that showed the schools to be enormously effective as devices for maintaining religiosity or promoting occupational success.

From these considerations a strategy for evaluation research emerges. The strategy involves two successive phases: First, a "reconnaissance" phase in which "soft" correlational, ex post facto or before-and-after designs are used to screen out those programs worth being investigated further. Second, an "experimental" phase in which powerful controlled experiment designs are used to evaluate the differential effectiveness of those programs that survive the first phase. In this connection, it is worthwhile to consider the use of social placebos to achieve more political acceptance for controlled experiments.

This is a strategy that is designed to provide hard knowledge in time enough to guide policy makers toward ever increasingly effective social-action programs.

Notes

1. WPA clerical assistance made possible such studies as St. Clair Drake and Horace Cayton's *Black Metropolis* (Chicago: University of Chicago Press, 1945) and Robert E. L. Faris and Warren Dunham's *Mental Disorders in Urban Areas* (Chicago: University of Chicago Press, 1939), but social science contributions to our understanding of the Great Depression were confined mainly to a Social Science Research Council monograph series on the effects of the depression (for example, on the family and on migration) with little or no attention paid to the effects of ameliorative programs.

2. Karen Rosenbaum "A Second Chance for Youth: A Comparative Study of Federal Youth Programs in the 1930's and the 1960's," Educational Research Associates, 1966.

3. The writer was director of the National Opinion Research Center (NORC) at the University of Chicago between 1960 and 1967.

4. This is not to deny that such programs could have favorable cost-to-benefit ratios as Robert A. Levine's chapter in this volume suggests may be the case for the Job Corps. It means primarily that a program like the Job Corps will have lower ratios than traditional approaches to training adolescents for the labor force.

5. The survey was conducted by Mr. Paul T. MacFarlane, a graduate student in the Department of Social Relations at Johns Hopkins University, whose help is gratefully acknowledged.

6. The remaining 829 had either not yet produced reports or had produced

such skimpy reports (one- or two-page summaries) that they were not catalogued by the library.

7. Daniel Yankelovich, "Detailed Findings of a Study to Determine the Effects of CAP Programs on Selected Communities and Their Low Income Residents," unpublished report, March 1967.

8. Kirshner Associates, "Description and Evaluation of the Economic Opportunity Loan Program," unpublished report, February 1966.

9. See account in Chapter 9 in this volume.

10. See for example, Frances D. Horowitz and Howard M. Rosenfeld, "Comparative Studies of a Group of Head Start and Non-Head Start Pre-School Children," University of Kansas, January 1966.

11. This statement can only be taken to mean that controlled experiments are very rare in the total universe of OEO evaluation studies. Levine (see chapter in this volume) reports on a controlled experiment currently being undertaken to evaluate the effects of a negative income tax policy.

12. This interested reader can find a masterful exposition of the relative utilities of research designs in Donald T. Campbell and Julian C. Stanley, *Experimental and Quasi-Experimental Designs for Research* (Chicago: Rand McNally, 1963).

13. Reported in James A. Davis, *Stipends and Spouses* (Chicago: University of Chicago Press, 1962).

14. In Chapter 9 in this volume, Levine notes that the Kirshner evaluation of the small-business-loan program is being ignored by Congress in favor of the benefits that might accrue to the small businessmen involved, even though they are not the target population (the poor) for whom the program was originally set up.

15. Even in the controversy over whether there is some causal link between smoking and lung cancer, both sides were able to muster experts of considerable stature.

16. Donald Ross, *Administration for Adaptability* (New York: Metropolitan School Study Council, 1958).

17. There is, of course, the danger that a program that shows only marginal increments over a placebo treatment might be shown to be quite effective as compared to no treatment at all. To guard against the possibility and to maximize the information to be obtained in such social-action experiments, the placebo treatment should be conventional and of minimum cost. The reasoning behind this recommendation is that an experimental treatment to be worthwhile should do better than relatively inexpensive conventional treatments.

18. That these obstacles may be peculiar to the American political system and ethos can be seen in the fact that large-scale experimentation is possible in at least one other Western society. For several years now Sweden has had underway a large-scale experimental evaluation of the relative merits of comprehensive versus traditional high schools. The high-school population of Stockholm was divided in half, one going to a traditional high-school system and the other attending comprehensive high schools.

19. Another possible direction would be to set up generalized control groups, for example, a continuing study of poor youth that could be used as control groups for a wide variety of social-action programs. Levine indicates that such a program is presently underway at OEO which is setting up a panel of poor youths to serve as controls for youth programs.

20. An ingenious design was employed in the evaluation of a manpower-retraining program in which participants in the program were matched with their unemployed friends, the assumption being that the correlation between friends in important respects was high enough to eliminate much of the bias in self selection. Obviously, while this is an ingenious attempt, it is hard to evaluate the extent to which it has reduced self-selection biases.

21. Even though possible, complex interaction effects of this sort have been found to be extremely rare.

22. U.S. Civil Rights Commission, *Racial Isolation in the Public Schools,* 1967.

23. Note that controlled experiments can hardly be done on this problem since we cannot experimentally control smoking habits of subjects. Indeed, there are very wide classes of topics to which common decency, if not more cogent human rights arguments, bars the use of human subjects.

24. Andrew M. Greeley and Peter H. Rossi, *The Education of Catholic Americans* (Chicago: Aldine Press, 1966) .

ᴄᴅ *The End of the Experiment?*

Jᴀᴍᴇs L. Sᴜɴᴅǫᴜɪsᴛ

A change of national administrations is a time of reappraisal and redirection. Historically, when the power shift is from Democrats to Republicans, the redirection takes the form of a sorting out of Democratic ideas and programs—the discarding of some, the acceptance of others and through that means their admission into the national consensus, the tidying-up of management. The Democrats innovate, the Republicans consolidate. The contribution of Dwight Eisenhower was to put finally beyond the range of political attack the New Deal of Franklin Roosevelt; the role of Richard Nixon will be to consolidate those social and economic innovations of the New Frontier and the Great Society that he and the country accept. And perhaps no incoming Republican President has ever found such a lush growth—one wants to say, such an anarchy—of experiments, innovations, bold beginnings, and promising but not fully-tested designs for action as in the programs that now come within the broad definition of the War on Poverty.

But it is not so easy for Nixon as it was for Eisenhower. For, to a far greater extent, the Roosevelt innovations had been completed and could be surveyed intact. The Kennedy-Johnson revolution was left unfinished. Hardly had its central theme, the War on Poverty, been accepted by Congress and enacted into law than funds, attention, and leadership were diverted to the morass of Vietnam. One final measure got under the wire—model cities—because the planning period would be long and financial commitments at the outset low. But more costly measures, such as large-scale public employment programs, income maintenance plans, and fundamental reform of the public welfare system, were referred to study commissions or simply deferred. If Hubert Humphrey had been elected, a third phase of the Kennedy-Johnson revolution would have been in prospect as the demands of Vietnam lightened. Humphrey had specific plans for new emphases and new directions.

Nixon promised in his campaign to review the Democratic programs, to select, consolidate, coordinate, and manage, but he made no promise to expand. Indeed, his comments about budget and fiscal policy followed the traditions of Republican conservatism and carried at least a suggestion that the War on Poverty would, in terms of federal expenditures, be curtailed. He would do more, not less, for the poor but, by mobilizing private enterprise and voluntary action; he would do it with less burden on the federal budget. Meanwhile, most of the specific proposals for mobilizing the private sector emanating from Republicans on Capitol Hill and from the private sector itself turned out to involve tax concessions—which are a burden on the federal treasury no less heavy (and probably more heavy, because of the nature of tax concessions) for being concealed. So the question is still how much of the national resources to allocate to the War on Poverty, under what strategy, and through what means.

And here President Nixon faces more than a review and consolidation of Democratic programs. He must look at those parts of the Kennedy-Johnson revolution that were still unattended to when Johnson went home to Texas as well as at those parts that had been enacted into law.

THE FUTURE OF COMMUNITY ACTION AND OEO

The first questions Nixon must face are organizational. Issues of money and of new programs may be put off until next year's budget, but what to do with the Office of Economic Opportunity (OEO) and its raucous offspring—the community-action agencies—must be settled before their statutory life expires on June 30, 1969. By the time these words appear in print the President may have chosen his course and Congress may have concurred in it, but the issues involved will persist in any case and are worth discussing.

No one who has read the preceding chapters of this volume can question that the community-action idea was launched on its nation-wide scale precipitously, without much pre-testing or any clear idea of the direction it would take. Certainly Congress did not know, nor did the President, as is evidenced by their pained surprise when they found out what manner of institution they had begotten. The sugges-tion has been made that within Sargent Shriver's task force there were those who did know but did not tell—that they smuggled into the Economic Opportunity Act the three big words "maximum fea-sible participation" knowing well the trouble they would cause but explaining them away (in the terms that Adam Yarmolinsky under-stood them at the time) as meaning simply that poor people would be given jobs as neighborhood workers. The conspiratorial interpre-tation of history is always tempting, and the accused sometimes give it credence by happily accepting credit for prescience. But did they possess it? Was community action a pre-planned or an accidental revolution?

To be sure, the task force members who wrote the community-action section of the President's bill were unhappy with the status quo in most communities. They made no secret about that. After all, they were engaged in experiments, sponsored by the Ford Founda-tion and the President's Committee on Juvenile Delinquency and Youth Crime, which were openly dedicated to the concept of "insti-tutional change." That concept was always a bit ambiguous, but fundamentally the change was to be in the direction of greater responsiveness. Anyone who had listened sympathetically to the poor had heard the story that Paul Jacobs detailed in *Prelude to Riot*: The poor found the public and private agencies with which they dealt to be remote in their physical location, rigid in their pro-cedures, difficult to establish communication with, unempathetic and often hostile (especially the police) in their attitudes, and, in the South and sometimes elsewhere, openly racist. To change all this, bureaucracy and professionalism had to be diluted; people who spoke the language of the poor, who could communicate with the poor, who were *of* the poor, had to be brought into participation with the professionals to communicate for them, interpret for them, and—through the reverse flow of communication and interpretation —influence them. In participation theory, the use of the poor as aides and subprofessional employees came first, then their development as lower-level administrators, and beyond that there was speculation about the poor taking responsibility in the design of programs and even in their direction.

The protagonists of participation who drafted the community-action language wanted plenty of room for experimentation with a variety of forms of community organization and a broad range of roles for the poor and their representatives. But, as faithful social scientists, they were the principal advocates also of starting the community-action experiments slowly and building a broad nation-wide program only as fast as experience could be evaluated. If they were revolutionary conspirators, they were singularly inept ones—any experimental program that developed radical manifestations could easily enough be throttled in its infancy by the administration and Congress. The decision to set the new and revolutionary institution in the midst of every American community, all at once, was made not by social theorists but by politicians—or, more precisely, their speech-writers. The key word that ordained all that followed was neither "maximum," "feasible," nor "participation" but "unconditional," from President Johnson's declaration of an "unconditional war on poverty." That set the tone from which there could be no retreat. That this would mean the organization of the poor for a frontal assault on the power structure in city after city—merging inevitably into racial conflict—was not planned by those who wrote the Economic Opportunity Act any more than it was foreseen by those who accepted and enacted it.

In any case, though all may be fair in war and legislative draftsmanship, the proponents of participation played fair enough by any standard. The concept was not concealed in the bill; the requirement that the community-action programs be "developed, conducted, and administered" with "maximum feasible participation" of the poor was plain to be seen, in unambiguous language. Anybody who pondered for more than a moment the implications of maximum participation in program development and administration would be bound to envision poor people on boards of directors of community-action agencies and as administrators of programs. Members of Congress, particularly the committee Republicans, were combing the bill's language for any and every weakness they could find to exploit. Yet the phrase was not protested.

The only possible conclusion is that the whole idea of participation, in all its ramifications, was plainly unexceptionable to those who considered it. The poor *ought* to participate, as a matter of equity and as a means of developing competence. If they were capable of taking on subprofessional duties, that was all to the good, and if they were capable of exercising power—well, more power to them. That OEO shortly developed guidelines suggesting that the poor be granted one-third of the seats on community-action boards was a logical and inevitable development. But, be it noted, the guidelines still reserved for the power structure two-thirds of the seats on the boards. A literal interpretation of "maximum" would have been all, not one-third. The OEO guidelines were, then, a moderate interpretation of the legislative language—one more moderate, surely, than would have been proposed by conspirators bent on fomenting community revolutions.

So much for the conspiratorial interpretation of the history of community action. That is not the question for 1969 anyhow. The issue now is not whether the idea *was* wise but whether it *is* wise. If the program is doing more good than harm, and if the potential for improvement exists, then nothing much is gained by destroying it just to chasten its creators. No single appraisal of community action is possible, because the one thousand CAAs include all kinds—the militant and the tame, the rigorously managed and the sloppily managed, the professional-dominated and the poor-dominated, the centralized and the decentralized, the respected and the disdained, and all the shadings in between all these poles. Beyond that, what is good and what is harm will depend upon the viewpoint of whoever makes the judgment. Given those qualifications, let us attempt a summing-up.

Weighed on the positive side must be the design and introduction of new services that poor communities had not known before—Headstart, legal services, neighborhood health services, and manpower services, all the innovations of which Gregory Farrell eloquently writes. On the plus side also must be the unquestioned impact of community action on the institutions of which it has been a critic and a rival: they are more sensitive now to the needs and problems of the poor; they are setting up outreach stations; they are employing and training subprofessionals from the ranks of minorities. The administrators of welfare departments, health departments, school systems, and other public services may look upon the community-action agencies as brawling nuisances, but they are bringing the participation philosophy into their own professional doctrines and administrative practices. Throughout America the most common phrase on the lips of those who talk of community action is "this town will never be the same again." On the plus side, finally, must be weighed the contribution of participation to the competence of the poor—the personal growth (of which Robert Coles so sensitively speaks) and the growth in the capacity of the poor for collective endeavor. No one who has walked through a neighborhood center can doubt that the experience of organizing and operating such institutions has been an intensive learning process for those of the poor who have been engaged. Out of the community-action milieu are rising political candidates, public office holders, and entrepreneurs as well as agitators and prophets.

On the negative side, there is no gainsaying that community action has disturbed the peace. It has created discord. But even that is not all negative. In rural communities that are not communities at all in the sense of people living *together,* that are the fiefs of callous and remote power structures, the peace ought to be disturbed; maybe it is impossible as a political matter over the long run for the federal government to instigate the disturbance, but as an intellectual matter the federal government can well be encouraged to try so long as it can get away with doing so. And the same goes for urban places. A community living without discord may be living without justice. As the Supreme Court told us in the school cases a decade and a half ago, the suppression of conflict is not an end above all others. With luck, discord will be brief and mild and it will lead to justice.

In the cities, in the past half-dozen years, the discord has not always been mild; it has spilled over into blood and fire. But those who have tried to lay the blame for the urban riots upon community action have not mustered proof. There is more evidence the other way. Paul Ylvisaker has defined riots as "unstructured conflict"; the object of community organization, he says, must be to recognize the fact of conflict and provide structure. Administrators of many kinds of programs have long recognized that the public hearing is indispensable: It gives people a chance to "blow off steam"; it gives them a sense of participation, if not the fact of it. Is there not a lesson in this? Does not the metaphor that equates participation in community affairs with the safety valve in engineering arise from a great depth of human experience?

But if the President and Congress decide this year that community action has had its day, its protagonists can take heart that their contribution has been indelible. The principle is now written into other laws, notably the model cities law. If model cities come to supersede community action as the federal government's chosen instrument for organizing slum communities, then the body of community action may moulder in the grave but its soul will go marching on. Things will not be the same again.

Yet it may well be that, when the showdown finally comes, community action will survive in much its present form. There is a clue in William Selover's account of the 1967 legislative battle. Although the Senate expressed no qualms, the House of Representatives wanted the program tamed, no question about that. In the Green Amendment, Congress provided for the taming by authorizing public officials to take over community-action programs. But in fewer than 5 per cent of the communities have public officials elected to do so. In the others, either the program was under their control already, it was so innocuous that it did not matter, or it had such power that they dared not move against it. The same considerations will bear again. Each congressman, when he faces the question, will be looking to his district: Will he make more enemies if he destroys the community-action agencies than if he saves them? Where they are tame or innocuous, to destroy them would make enemies of those directly involved and yet might inspire no particular applause from the rest of the community. Where they are powerful, the congressman might feel the same inhibitions that the mayors and county commisioners have felt.

President Nixon and the Congress must choose their course in the light of the fact that OEO and the community-action agencies have become, in Marian Wright Edelman's phrase, "the visible symbol" that the government cares about the poor—which, translated, means about Negroes, Mexican-Americans, Puerto Ricans, Indians, and other minority groups whose members are mostly poor. The Republican party, if it is ever to become the majority party, needs desperately to dispel the vast distrust in which it is held by minorities and the poor and their organizations and sympathizers. Nixon is nothing if not a political realist. Nobody understands more fully, or more personally, that it was Eisenhower's inflexibility on just such matters that cost his party the 1960 presidential election. Will Nixon choose at the outset of his administration to destroy the visible symbol and make a host of enemies he need not have? Will he take any course that might risk a chance—even a remote chance—of igniting the urban tinderbox? OEO's obituaries written in the pre-inauguration days may prove to have been premature.

A name change for OEO, a gradual redirection of its energies, a new emphasis upon the private sector—these are something else again. Too many Republicans are on record as being against the way that OEO has been organized and administered, perhaps, to permit a new Republican administration to leave it wholly undisturbed. And an objective observer would have to discourage the Republicans from doing so. There are many improvements that can be made. Most notably, government-wide coordination of the War on Poverty, which OEO has never assumed and as a program-operating agency could not assume, should be transferred to an element in the White House or elsewhere in the President's executive office which is organized and staffed for the express purpose of helping the President coordinate his domestic programs. And the Republicans have been right in emphasizing (as Hubert Humphrey emphasized, too) the need for a new and dynamic economic component to the War on Poverty. New ideas and programs are emerging for government aid to community corporations, minority entrepreneurs, and established firms that may be willing to locate new enterprises in urban and rural slums. If the mission of OEO were to be so broadened, then a new name and a reorganization—encompassing also a careful transfer to the old-line departments of more routinized programs, such as Headstart—would be in order. The visible symbol would remain—refurbished perhaps, wiped clean of the accumulated tarnish of the years.

COMMUNITY ACTION IS NOT ENOUGH

Part of the criticism of community action rises from a broader context of strategic thinking. It is argued that community action should be de-emphasized, or eliminated, because it is intrinsically of lower priority than other measures that, because of the stress on community action, are being neglected. The effects of community action upon the poverty statistics are at best indirect and, in the case of programs like Headstart, far in the future. To center the national energies upon community action is only feinting at the enemy when a frontal assault is called for. What is needed is a new approach—one that would emphasize jobs and income *now,* that would lift people out of poverty simply by putting money in their hands. So the argument runs.

When the War on Poverty was launched, its planners thought they were embarking on a dual strategy—jobs plus services. They had a job-creation measure of unprecedented boldness, President Kennedy's $11 billion tax cut, then pending. But expansion of the economy would not in itself suffice to create opportunity for poor people. Experience under the Manpower Development and Training Act had dramatized the wide gap that could exist between the skill requirements of new jobs that were created and the competence of persons available to fill them. The poor had to have education, training, health services, counseling and placement, and perhaps a range of other services yet to be discovered and defined. Many of the services were remedial, designed to equip the present generation of working adults for jobs, but if one looked ahead it was plain that preventive services were to be preferred—those that affected young people long before they entered the labor market, beginning even in the preschool years. For full employment, then, job-creation measures—what at the time meant fiscal policy measures—had to be accompanied by other actions designed to prepare the poor to grasp the economic opportunities that would be opened to them. So the other actions were written into an Economic Opportunity Act, to be administered by an office of the same name.

Given that conception of its purpose, no employment or income supplements as such were proposed in the bill that launched the War on Poverty. Sargent Shriver boasted in his congressional appearances that his bill contained no "handouts." What jobs it did provide were concealed in the disguise of training. Thus the Neighborhood Youth Corps, essentially an employment scheme, appeared under the heading of "work training" and the adult employment programs under the heading of "work experience"—all still in the context of making the poor employable. There was only one moment when a large scale job-creation measure beyond the tax cut was seriously considered—when Shriver, backed by Labor Secretary Wirtz, presented to the Cabinet a public-employment program to be financed by a special tax on cigarettes. But the President saw no political sense, whether or not he saw economic sense, in both raising and lowering taxes for the same general purpose in the same year. He rejected the Shriver proposal and that was that. The tax cut was enacted and, as Wirtz had insisted would be the case, it failed to wipe out unemployment. Using a new index called "sub-employment" (a number derived by counting workers who suffer long-term unemployment plus those who work but earn only poverty wages), the Labor Department found that 34 per cent of the potential labor force in the slums of the big cities was sub-employed in the fall of 1966. But President Johnson still did not propose a large-scale public employment program, and when such a program was put forth by others he publicly condemned it as "make work." OEO became an advocate within the administration of an income maintenance plan—a negative income tax or some variant thereof—but this was referred to a Presidential commission for study and report. So the War on Poverty remained harnessed exclusively to the "services strategy" or "opportunity strategy."

The members of the seminar out of which this volume grew were united in their judgment that a "jobs and income strategy" has to be adopted. Our policy discussions, whenever we talked about policy (and that was not the purpose of the seminar) were focused on that issue. "Regardless of how poverty is defined, we cannot rely on either a services strategy or an opportunity strategy," said Daniel Patrick Moynihan, the seminar's chairman, in summarizing the conclusions of ten weekends of discussion. "What we must have is income redistribution. After long hours of sociological discourse, one fact remains clear: The poor do not have enough money." From that point of consensus, the members moved quickly to positions of sharp divergence as to what the "mix" of the various strategies should be: how much emphasis upon jobs and income, how much (if any) on services and opportunity programs and community organization. The varied viewpoints reflect the alternatives available to Nixon's strategic thinkers and suggest the considerations that must be weighed in the selection.[1]

Some of the members go so far as to argue that the new strategy should be wholly substituted for the old. Lee Rainwater holds that

The popular "services strategy" is and will continue to be a bust judged in the light of sociological analysis, the dynamics of the lower-class culture and behavior, or from the evidence of performance of government programs to date. The only kind of strategy that has a chance of really working is a "resource strategy" that directly alters the life situation of poor people.

The poor, or many of them at least, differ from the middle class not just in income but in some aspects of behavior, which set them apart as a "lower-class culture," in Rainwater's phrase, or as a "culture of poverty," in the words of Oscar Lewis. But the question is one of cause and effect. Are people poor because they behave differently, or do they behave differently because they are poor? The "services strategy" rests on the former view, argues Moynihan, and therefore it seeks to lift people out of poverty by altering their behavior. This is the rationale for social work and for emphasis upon education. "But by and large," says Moynihan, "that strategy has not worked. Not only is it true that the traditionally defined social work services produce little in the way of results, but we are also finding that education is a process which has little impact on students."

Rainwater questions whether the cultural patterns of the lower class can ever be changed by outside intervention so long as there remains a lower class in terms of income. The cultural patterns of the poor represent, after all, an adaptation by people to their social and economic circumstances, an adaptation that is essentially successful and that is reinforced through daily experience. But provide the poor with middle-class incomes, and middle-class behavior will follow—even though slowly—because poor people share the conventional values of the middle class and, basically, desire to conform.

Moreover, contends Peter H. Rossi, a strategy that offers services specifically for the poor is "in error primarily because they stigmatize the condition of being poor." A Headstart program would be acceptable if offered to everyone in the form of a general nursery school program, but a Headstart program for the poor alone is not.

Rainwater agrees:

There is a remarkable degree of consistency in sociological findings that special services for the poor inevitably become stigmatized services. No matter how hard governments might try, and no matter how good and pure their intentions, it is not possible to develop special services for the poor that do not stigmatize those who make use of them.

Zahava D. Blum also objects to the "labeling" of the poor through special programs. "The dignity and self-respect we so often demand for ourselves (and consider as part of our rights) are so often denied to the 'poor' by forcing them to admit personal failure the very moment we ask them to participate in a 'poverty program,'" says Mrs. Blum. Moreover, she reminds us, people move from one economic status to another. "It may, after all, be a family that is currently ineligible for a given program that may be downwardly mobile and below our 'poverty line' next year." So her logic, like Rossi's, leads toward meeting the needs of the poor through programs of general applicability, while recognizing that these would be more costly and would probably be more difficult to enact than specific "help the needy" programs.

Those who downgrade the services strategy argue further that, when the poor are lifted out of their poverty through job and income measures, they will be able to buy many of the services now provided by OEO and other agencies. And because they will have bargaining power, they will get better services. When housing, for example, is provided as a service, the poor are concentrated into huge, institutionalized public housing projects where individual and family problems, and problem behavior, are reinforced. Given money to shop for housing, they will spread throughout the stable working-class neighborhoods and be more likely to adopt the behavior patterns of those communities.

While the seminar did not consider the relative merits of various income maintenance schemes,[2] guaranteed employment for those able to work drew the widest endorsement. For those not able to work, the family allowance plan has been advocated by Moynihan, but Rossi and Mrs. Blum took occasion to disagree. "I am opposed to a family allowance program which would in any way reward large families," says Rossi. "We have a burgeoning population problem on our hands that also has to be handled."

At the opposite end of the spectrum stand those who place the highest value upon the services strategy, notably Oscar Lewis. He is for employment and income measures, but

jobs, occupational retraining, and an annual minimum family income will in themselves not eliminate the pathology associated with the Culture of Poverty. They will not eliminate poor mothering, free unions, illegitimacy, alcoholism, gambling, wife-beating, present-time orientation, impulse spending, and provincialism, to mention only a few traits.

Lewis concedes that some of the poor still subscribe to the basic values of middle-class society, but he argues that to others poverty has given "a whole way of life." The War on Poverty must distinguish between those who are outside and those who are inside the culture of poverty, and for the latter must devise service programs far more intensive than those now being carried out under the Economic Opportunity Act—"mass, socialized therapeutic measures," he calls them. "Increased income in the families that I've studied hasn't really changed anything," Lewis observes; the families may have better furniture but the treatment of children is the same. The people are still unorganized, still without faith in the future, still without "a sense of belonging to the United States," still essentially dependent. Lewis's solution is intensive case work with individual families, undertaken by middle-class people who have been trained "to overcome the great sense of distance they feel toward the poor," with no more than two or three families to the worker. If the workers remained with the same families for five years, Lewis contends, "startling and remarkable results in human rehabilitation" would be shown.

S. M. Miller shares some of Lewis's skepticism of the impact of the "jobs and income strategy" by itself. Though he supports a shift in emphasis toward that strategy, "it is not a panacea for the problems of the poor," he holds.

Poverty is a condition not only of income insufficiency but also of insufficiency of housing, basic services, education, and political and social participation. Marginal improvements in income will neither solve the health, housing, and educational problems of the poor nor guarantee a high level of participation within the society. Improving income will not automatically produce educational gains for the children of low income nor will it change by itself power relations in society. It can do much about the problems of inequality; it cannot do all.

The War on Poverty should enter a second phase, built upon guaranteed employment and new forms of welfare or income maintenance but also aimed at affecting the institutions that deal with the poor. In particular, existing poverty programs should be extended more effectively to the non-Negro poor and to the rural poor.

After a job program and an income distribution program—to which he would add a national housing program—are adopted, Sanford Kravitz still finds a "vital" role for the services of community-action agencies. They can

link low-income people to critical resources—education, training, counseling, housing, and health. They can increase the accessibility of available critical services that the poor still often find beyond their reach or blocked off from them. They can create competent communities by developing in and among the poor the capacity for leadership, problem solving, and participation in the decision making that affects their lives. They can restructure community-service institutions to assure flexibility, responsiveness, respect, and true relatedness to the problems faced by the poor.

Herbert J. Gans puts his emphasis upon the jobs and income strategy and sees it as sufficient in itself for many of the poor—though not for all.

Poverty is fundamentally economic in origin, and therefore the most necessary policies in the elimination of poverty are economic. These policies—jobs for the unemployed, better jobs for the underpaid and underemployed, and higher income grants for those who cannot work—are not only *necessary* but even *sufficient* for many presently poor, although we do not know for how many. If they have sufficient economic resources, the vast majority does not need any cultural training in order to "behave." Moreover, cultural training works in mysterious ways, and I do not believe we know how to program it for those who need it most. I am not even sure that we ought to know, for I suspect it involves a kind of brainwashing that goes against the democratic grain.

It is noteworthy that while several sociologists—Rainwater, Rossi, and Mrs. Blum—were among those who would supplant the social services strategy in favor of the economic (or jobs and income) approach to poverty, some of the firmest support for the non-economic, or services, approach came from the seminar's economists. Gerald Rosenthal reminded the group that the War on Poverty sought not merely to raise people's incomes but to improve "the quality of life." "Even if everyone had an income above the poverty level," he contends, "opportunity programs would still be necessary to help people get more out of society." And while make-work programs may have the greatest payoff in the short run, over a longer time span investments in education may have the most decisive impact upon poverty.

And the economist Robert A. Levine decries the "social simplification" that he detected in the seminar's discussions.

Academicians, tend to look for single causes for social problems and single cures to solve the problems. They talk too frequently about alternative "strategies" in which a choice must be made between this way or that way of solving a problem, when in this real world it will take both ways and probably a half dozen others to accomplish anything.

In OEO, we divide anti-poverty programs among four categories— employment, education, community change, and income maintenance. These are complementary rather than exclusive alternatives. What we need, and what we are working toward, is a complex strategy with a proper mixture of programs of each type. The belief of some, that an "opportunity" strategy is an alternative to an "income support" strategy, is as naive as any other set of exclusive alternatives. About half the families in poverty cannot take advantage of opportunity and can be lifted out of poverty only through better income maintenance. But, if the children of these families are to be self-sufficient in the next generation, income support is no substitute for training, education, and other services. Poverty in the United States is a problem with many causes; the one thing which is least likely to work is an approach along a single line, appealing though its intellectual simplicity may be.

In rebuttal comes the reply that to advocate "complementary strategies" may simply be a cloak for failing to come to grips with issues and deciding priorities.

The editor, as will be clear from the earlier pages of this chapter, takes his stand with Levine. So does Adam Yarmolinsky, who explains: "Though I think jobs are the key, poor people can only find and get adequate jobs if the service approach is used in helping them to do so." Harold W. Watts shares Levine's impatience with "pure strategies" as opposed to mixed ones but thinks the current mix is "quite deficient in the weight it places on jobs and incomes."

Watts emphasizes however, that new jobs can be created and higher incomes attained

without the creation of *any* new programs or bureaucratic structures. It merely requires the determination to use fiscal and monetary measures to depress the unemployment rate down to 3 per cent or below. . . . This is not a strategy calculated to maximize happiness in Zurich, and it might cause some heart failure amongst fiscal conservatives here. But it would, without question, benefit the poor as a group—regardless of what it does to the price level. Moreover, it is hard for me to see how any of the other strategies could be sustained at any level of effectiveness without a strong, expansive and manpower-hungry economy.

One can quickly check off manpower training, current welfare (and any future transfer mechanism), employer of last resort, and even community action, as being either impossible, expensive, or completely ineffective without such a buoyant level of demand. I don't believe that demand by itself is a sufficient answer, but it almost certainly is a necessary component of a complete answer.

A NOTE OF URGENCY

Finally, the seminar was deeply concerned—even alarmed—at the loss of momentum so apparent in 1967 and 1968 of the national effort to have done with poverty. Whatever their individual views as to the wisdom of the government's Vietnam policy, the members were unanimous in deploring the consequences of that policy in taking resources and attention from the domestic problems of race relations and of poverty. In Stephan Thernstrom's words: "We need only open our eyes to see that we are in a crisis. Something fundamental has to be done to avert calamity."

The record of the American people in averting calamity is not a reassuring one. We did not avert the Civil War even though few failed to see it coming. We did not avert the Great Depression. We did not prevent the formation of the ghettos or act to prevent their misery from worsening. And when they exploded, which should have been predictable enough, we failed to avert the subsequent polarization of the nation on class and racial lines.

The War on Poverty needs research, yes, and experimentation and evaluation. But already much more is known about how to conquer poverty than is being used. The general directions in which the country has to move are clear enough: the creation of jobs for the poor, the maintenance of income, the improvement of services, the development of competence among the poor as individuals and communities, and the abolition of the ghetto and all that it stands for. All of these have been urged upon the country many times, most forcefully of late by the National Advisory Commission on Civil Disorders.

The trouble is that there has been no decision to allocate enough of the nation's resources for employment programs, better education, better housing, better health, better cities, and all the other things that must be done. If the nation fails, this time, to avert calamity, it will not basically be for lack of knowledge. It will be for failure of the nation's political leadership to muster the nation's will.

Notes

1. The quotations that follow are based upon comments made during the American Academy of Arts and Sciences seminars that were the genesis of this volume and upon written communications received from the participants after the seminars were over, in response to an invitation to each to summarize his views upon the policy implications of the entire series of discussions.

2. These are defined and compared in a number of recent publications. Among them are James Tobin, "Raising the Incomes of the Poor," and James L. Sundquist, "Jobs, Training, and Welfare for the Underclass," in Kermit Gordon, ed., *Agenda For the Nation* (Washington, D.C.: Brookings Institution, 1968).

Index